THE BREATHLESS ZOO

ANIMALIBUS
OF ANIMALS AND CULTURES

Nigel Rothfels and Garry Marvin
GENERAL EDITORS

ADVISORY BOARD:
Steve Baker
University of Central Lancashire

Susan McHugh
University of New England

Jules Pretty
University of Essex

Alan Rauch
*University of North Carolina
at Charlotte*

*Books in the Animalibus series share a
fascination with the status and the role
of animals in human life. Crossing the
humanities and the social sciences to
include work in history, anthropology,
social and cultural geography, environmental studies, and literary and art
criticism, these books ask what thinking
about nonhuman animals can teach
us about human cultures, about what
it means to be human, and about how
that meaning might shift across times
and places.*

THE BREATHLESS ZOO

TAXIDERMY AND
THE CULTURES
OF LONGING

Rachel Poliquin

THE PENNSYLVANIA
STATE UNIVERSITY
PRESS
UNIVERSITY PARK,
PENNSYLVANIA

Library of Congress
Cataloging-in-Publication Data

Poliquin, Rachel, 1975–
The breathless zoo : taxidermy and the
cultures of longing / Rachel Poliquin.
       p.   cm. — (Animalibus : of
animals and cultures)
Summary: "A cultural and poetic analysis
of the art and science of taxidermy, from
sixteenth-century cabinets of wonders to
contemporary animal art"—Provided by
publisher.
Includes bibliographical references and
index.
ISBN 978-0-271-05372-1
(cloth : acid-free paper)
1. Taxidermy—History.
2. Taxidermy—Social aspects.

3. Taxidermy—Psychological aspects.
4. Human-animal relationships.
5. Desire—Social aspects.
6. Animals in art.
7. Animals in literature.
I. Title.

QL63.P65 2012
590.75′2—dc23
2011045700

The Pennsylvania State University Press
is a member of the Association of
American University Presses.

It is the policy of The Pennsylvania State
University Press to use acid-free paper.
Publications on uncoated stock satisfy the
minimum requirements of American
National Standard for Information
Sciences—Permanence of Paper for
Printed Library Material, ANSI z39.48–
1992.

Designed by Regina Starace

CONTENTS

ILLUSTRATIONS

ACKNOWLEDGMENTS

This project would not have been possible without a postdoctoral fellowship from the Social Sciences and Research Council of Canada. I would like to thank Harriet Ritvo and the History Department of the Massachusetts Institute of Technology for hosting me, however briefly. A special thank you to all the librarians and archivists who helped this project along, particularly James Hatton at the Natural History Museum in London, Sarah Kenyon and Claire Pike at the Saffron Walden Museum, Nina Cummings and Armand Esai at the Field Museum, and Dana Fisher at the Ernst Mayr Library at Harvard University's Museum of Comparative Zoology. For their encouragement, support, and assistance, I would also like to thank Nigel Rothfels, Garry Marvin, Kendra Boileau, Steve Plant, Lisa Grekul, Eva-Marie Kröller, and, of course, my family, Tobias, Duane, Judy, Morgan, Erin, and Beatrice.

In 2004, Nanoq: Flat Out and Bluesome opened in Spike Island, a large, white-walled art space in Bristol, England. On display were ten taxidermied polar bears, each isolated in its own custom glass case, all transported from separate locations across Great Britain to exist briefly together yet solitary. The exhibition marked the conclusion of Bryndís Snæbjörnsdóttir and Mark Wilson's quest to find and photograph every mounted polar bear in the United Kingdom, a three-year journey that unearthed thirty-four bears. Most were located in natural history museums, some on display, some in storage, boxed in among filing cabinets and other discarded displays. Other bears stood in parlors and hallways of private homes or blended with the eclectic décor of a country pub.

Each of the bears was photographed in situ where Snæbjörnsdóttir and Wilson discovered them, captured in the mix and muddle of their dwellings, not their native environment, to be sure, but their second and more permanent home. Although the photographs exude a colorful vitality, there is also an indeterminate wistfulness to the images, a sense of lingering or waiting: the gentle sadness of the bears' stoic persistence in the face of artificial ice floes, bottles of beer, and African animals. One of the bears holds a wicker basket of glowing plastic flowers; another is penned in between a wallaby and a tiger; yet another has been forgotten behind a dust-covered bicycle and a child's rocking horse. The compromising situations envelop the bears in a vague sense of noble tragedy, an aura captured by the project's ambiguously melancholic title: Nanoq: Flat Out and Bluesome, "nanoq" being the Inuit name for polar bear. "Flat out" implies death, fast forward, and flatten like stretched skins, while "bluesome" suggests both the bluish light of Arctic snow and the weight of melancholia.

The wistfulness of the photographs and exhibition title was sharpened by the display of the ten bears themselves. The atmosphere of the gallery was marked by

1   Bryndís Snæbjörnsdóttir and Mark Wilson,
     Somerset, from Nanoq: Flat Out and
     Bluesome, 2004. Photograph. Photo
     courtesy of the artists.

a sense of absence, an uneasy silence, a loneliness and longing. Perhaps it was the austerity of the space, with its white walls, white floor, glass, clean white metal, and isolated honey-white bears. Or perhaps the sheer physical presence of the bears captured and communicated something that two-dimensional photographic images never could.

As part of their project, the artists researched the personal history of each specimen. The bears were variously shot during Arctic adventures or euthanized in zoos. One died of old age; another traveled with a circus. But whatever their precise story and route, polar bears are aliens to Great Britain; they were all taken from their native landscapes at some stage of life or death and manhandled into everlasting postures. The artists' choice to document specimens of an Arctic species, rather than creatures indigenous to Britain, adds an additional layer of significance to the polar bears. These are not "common" indigenous creatures. They are not unwanted invasive species but coveted imports, and as such are necessarily endowed with longing. Without the desire to capture, to kill, to see, to document, these bears would not be in Britain and certainly would not have been taxidermied.

Many of the bears date to the mid-nineteenth century and linger as relics of Victorians' fascination with the Arctic. The bear at the Natural History Museum in London may have been killed during Captain Parry's efforts to find the Northwest Passage in the early 1820s. The National Museum of Ireland's bear was shot in 1851 in Baffin Bay during a reconnaissance mission to discover the fate of the Franklin expedition. The bear in the Kendal Museum was shot by the earl of Lonsdale on an Arctic voyage prompted by the request of Queen Victoria, and the bear in the Dover Museum was one of sixty shot during the Jackson-Harmsworth Expedition, which unexpectedly encountered Norwegian explorers Fridtjof Nansen and Hjalmar Johansen from the *Fram*, who had survived overwinter on polar bear and walrus meat.[1] And with this early history, the bears also evince the Victorian infatuation with taxidermy itself. Some of the bears were preserved by the greats of late Victorian taxidermy, most notably Rowland Ward and Edward Gerrard & Sons. The bears' aggressive standing poses make clear the era's reveries of exotic animal dangers in distant lands. As such, the bears are documents of a British cultural imaginary which has slipped—thankfully or not—forever into history.

More pressingly, from a contemporary perspective, the bears can also be read as an anxious narrative of global warming. Here are so many bears from territories under threat. But if the bears are troubling environmental documents, they also stand as quiet educators. They offer visitors an opportunity to experience the majestic size of polar bears and to appreciate personally, intimately, the dignity and exceptionality of the species. If the bears provide a critique of past collecting practices, they also make material the intrinsic worth of preserving animals. If a creature becomes extinct, no matter how much video footage and photographic images may have been amassed, nothing can ever compare to the physical presence of the animal, admittedly dead and stuffed, but a physical presence nonetheless. The taxidermied remains of passenger pigeons, quaggas, great auks, and all other extinct species are precious beyond words. They are the definition of irreplaceable.

On display in Spike Island, the bears are also purloined objects of science. The majority were taken from natural history museums where they stood as examples of their species and representatives of Arctic whiteness. The display of ten polar bears is most probably a unique historical occurrence. It would be rare to see ten polar bears—a typically solitary species—together in the wild, and such an assembly would never occur in a natural history museum. Most museums have a solitary bear, having neither the space nor the educational need to display more than one. More than one is unnecessary repetition. Amassed together within the neutral space of an art gallery, disconnected from the didactic trappings of a natural history museum, the polar bears are transfigured by their multitude and setting, together becoming animal-things that are neither fully science nor fully art: mysterious, unsettling, provocative, and overwhelmingly visually magnetic.

A one-day conference held in the gallery, titled "White Out," engaged speakers to discuss the bears' significance. The title suggests a blizzard, an environmental obliteration, a toxic erasure of words and meaning, a blank slate, a new beginning, always with the bears as off-white canvases on which humans have inscribed meaning. The ambiguous title is fitting: the physical presence of the bears cannot be entirely explained with language. Even living bears present a complex of interpretations. "We have witnessed how in living human memory," Snæbjörnsdóttir and Wilson write in the exhibition catalogue, "the image of the polar bear has been appropriated and put to the most varied and unlikely purposes—selling dreams, sweets, lifestyles, travel." A formidable predator and a Coca-Cola icon of kitschy winter wonderland fantasies, the polar bear is "a catalogue of paradoxes," a "prism with the capacity to contain and refract all manner of responses in us: fear, horror, respect, pathos, affection, humour."[2] How much more complex are taxidermied polar bears? From one angle, the polar bears are trophies of nineteenth-century

British infatuation with Arctic territories; from another, they are cautionary tales offering traces of human activity carved in nature. They are contemporary art, scientific specimens, natural wonders, and symbols of contemporary environmental anxiety. They offer the opportunity to observe intimately a fearsome man-eater and indulge in the sheer pleasure of looking at beasts that may be nearly two centuries old. At once symbolic and individual, both victimized and saved, the polar bears resist any easy interpretation. And it is this ambiguity that makes them such potent objects.

As dead and mounted animals, the bears are thoroughly cultural objects; yet as pieces of nature, the bears are thoroughly beyond culture. Animal or object? Animal and object? This is the irresolvable tension that defines all taxidermy. What, then, do the ten bears communicate to viewers? What, for that matter,

2   Bryndís Snæbjörnsdóttir and Mark Wilson, Nanoq: Flat Out and Bluesome, 2004. Photo courtesy of the artists.

can any piece of taxidermy offer? Do they talk about their makers, about human romances and obsessions with animals and nature? Or do they tell us something about themselves? As the following chapters demonstrate, with taxidermy there are no easy answers.

The reasons for preserving animals are as diverse as the fauna put on view: to flaunt a hunter's skill or virility, to contain nature, to immortalize a cherished pet, to collect an archive of the world, to commemorate an experience, to document an endangered species, to furnish evidence, to preserve knowledge, to decorate a wall, to amuse, to educate, to fascinate, to unsettle, to horrify, and even to deceive. This list can be simplified into eight distinct styles or genres of taxidermy: hunting trophies, natural history specimens, wonders of nature (albino, two-headed, etc.), extinct species, preserved pets, fraudulent creatures, anthropomorphic taxidermy (toads on swings), and animal parts used in fashion and household décor. A sportsman's trophy is a very different object from Martha, who was displayed alongside other extinct birds at the Smithsonian Institution: the last American passenger pigeon, a species shot to extinction by nineteenth-century hunters. And both are different again from *Misfits*, a disconcerting series of taxidermied animals by the internationally acclaimed contemporary artist Thomas Grünfeld, which includes such composite creatures as a monkey with a parrot head and a kangaroo with ostrich legs and a peacock head. Different again is a stuffed pet, or a herd of caribou posed in a "natural" scene behind museum glass, or a miniature diorama of kittens having tea. Despite the diverse reasons and causes for taxidermy and the plethora of genres, I argue that all taxidermy is deeply marked by human longing. Far more than just death and destruction, taxidermy always exposes the desires and daydreams surrounding human relationships with and within the natural world.

All organic matter follows a trajectory from life to death, decomposition, and ultimate material disappearance. The fact that we are born and inevitably disappear defines us, organically speaking. Taxidermy exists because of life's inevitable trudge toward dissolution. Taxidermy wants to stop time. To keep life. To cherish what is no longer as if it were immortally whole. The desire to hold something back from this inevitable course and to savor its form *in perpetuum* exhibits a peculiar sort of desire. Why this piece and not another? Why the yearning to detain what should have passed from view? Taxidermy is hardly a simple or swift practice. It takes patience, skill, time, and labor, all of which depend on an intense desire to keep particular creatures from disappearing. No doubt there are many idiosyncratic motives, but I offer seven incentives—what I call narratives of longing—that impel the creation of taxidermy: wonder, beauty, spectacle, order, narrative, allegory, and remembrance. The seven longings take different shapes. Some are aesthetic hungers; others are driven by intellectual concerns, memory, or the force of personality, but they share a similar instability. As the very word *longing* suggests, fulfillment is always just beyond reach.

Although each of the seven chapters draws out a particular longing, to a degree, all seven longings are palpable in all taxidermy. All taxidermy is a disorientating, unknowable thing. All taxidermy is driven to capture animal beauty. It is always a spectacle, whose meaning depends in part on the particularity of the animal being displayed. It is motivated by the desire to tell ourselves stories about who we are and about our journey within the larger social and natural world. It is driven by what lies beneath the animal form, by the metaphors and allegories we use to make our world make sense. And finally, taxidermy is always a gesture of remembrance: the beast is no more. In short, the chapters all attempt to get to the heart of taxidermy by answering the two fundamental questions: why would anyone want to preserve an animal, and what is this animal-thing now?

Longing is itself a peculiar condition. It works as a kind of ache connecting the stories we tell ourselves and the objects we use as storytellers. In a sense, longing is a mechanism for both pacifying and cultivating various lusts and hungers by creating objects capable of generating significance. And here, objects of remembrance or souvenirs are exemplary.

A souvenir is a token of authenticity from a lived experience that lingers only in memory: a shell from a beach walk, or a trinket purchased on holiday. Even simple objects embolden the longing to look back and inward into our past, to recount the same stories again and again, to speak wistfully, that gives birth to the souvenir: without the demands of nostalgia, we would have no need for such objects of remembrance. But nostalgia cannot be sustained without loss, and souvenirs are always only fragments of increasingly distant experiences or events, and so are necessarily incomplete, partial, and impoverished. Yet this loss is precisely a souvenir's power: never fully recouping an event as it actually was but resonating with golden memories. In other words, a souvenir is a potent fragment that erases the distinction between what actually was and what we dream or desire it to have been. Equally important, its existence depends on the impossibility of fulfillment. The longings and daydreams encapsulated by souvenirs can never be fulfilled—the cherished experiences exist forever in the past.[3]

Remembrance is only one of the narratives explored in the following chapters, yet it offers a solid illustration of the relationships between storytelling, potent objects, and the uncertainty (or impossibility) of complete satisfaction that underlie all taxidermy. Taxidermy is motivated by the desire to preserve particular creatures, but what motivates *that* desire is something far more nebulous than the animal on display: the coveted object both is and is not the driving impulse. As with objects of remembrance, all narratives of longing and their taxidermied animals work together in curious circular tension. On the one hand, desire creates its objects: taxidermied animals are not naturally occurring. On the other, it is the animal itself that activates, substantiates, and perpetuates human craving for its vitality and form. This unfulfillable desiring permeates all taxidermy: the longing for the beast (for its beauty, menace, or familiarity) scars the beast's beauty, menace, or familiarity.

The seven longings take their own shape and emphasis, but they are all driven to capture and make meaningful the potency of nature. If we were unaffected by nature, we would have no need to render it immortal. It is this simultaneous need to capture pieces of nature and to tell stories—whether cultural, intellectual, emotional, or aesthetic—about their significance within human lives that marks taxidermy so deeply with longing. We do not desire souvenirs from unmemorable events, and the same is true of all pieces of preserved nature: we do not need or desire parts that cannot speak to us of where we are, what we think we know, and who we dream ourselves to be.

Storytelling, as we will see, is an important component of all encounters with taxidermy and, for that matter, most encounters with nature. By storytelling, I mean human interpretation and the creation of significance: the way we pull pieces of the world into meaningful and eloquent shapes. From cave paintings of animal spirits to zoos, from pets to hunting trophies, nature and all its nonhuman inhabitants have remained vital to the human search for significance and fulfillment. As Stephen Kellert writes, the "human need for nature is linked not just to the material exploitation of the environment but also to the influence of the natural world on our emotional, cognitive, aesthetic, and even spiritual development. Even the tendency to avoid, reject, and, at times, destroy elements of the natural world can be viewed as an extension of an innate need to relate deeply and intimately with the vast spectrum of life about us."[4] The parts of nature we fear or admire, the ways we connect with animals, the philosophies we project over the natural world, and the hierarchies we build are all forms of human striving to make sense of our world and our place within it. Yet nature is its own abundance and exists beyond "meaning," which is forever a human urge and imposition. More often than not, what we choose to say about nature reveals more about human beliefs, desires, and fears than it does about the natural world. This is not to say that nature is forever trapped beneath a murky human-painted veneer and always best appreciated as a construction of cultural and political agendas. But it is to say that nature is a chaos of forms and colors and shapes and forces, and the various ways in which that chaos has been untangled and made legible should never be taken as nature's truth but rather as nature's possibility within a human imaginary.

Taxidermy is one medium for imposing the possibility of meaning or, more accurately, for exposing the human longing to discover meaning in nature, but always obliquely and often in contradictory ways. There is nothing unequivocal about the practice except that the animals are dead but not gone. In writing this book, I hope to clarify what sort of thing a preserved animal becomes—what does it mean to be dead but not gone?—and also to explore why anyone would desire such an animal-thing to exist.

Taxidermy has a rich history. Most Western cultures have their own particular taxidermy traditions, their own taxidermists, their own collections and creatures. All natural history museums likewise have their own institutional histories and display tactics. The subject is simply too broad, too nuanced, and too detailed to discuss in full. In part to negotiate such "arkish" proportions, several of the chapters deal with only one species. "Beauty" focuses on hummingbirds, "Spectacle" on lions, and "Order" on zebras. Other creatures were hardly unaffected by those particular longings, but I hope that these particular creatures offer exemplary windows onto the particular narrative of longing. Although I make excursions into various eras and cultures, the heart of this book rests in nineteenth-century

England. This focus is partly driven by my own interest and expertise and partly because taxidermy achieved its apotheosis in the Victorian imagination. Certainly other nineteenth-century traditions similarly elevated taxidermy as a superior technology for making nature visible, but it is, I believe, the heritage of Victorians' attitudes and assumptions that in great part shapes how taxidermy is understood (and perhaps misunderstood) today.

Derived from the Greek words for order, *taxis*, and skin, *derma*, taxidermy literally means the arrangement of skin, but the practice has never been a pragmatic process of assembly. How could it be? It requires the death of our closest compatriots—our fellow sentient creatures. Looking at dead animals necessarily engages our emotions. The following chapters explore this engagement from a variety of aesthetic, intellectual, cultural, and ethical perspectives, but whatever the analytical angle, the raw fact is that taxidermied animals carry their deaths with them.

Death is what makes taxidermy possible, but taxidermy is not motivated by brutality. It does not aim to destroy nature but to preserve it, as if immortally, and to perpetuate the wonderment of nature's most beautiful forms. As such, taxidermy always tells us stories about particular cultural moments, about the spectacles of nature that we desire to see, about our assumptions of superiority, our yearning for hidden truths, and the loneliness and longing that haunt our strange existence of being both within and apart from the animal kingdom.

WONDER

1

A REPOSITORY OF WONDERS

On October 5, 1687, after a month of delays due to contrary winds, the *Assistance* at last put out from Plymouth and set sail for Jamaica with Sir Hans Sloane aboard. Earlier that year, Sloane had accepted the position of personal physician to Christopher Monck, the second duke of Albemarle, who had been appointed governor of the island. As a young physician in his late twenties and a passionate naturalist, Sloane was more than willing for the adventure. Since his youth, he had avidly studied nature's most wondrous parts, particularly exotic creatures from distant, barely known geographies. "I had seen most of those Kinds of Curiosities," Sloane wrote, "which were to be found either in the Fields, or in the Gardens or Cabinets of the Curious," yet explanations of such "Strange Things, which I met with in Collections, and, was inform'd, were common in the West-Indies, were not so satisfactory as I desired."[1] The appointment was exactly the opportunity to investigate such "Strange Things" for himself. As Sloane admits, "next to the serving of his grace and family in my profession, my business is to see what I can meet withal that is extraordinary in nature in those places."[2]

A salamanders egg from the East Indies. The young one seen in it. . . .
A ratt which was starved to death in a wall given me by Mr Fowler. . .
The fore Paws of an Orang Outang or Chimpanzi from the Duke of Richmonds Sale. . . .
A very large Sea horses tooth. . .
The skin of a black fox from Carolina where they are very rare & found only on the mountains. . .

—FROM THE UNPUBLISHED CATALOGUE OF SIR HANS SLOANE'S COLLECTION, 1680–1753

Even before the *Assistance* had left English shores, Sloane was already at work observing and describing anything and everything that caught his attention, beginning with a viscerally detailed discussion of seasickness, its causes, effects, and various remedies. (Sloane recommended that his patients drink a little warm water or beer "to make all come up easily, on which they found Relief." Nothing worked for Sloane himself, who was immediately sick "upon the least puff of Wind extraordinary.") During the three-month voyage south, Sloane captured phosphorescence with a bucket, concluding that the "Sparkles" were probably caused by tiny decaying particles of fish. He noticed that sharks came about the ships when the fleet was becalmed. He detailed interesting plants native to the islands of Madeira, and while still five hundred leagues from Barbados, he captured a large live grasshopper that had blown out to sea.[3]

The duke died within ten months of landing in Jamaica, a sad fact that cannot be blamed entirely on his physician: the duke was a notorious drinker. Sloane dutifully embalmed the body for travel, and he, the embalmed duke, and the duke's widow would have immediately returned home if not for the political turmoil surrounding the throne in England. But Sloane's interlude was hardly idle. During his fifteen months in Jamaica and his travels to neighboring islands, Sloane collected, preserved, sketched, and documented an abundance of "Strange Things," returning home with more than eight hundred specimens of animals, plants, and minerals, which established Sloane's early collection.

Over the following decades of his life, Sloane's collection became something of a wonder itself. It grew to astonishing size and range, encompassing all things of human or natural origin, including natural history specimens, coins and medals, antiquities from Egypt, Greece, and the Orient, books and manuscripts, prints and drawings, and various ethnographic collections from Africa, the Americas, Asia, and the West Indies. It was a cabinet of curiosities beyond compare, attracting admirers from across Europe. And when visitors described the contents of the eleven large rooms housing the collection, they invariably fell into swollen list making in the effort to encompass the superabundance of "extraordinarily curious and valuable things," as Zacharias Conrad von Uffenbach put it in 1710.[4] There were simply too many wonders, too many visual delights to describe.

Sloane's natural history collection contained specimens from the far reaches of the known world, from the stuffed skin of a zebra to a white swallow from

Buenos Aires, from a New Guinean bird of paradise and eggs from a Chinese pheasant to a great auk from northern Scotland. It grew to be one of the most significant collections ever amassed by one individual.[5] At the time of his death in 1753, Sloane's vertebrate collection (not to mention his collections of insects, shells, sea urchins, crustaceans, and eggs) encompassed 1,886 specimens of "Vipers, Serpents, &c.," 2,076 specimens of fish, 1,172 birds, and 1,886 animals, some whole, but most in fragments, or, as the catalogue describes them, various animals "and their Parts."[6]

Indeed, snippets of fish, leg bones, horns, and loose feathers composed the majority of natural history specimens in early modern collections. As we will see, early preservation techniques were hardly capable of capturing specimens that matched collectors' ardor for exotic wonders. Besides a limited number of birds and beasts preserved whole, Sloane's vertebrate collection was divided into smaller assemblies of parts from divers animals: a collection of teeth, a collection of feathers, one of beaks, another of skins, and an assortment of horns.[7] If naturalists and collectors did not travel to see exotic nature for themselves, what arrived from distant lands invariably arrived as enigmatic bits and pieces. Among the more intriguing items in Sloane's collection were two cataracts taken out of the eyes of a Greenland fox, the bill of a toucan, the back part of an ostrich's eye, the skin of a polecat, a condor feather, the head and hock of a red-headed Bengal crane, the trunk and eyes of an elephant, a buffalo horn, a beaver's tail and the pickled remains of her genitalia in a glass jar, a patch of skin from a lion, and a hair ball from the stomach of a local cow—shards, morsels, wondrously strange fragments of nature that teased along the edges of reason and confounded all belief.[8]

This first chapter examines the natural wonders in sixteenth- and seventeenth-century collections, particularly how the materiality, the *thingness* of these rarities, provoked creative thought. It is true enough to say that taxidermy evolved from rude preservation precisely to preserve such wonders of the natural world. If collectors and naturalists had not been amazed at the eccentric varieties of nature's forms, the art of taxidermy might not have been developed until the eighteenth century, when taxonomy and classification of the ordinary—not extraordinary—arose to hold sway over human imaginations. But with wonder came the desire to possess and revisit, and rough-and-ready preservation techniques slowly matured into what we now call taxidermy.

A strange fish! Were I in England now, as once I was, and had but this fish painted, not a holiday fool there but would give a piece of silver: there would this monster make a man; any strange beast there makes a man.

—TRINCULO, on first setting eyes on Caliban (Shakespeare, *The Tempest*, 2.2.27–32)

For medieval and Renaissance Europeans, natural wonders included all strange phenomena—some real, some mythical. Wonders did occasionally spring up in Europe—abnormal births such as conjoined twins, two-headed calves, or the hermaphroditic child born in Italy in 1512 with wings instead of arms and a horn growing from its head.[9] Most wonders, however, were engendered somewhere over the horizon. Before Columbus opened a route to an unknown continent and initiated the flow of birds of paradise, hummingbirds, and armadillos, and, in time, new routes to wombats, kangaroos, and platypuses, the wonders that cluttered up the antechambers of princes and the cabinets of curious collectors had been mainly of Asian origin: the claws and eggs of the mythical beasts known as griffins (part lion, part eagle), crocodiles, unicorn horns, ivory tusks perhaps ornately carved into drinking horns, sharks' teeth, lion skins, and serpents' tongues. The East was surrounded by exotic romance, and medieval writers envisioned a topography of wonders along the fringe of the known world beyond which nothing existed but a giant blue encircling sea.[10]

Transported back from the edge, exotic curiosities were portals to those distant lands, offering enticingly incomplete visions of worlds filled with incalculable strangeness. Medieval rhetoric of the marvelous, as Lorraine Daston and Katharine Park explain in *Wonders and the Order of Nature, 1150–1750*, was "first elaborated in the twelfth- and thirteenth-century literature of romance—in its rhapsodic descriptions of Eastern luxuries, its emphasis on quest and adventure, its exploitation of the unexpected, its taste for exotic settings, its reliance on magical natural objects, its constant invocation of wonder and wonders, described in terms of diversity, and its association of those wonders with wealth and power."[11] The fabulous tales of Marco Polo took the romance of exotic travel writing to new heights. During his twenty-four years in Asia, he traveled the Silk Road, became the confidant of the Kublai Khan, and amazed his readers with extraordinary tales. Describing the Indian kingdom of Kollam (Quilon) in 1294, Marco Polo writes:

> The country produces a diversity of beasts different from those of all the rest of the world. There are black lions with no other visible colour or marks. There are parrots of many kinds. Some are entirely white—as

white as snow—with feet and beaks of scarlet. Others are scarlet and blue—there is no lovelier sight than these in the world. And there are some very tiny ones, which are also objects of great beauty. Then there are peacocks of another sort than ours and much bigger and handsomer, and hens too that are unlike ours. What more need I say? Everything there is different from what it is with us and excels both in size and beauty. They have no fruit the same as ours, no beast, no bird.[12]

Bigger, more beautiful, strangely colored and patterned. Azure breasts, flushed beaks, tufts, plumes, rosy throats, and vermilion eyes. As Sir John Mandeville (perhaps the supreme medieval spinner of travel tales) wrote, in the Eastern parts of the world, beyond lands known to Europeans, lived many strange and marvelous things: "it behoves a man who wants to see wonders sometimes to go out of his way."[13] Diamonds grew as big as hazelnuts, and giant shrubs were bent low with fragrant spices; there were self-sacrificing fish, blue elephants, wild geese with two heads, and races of pygmies that lived on the smell of wild apples.[14] The marvels of the East streamed in an endless current of wonder. Anything, it seemed, could exist, any combination of colors, any variation in form.

Such rare exotics were appreciated as part of the natural world, yet they quivered at the edges of human comprehension. They suggested that untold forces were at work in the earthly realm, and they became vehicles for infinite reveries of possibility, expectation, and hope in a way that lowly nature, abundantly available—cows, pigs, and cabbages—never could. And certainly, as Jacques Le Goff suggests in his classic work *The Medieval Imagination*, the exaggeration of marvelous qualities was delicious compensation for the banality and harsh rigors of daily life. "It is no accident," Le Goff writes, "that one of the few medieval inventions was that of never-never land, which first appeared in the thirteenth century. One can trace earlier roots or roughly equivalent notions, but the thing itself was a creation of the Middle Ages."[15] Exotic marvels inflamed the imagination. Just a piece of a crocodile or a hippopotamus tooth would do, not to mention a crust of griffin's hide or a unicorn horn. From snippets entire landscapes were imagined, each with its own unique organic rhythms, places where men metamorphosed into storks, and herbs were cultivated to restore sight to blind sheep.[16]

And when outlandish creatures began surging into Europe in the sixteenth century from a previously unknown continent to the west, nothing, it seemed, was impossible. As Lawrence Weschler puts it, "*Europe's mind was blown*" by the sheer volume of wondrous things inhabiting the Americas. It was not simply the number of unknown creatures flooding into European ports; it was "how the palpable reality of such artifacts so vastly expanded the territory of the now readily conceivable."[17] Wonder became the predominant European response to the radical difference offered by the New World.[18] If an entire continent had lain hidden from Europe, filled with strange beasts unknown to even the great ancient naturalists Aristotle and Pliny, what limits could be placed on nature's creative potential? Intoxicated by the seemingly endless discoveries of new lands, new people, new plants, herbs, spices, animals, and birds, all with untold potential and powers, the curious elite of Europe could scarcely satisfy their thirst for more wonder, more unknowing. The age of wonder was insatiable.

By the mid-sixteenth century, exotic and wonderful things were literally spilling out of European ports and into the collections of anyone who could afford them. Whatever was rare in occurrence, exotic in origin, or in any way unusual or curious, prodigious, or outlandish was avidly collected. Collectors mingled artifacts indiscriminately in chaotic displays of visual delight. Strange fish and mummified reptiles hung from the ceiling, stuffed birds and mammals lined the walls, shells and dried reptiles were arranged in drawers, and pickled sea creatures stood in glass jars in open cabinets. After all, the driving momentum behind such cabinets of wonder, or *Wunderkammern*, as early collections were known, was to provoke wonder at the dizzying variety of nature. To collect is not to mirror the world but to remake it, and cabinets of wonder did not create mundane, ordinary worlds but worlds filled with fantastic creatures and infinite possibility. The collections exposed their creators' yearning for wonder: wonder at the diversity of nature, wonder at the shapes and colors of exotic creatures, and wonder aroused by the secret workings of the natural world, only ever half-revealed.

The collection established by the Holy Roman emperor Rudolf II in the late sixteenth century in Prague Castle contained the leg of a cassowary, a dodo, various parts of twenty birds of paradise, an embalmed hen with three legs, and the pelt of a white vulture from India. Among the curiosities of the sixteenth-century Veronese apothecary Francesco Calzolari were a mummified deformed human head, a bat, a flying fish, an assortment of eggs, and a spotted creature with enormous claws. The museum of Ferrante Imperato, an apothecary in Naples and a

RITRATTO DEL MVSEO DI
FERRANTE IMPERATO

close contemporary of Calzolari, was described as a "repository of incomparable rarities," among which were a male and female chameleon, "an extraordinary greate crocodile," a salamander, an armadillo, what appears to be a small walrus, a two-headed dog, a two-headed snake, and a lizard with two bodies.

Displayed in the entrance of the Leiden anatomical theater in 1659 were an elephant's head, the skin and horn of a rhinoceros, a dog's skeleton, a heron, the snout of an unknown fish, and the bristly skin of an unidentified Brazilian beast. Affectionately known as "the Ark," the seventeenth-century collection of John Tradescant

3 The museum of Ferrante Imperato, in Ferrante Imperato's *Dell'historia natural* (Venice, 1672). From the collections of the Ernst Mayr Library, Museum of Comparative Zoology, Harvard University.

and his son contained a flying squirrel, the testicles of a beaver, a pelican, a dodo, a wildcat from Virginia, and an egg that was suspected to be from a dragon.[19]

Wonders were turbulent, category-shattering, awe-inspiring, intoxicating objects, but they were not outside culture. They belonged to an affective category of things that functioned symbolically, allowing the collector to harness and display physical invisibilities in concrete items. As Krzysztof Pomian notes, "Objects were not seen but seen *through*." In a sense, curiosities were collected because they acted as portals through which Europeans could experience and, in a sense, possess exotic lands, different societies, and outlandish creatures without traveling.[20] Considering the difficulty of accessing those distant lands—the months of sea travel, the networks of explorers, traveling naturalists, merchants, and transport ships—the fact that specimens arrived in Europe at all provoked wonder and delight. Within the economy of wonders during the late Renaissance and early modern period, such awed appraisal was transferred to collectors' good taste and wealth. Eliciting amazement through the conspicuous display of wondrous objects—at least to one's privileged guests—was a means of endowing oneself with prestige. Possessing a museum of eccentric rarities was a means of climbing the social ladder.[21]

But more than an index of civility and wealth, from what might seem a promiscuous hoarding of raucous objects, historians have teased out particular processes of Western intellectual and cultural formation. Spanning the early development of modern scientific thought in Europe, from the mid-sixteenth century to the early decades of the eighteenth century, cabinets of wonder stand on the cusp of two separate but intimately entwined traditions of collecting. One led backward in time to a world resonant with the power of relics, mystical visions, and mythological lore; the other pointed toward what would slowly germinate and sprout into the ordered field of science based on empirical observation. The period has been described as an interim between the rule of religion and that of science, a period over which curiosity held sway and, even more particularly, an age in which things themselves were crucial for knowledge. Inquiry necessitated a collection, and collections exuded a vibrant interest in things as *things*, a tactile, theatrical world of materiality.[22] In short, the act of collecting became an essential practice for naturalists, who hoped that possessing nature would lead eventually to an understanding of her contents.[23]

Culture always shapes infatuation. Sloane, Calzolari, Imperato, and the Tradescants were all men of their age, addicted to the unknown and obscure. Still, despite such cultural motivations, some things are particularly potent, particularly mesmerizing. Parts of nature that are rare, exotic, or otherwise radically unknown configure precisely such a category of intoxicating things. After all, a wonder is simultaneously an object *and* the reaction it inflames. A wonder is not a wonder if it fails to startle and disrupt expectation. In a sense, preserving a strange creature was as much a means of prolonging the emotional encounter of unknowing as it was a method of hindering natural decay. Hovering between materiality and emotion, some objects have an intrinsic power to disorient, provoke, and excite.

As part of his larger work on poetry, *La deca ammirabile*, published in 1587, Francesco Patrizi lists twelve sources of wonder available to the poet: ignorance, fable, novelty, paradox, augmentation, departure from the usual, the extranatural, the divine, great utility, the very precise, the unexpected, and the sudden.[24] For Patrizi, wonder was a shocking encounter with obscurity tinged with delicious anticipation. It was the tingling experience of going back and forth between what our reason tells us cannot be so and what our eyes cannot deny is so. When something new and unexpected appears before us, Patrizi explains, it "creates a movement in our soul, almost contradictory in itself of believing and not believing. Of believing because the thing is seen to exist; and of not believing because it is sudden, new, and not before either known, thought, or believed able to exist."[25] Even the usual could provoke wonder if its appearance was somehow unexpected: a shadow, for example, strangely enlarged and looming up a wall could momentarily disorient. In other words, wonderful objects were not merely seen but *experienced* as visceral and emotional events.

Writing for poets, Patrizi encourages an indulgence in such a poetics of strangeness to create startling scenarios and dramatic tension. Another, parallel tradition of wonder was hardly so enthusiastic. Like Patrizi, the seventeenth-century French philosopher René Descartes described wonder as a "sudden surprise of the soul" when one encountered something rare and unknown. "When the first encounter with some object surprises us, and we judge it to be new or very different from what we formerly knew, or from what we supposed that it ought to be, that causes us to wonder and be surprised." But in contrast to Patrizi, Descartes considered wonder constructive only if it led to knowledge. Otherwise, like all addictions, too much wonder muffled clear thinking and stupefied reason. If indulged, wonder became a sickness, "the malady of those who suffer from a blind curiosity—that is, who seek out things that are rare solely to wonder at them, and not for the purpose of really knowing them."[26] Descartes's sickness was perhaps Patrizi's ideal state of poetic creation: an awestruck loosening into unknowing.

By aligning wonder and ignorance, Descartes was following the ancient philosophy of Aristotle, who described wonder as an initial step toward knowledge. Wonder, Aristotle claimed, was the seed from which our interest in anything was first aroused. "For it is owing to their wonder that men both now begin and at first began to philosophize; they wondered originally at the obvious difficulties, then advanced little by little and stated difficulties about the great matters."[27] The unknown qualities of strange objects hinted at a hidden but rational design, which if understood could explain the object's existence. In a sense, Descartes and Aristotle sought to domesticate wonders, to make them comprehensible and to normalize their mystery.[28] In contrast, Patrizi sought no explanations: wonders were simply experienced as provocatively, enticingly unknowable entities.

The theories of Descartes and Patrizi lie at opposite ends of the intellectual spectrum that connects sixteenth-century collections of marvels and early eighteenth-century repositories of natural specimens. Over the course of the seventeenth century, an increasingly sophisticated culture of wonder emerged, or rather, wonder was superseded by curiosity, and curiosity spawned natural facts. Yet poetic explanations of phenomena were not necessarily incompatible with rational investigation. Some things, as we will see, were too obscure to decipher by purely empirical means.

In examining the properties of particularly compelling things, historian of science Lorraine Daston notes that some things "speak irresistibly, and not only by interpretation, projection, and puppetry. It is neither entirely arbitrary nor entirely entailed which objects will become eloquent when, and in what cause. The language of things derives from certain properties of the things themselves, which suit the cultural purposes for which they are enlisted."[29] That is, the language of things arises as much from their physicality—their shape and size, their shininess or perfection—as from their particular meaning within a cultural moment. Although their voices may grow fainter or louder as culture shifts and decades pass, although they may be ignored or discarded by subsequent generations, certain things are inherently charismatic. These elusive and somewhat magical things reverberate with a multiplicity of significances that always hover just beyond full explanation. "As they circulate through our lives," cultural historian Bill Brown writes, "we look *through* objects (to see what they disclose about history, society, nature, or culture—above all, what they disclose about *us*), but we only catch a glimpse of things."[30] Simply put, like an extraordinary work of art, things possess us. They resonate deeply within us. They cannot be ignored.

As the following chapters demonstrate, all taxidermied animals are such things, and they are always surrounded by a poetics of strangeness. They exist just beyond full elucidation; they are always more than mere objects fully explainable by their cultural moment. But then, animals—whether living or dead, wondrous or familiar—are always so much more than any imposed human meaning could possibly explain.

Consider, for example, a two-headed kitten or a brain coral. Perhaps we can explain why the coral is so fabulously shaped or why a fetus mutates, but does an explanation make these animal-things any less mysterious, any less visually arresting? This obdurate materiality that resists full disclosure is precisely the source of a wonder's imaginative potency: if it could be fully known, if we could fully account for its qualities, form, and reason for existence, it would lose its mesmerizing quality and become just another object. Our twenty-first-century science tells us that an anomalous birth is just a random genetic misfire. But for all the biological explanations, a two-headed cat will always suggest an underlying mystery. If such a creature was born, what other shapes and combinations could also be produced? Nature suddenly seems more alive with its own autonomous and creative potential, albeit with more disturbing anatomical possibilities than we might like to consider. As always, the wonderful casts a spell, momentarily transporting viewers out of themselves, out of their confident knowledge of the workings of the world, and like a sudden tempest scatters everything they believed to be true.

And it is perhaps only when confronted with a monstrous birth that contemporary viewers can even begin to understand the enthralling experience of stepping into early collections. In a room filled with exotic, unknown, and abnormal creatures jumbled together in provocative groupings, there is the sense that anything might exist somewhere in the world, any combination of parts, any size, shape, or structure. If wonder can be an initial step toward curiosity and erudition, it can just as well lead toward explosive imaginings. But still, what did these animal pieces actually look like?

From princely antechambers and baroque cabinets of wonder to the gatherings of pharmacists and early modern repositories of material facts, whether private or institutional, whether spurred by natural philosophy, curiosity, or social prestige, two features remain constant in all such collections. First, what was gathered was deemed to be visually and viscerally fascinating.[31] More important, what lingered on display was dependent on the appetite of moths, ants, and maggots and the progress of rot, dampness, and mold. The bits and pieces composing early collections offer only the barest glimpse of nature's forms. Snouts, testicles, feathers, and bristly skins are objects more inclined to breed awe and mystery than clear-eyed facts. As much as exotic creatures, collections exhibited nature's organic urge toward dissolution and decay.

GRAPPLING WITH NATURE

...another paradise bird in a very bad state and eaten by moths ...

—FROM THE INVENTORY OF RUDOLF II'S CABINET, 1607–11

Early taxidermists did not start from scratch but expanded on the preservatives and techniques of several other trades, namely, those of tanners, upholsterers, saddlers, furriers, and clothing makers who had long since perfected the art of preparing animal skins for their various uses. Taxidermists simply elaborated on their arts by shaping dried skins into some semblance of animals. In fact, well into the nineteenth century, much taxidermy was really a fancy species of upholstery: a tanned skin stuffed with soft material sometimes held in form by wires bent and looped into stiff backbones. And, of course, there was the ancient knowledge of mummification.

The Egyptians perfected a highly sophisticated method of bodily preservation, which they used on humans as well as animals. Cats, dogs, bulls, mice, hawks, ibises, crocodiles, and other sacred animals or pets of rulers were carefully preserved and entombed alongside their human companions. After the brain was removed through the nose and other internal organs through small incisions, the body was washed inside and out with astringent palm wine and then filled with pounded aromatics such as myrrh, cassia, camphor, and cinnamon. The body was then covered in natron, a type of salt mined from dry lake beds near the Nile River, which accelerated the dehydration of the body. After a period of several months, the body was washed again and wrapped with bands of fine linen smeared on the inside with a gluelike gum. Essentially, mummification prevents putrefaction by allowing the body to release moisture slowly; the skin and muscles become rigid and the tissues shrink, adhering to the skeleton. Preventing rehydration was just as important as the initial dehydration, and at various stages of the process water-repelling products such as oils, beeswax, and resins were rubbed over the bodies. Many creatures spilling out of early cabinets of curiosity were prepared by some process of mummification. Fish, snakes, and lizards were commonly dehydrated—either air-dried or slowly baked in ovens—rubbed with various astringent substances and salts to cure the skin and deter insects, and then lacquered into a hard and shiny shell.

Because mummification leaves the skin intact and in place, the process cannot properly be considered taxidermy. Crucially, taxidermy involves *removing* skins from bodies, discarding all flesh and viscera, and rearranging the skins in a life-like manner. The word *taxidermy* literally means the arrangement of skin, and it applies to creatures that are preserved *as if still alive*. Neither mummification nor other forms of bodily preservation, such as shrunken heads, strive for a liveliness in form, although the techniques preserve anatomical features with a high degree of precision.[32] And this leads to perhaps the most acute difference between taxidermy and most other processes of bodily preservation: the distinction between the palpable world of materials and the spiritual otherworld of invisible forces.

The techniques developed by various cultures to preserve the bits and pieces of dead humans and animals were secret arts, frequently associated with religious ceremonies and mystical rites. Protecting the dead from decay was variously understood as a means of easing the spirit's transition between this world and the next, harnessing unnatural forces, or accessing secrets known only to the gods. Preserved body parts were links to the afterworld and were accordingly revered as symbols of strength and worldly representations of unworldly powers. In an effort to ensure abundant harvests, the Maori sometimes placed the skull, bones, and dried heads of ancestors on the perimeter of their fields in the hope of recruiting ancestral aid. Some North American First Nation peoples were known to use the preserved heads of porcupines, foxes, raccoons, and eagles to decorate their clothing and equipment. The Western Christian tradition also has its share of revered relics. The shriveled toes and fingers, vials of blood, and preserved hearts or other body fragments of saints were displayed in early Christian churches and venerated by pilgrims who believed in the power of a saintly morsel to alleviate suffering or simply to transport worshippers to a higher spiritual plane from which to contemplate the divine.

The common Flying-fish (*Exocœtus evolans*) is a marine species of gregarious habit, and remarkable in being able to take a skimming flight, from which it derives its name.

The ordinary length of a Flying-fish is from ten inches to a foot, its chief characteristics are the great length of the pectoral fins, and the blunt head. It is quite certain that these fish take their flights to escape from their enemies. It must be clearly understood that the flight is not prolonged by any flapping of the fins, its continuance being entirely due to the original impetus of the leap.

4 Dehydrated flying fish from the nineteenth century. Photo courtesy of Craig Finch / Finch & Co.

But, technically speaking, none of this is taxidermy. Taxidermy originated as and has remained a secular art for portraying the physical shapes and sizes of animals. Almost without exception, the practice has never been used for spiritual intercessions.[33] And while various bits and pieces of taxidermied creatures in the medieval and Renaissance periods suggested that divine forces were at work in the natural world, and sometimes lifted the minds and hearts of observers to contemplate God's wondrously creative powers, these early wonders are best described as evocative and provocative entities. For example, in 1260 a crocodile was given to King Alfonso X by the sultan of Egypt. When the animal died, its body was dried and hung in the Portal of the Lizard (named for the reptile), which leads from the cloister to the Cathedral of Seville. The crocodile eventually decayed, however, and was replaced by a wooden replica. But still the creature was not worshipped as a god; preserving its body was not understood as a way of preserving any mystical powers. Rather, it was a potent *thing*, mysterious and entrancing, but a material presence that offered a palpable expression of God's manifold creative acts on earth. In other words, taxidermy has always striven, simply and rather mundanely, to perpetuate the ability to look at animals.

The astringent barks, salts, spices, resins, and gums used in mummification were also crucial to the process of taxidermy. The most popular included salt and hot spices like pepper, cinnamon, sulfur, potassium nitrate (known as saltpeter), potash, alum, tobacco, frankincense, and myrrh. Many spices not only cured skins and masked bad smells but were also natural antifungals, insecticides, and antiseptics. Myrrh was among the most effective (and most expensive) preservatives. The dried red-brown sap of *Commiphora myrrha*, a tree indigenous to Somalia and Ethiopia, myrrh has antifungal and antiseptic properties and a pungent, bitter smell that masks the stench of corpses. Similarly, frankincense, the white sap from a family of trees indigenous to arid climates, is an effective insecticide. It was used in ancient Egypt to fumigate wheat silos and to repel moths, mosquitoes, and sand flies. Apart from the well-appreciated dehydrating effects of salt, however, there was no consensus among early naturalists as to which spices or solutions were the most effective, which is to say that ultimately none could stop insect attacks. Nevertheless, sixteenth-century French naturalist Pierre Belon swore by salt. The American naturalist Mark Catesby favored snuff, while Manasseh Cutler, an eighteenth-century American clergyman and nature enthusiast, suggested equal parts alum, saltpeter, and pepper.[34]

The spice trade in early modern Europe was a highly profitable business: nutmeg, frankincense, cinnamon, cloves, and even pepper commanded high, often exorbitant prices. Shrewd spice merchants often returned home with exotic creatures as well, which were eagerly purchased by apothecaries, since all sorts of creatures and plants, even parts of mummies, were used in their remedial preparations. It is hardly surprising, then, that some of the first large collections of natural specimens—most notably those of Ferrante Imperato and Francesco Calzolari— were established by apothecaries. William Shakespeare immortalized exactly such an intoxicating place in *Romeo and Juliet*. When Romeo determines to join Juliet in death, he visits an apothecary in whose shop "a tortoise hung, / An Alligator stuff'd, and other skins / Of ill-shaped fishes."[35] Add to this mysterious chamber the heavy pungency of spices and decomposition. Cabinets were holistic sensory experiences for the mind, the eyes, and the nose.

Among the first uses of rudimentary bird taxidermy were falcon lures and decoys. Live birds were more effective for attacking predator birds, but stuffed decoys were also used extensively to trap pigeons, doves, grouse, and waders.[36] Although the earliest reference to stuffed bird decoys dates to the thirteenth century, since lures had been used in falconry from at least the second century, it is tempting to suggest that taxidermied decoys are equally old. Perhaps the first such instructions are from a hunting manual written by Emperor Friedrich II of Hohenstaufen in the early thirteenth century. In the third book of his famous work *De arte venandi cum avibus* (On the Art of Hunting with Birds), Friedrich explains how to preserve a crane's wing to use as a falcon lure. The wing was disjointed from the bird, all the flesh removed, and the inside skin rubbed with potash to prevent maggots and decay. The wing was then "hung in the chimney until the moisture in the flesh has completely evaporated. Although those wings that are not smoked are always more beautiful and glossier they will not last as long."[37] The results were less than beautiful, but the method was ancient and proven.

Although the interest in preserving the forms of exotic creatures increased throughout the sixteenth and seventeenth centuries, this basic process of preservation hardly advanced until the mid-eighteenth century. Skins were scraped clean of fat and muscle, rubbed with pungent spices and salt, and smoked repeatedly to deter insects. In 1555 Pierre Belon suggested opening birds longitudinally, removing their innards, spreading salt in the cavity, and hanging them to dry, while in the same year Conrad Gessner (whose father was a furrier and so who was probably familiar with preserving skins and furs) suggested filling the cavity with wool and volatile oils to keep the creature as fresh as possible.[38] Another method of preservation was even simpler. After being skinned, birds were cut in half longitudinally. One half was filled with plaster and fixed at the back of a shallow box proportional to the bird's size. An eye was inserted, and the actual beak and claws of the bird were used or represented with paint.[39]

In 1696 the English naturalist and collector James Petiver drew up one of first sets of instructions for preservation, titled "Brief Instructions for the Easie Making and Preserving Collections of all natural Curiosities," which he published as an appendix to a catalogue of his museum.[40] Petiver was an avid collector of exotic nature, and he regularly issued requests to explorers, traveling naturalists, and merchants for rare specimens from abroad. His interests were so catholic that he even advised travelers to examine the stomachs of fish: "N.B. You may often find in the *Stomachs* of *Sharks,* and other great Fish, which you catch at Sea, divers strange *Animals* not easily to be met with elsewhere, which pray look for, and preserve."[41] Such letters of request were common enough, but Petiver helpfully provided detailed instructions on how to prepare specimens for travel.

European naturalists would of course have preferred to examine live creatures, to study their habits and behaviors, but exotic birds and animals frequently died at sea. Who could guess what seeds or insects strange birds fed on, or what temperatures they preferred? Or perhaps the crew just got hungry for fresh meat after weeks of salted pork and biscuits. Hans Sloane, a frequent correspondent and close acquaintance of Petiver, vividly described the difficulties of bringing living creatures to Europe from distant locations. On March 16, 1689, Sloane set sail from Jamaica for England with a small menagerie, including an enormous yellow snake, an iguana, and an alligator kept in a tub of salt water. His seven-foot yellow snake, which had been tamed by a native to follow him everywhere, "as a Dog would his Master," escaped from its jar and was shot by the duchess's footman. His "Guana," free to run about the ship at will, was frightened by a seaman one day, leapt overboard, and drowned. And on May 14, the alligator, which Sloane had kept alive with scraps of "Guts and Garbage of Fowl, &c.," finally died. "Thus I lost, by this time of the Voyage, all my live Creatures and so it happens to most People, who lose their strange live Animals for want of proper Air, Food, or Shelter."[42]

Sloane does not relate how his preserved specimens fared, but he probably would have followed instructions similar to Petiver's. In Petiver's opinion, the best method of protecting specimens on long sea voyages was alcohol. "*All small Animals, as Beasts, Birds, Fishes, Serpents, Lizards,* and other *Fleshy Bodies* capable of *Corruption,*" were to be preserved in rum, brandy, or any other high-proof spirit. If no alcohol was available, then a strong brine of seawater would do, supplemented with three or four handfuls of salt to every gallon of water, along with a spoonful or two of alum powder if possible. The specimen was then put in a bottle, which was corked and rosined.[43] With larger birds, the entrails were to be removed and their bodies stuffed with flax, hemp, or some other fibrous material mixed with pitch and tar—a mixture known as oakum and incidentally the same material that was used to plug holes in seagoing vessels. The birds were then to be dried in the sun, wrapped tightly, and kept from moisture, the last requirement being not an easy enterprise onboard a ship. If the bird was too large to preserve whole, Petiver suggested that just its head, leg, or wing would suffice. From these murky, oven-baked, tar-smeared, ambiguous lumps of fur and feathers, naturalists fashioned specimens for their cabinets.

Preservation techniques improved little well into the eighteenth century. René-Antoine Ferchault de Réaumur, the polymath French naturalist and owner of one of the largest bird collections in eighteenth-century Europe, dissuaded traveling naturalists from attempting even rudimentary taxidermy. And what Réaumur advised was indeed rudimentary: remove the skin of the bird, discard the fleshy parts, and either fill the skin with some soft material or stretch it over a mold of the bird's shape. "The foregoing Way of preserving the Shapes of Birds," Réaumur noted, "requires a Hand used to it, and even falls short of sufficiently imitating Nature," but, he added, there was "no great Skill required" to pickle a bird in brandy, Réaumur's second method of preservation. Réaumur's third method was to embalm the animal with various spices and powders, which was particularly useful for collectors in "Countries where the Spices are cheap." Although embalming did not completely deter ravenous insects, it was an effective means of slowing, even stopping, decay and resulted in specimens that "at least . . . will smell the sweeter, and become as it were a Piece of Perfume."[44] After the bird was gutted, its body cavity, neck, and bill were filled with hot spices and astringents, and the specimen was packed in a box filled with the same mixture of spices. Réaumur warned that during the first few days and even weeks, "the Birds may cast a bad Smell." But the smell would lessen as the bird dried, and, even better, Réaumur claimed that feathers would remain attached even during long journeys, a comment that suggests that it was only by luck that creatures arrived at European ports in good enough shape to even bother mounting. In fact, early taxidermy instructions frequently offer advice on how to rebuild a bird from a pile of feathers.

Réaumur's fourth preservative method was to bake specimens in an oven "after the Bread is taken out" in order to speed up dehydration and kill insects. The process was not without its risks, but Réaumur offered several hints. To prevent singed feathers, Réaumur suggested putting "Feathers into the Oven, and to take them out 5 or 6 Minutes after; if you find that they are not singed, nor turned red, you ought not to be under any Apprehension for the Feathers of the Bird, which is to be put into the Oven." Small birds required only an hour or two, but larger, fleshier birds required longer drying time and perhaps even several turns in the oven. And rebaking was always necessary "to stop the Progress of the Evil," that is, rot and insect attacks.[45] Unlike animals preserved with alcohol or spices, however, baked skins could not be relaxed and repositioned: like a crust of bread, they were forever fixed into shape. Réaumur's crude instructions offer a clear picture of the sort of shriveled, awkward specimens arriving from abroad. Réaumur offers no suggestions on how to craft animals' expressions or elegant postures. This was rudimentary preservation of specimens, hovering briefly before the inevitable insect damage and decay set in.

The exigencies of long-distance shipboard travel always fanned and frustrated collectors' desires for exotica. According to taxidermy lore, among the first taxidermied specimens was a preserved aviary of exotic birds from the West Indies owned by a wealthy Hollander around the turn of the sixteenth century. Apparently the birds died during the voyage home, and the owner, determined to reap some advantage from the disaster, had the skins preserved. The very fact that most early taxidermy instructions were written for travelers preparing specimens for shipment suggests just how much hope and disappointment surrounded opening shipping boxes that had been months in transport. How were species to be identified from such wizened specimens, with their spotty plumage and discolored skin? As late as 1774 John Lettsom, in his guide to collecting and preserving specimens, wrote that "a more general knowledge of a good antiseptic for animal substances has been much inquired after. Owing to a want of this, many curious animals and birds particularly, come to our hands in a very imperfect state: some from foreign parts entirely miscarry, and other of the finest plumage are devoured by insects."[46]

Once back in Europe, skins were unpacked and relaxed by soaking in various solutions. Skins were typically stuffed with soft materials or molded over forms of straw tied stiffly together with wires pushed through to keep the animal upright. The methods were rough and rude, but why labor to create an expressive mount when the specimen would surely disintegrate before long? Specimens grew rank and oozed fluids, becoming a breeding ground for maggots, or else they were dried, shriveled, and cracked. Although salt and pepper were the most commonly used preservatives, one naturalist noted that specimens "never fail to become humid in moist air . . . suffer the flesh to rot, and even corrode the wires . . . till the whole drops to pieces on the least touch or motion."[47] Another naturalist commented that salt "agglutinises the beards of the feathers, takes from them their velvet appearance, attracts and retains the dust; and in the dry seasons the birds appear grey from the crystallizations of alum, and other salts, which fix on their feathers."[48] Varnishes crumbled or became opaque with age.[49] While the etchings of early collections show a large number of whole creatures, the majority of early collections until the late seventeenth century were largely composed of fragments and parts not susceptible to decay or insects, such as horns, bones, beaks, antlers, teeth, claws, feathers, eggs, tufts and balls of hair, and calcitic deposits expelled or found inside human and animal bodies. Cabinets were invariably haphazard aggregations of what could be found, transported, and kept from decay.

Surprisingly few laments of loss were written by sixteenth- and seventeenth-century collectors. Perhaps collectors were resigned to the inevitable. A rare seventeenth-century acknowledgment of the ephemerality of specimens is found in the rules that Elias Ashmole drew up in 1686 for the governance and maintenance of the Ashmolean Museum, established at Oxford University with the contents of Tradescant's Ark.[50] Article 6 stipulated that "whatsoever naturall Body that is rare, whether Birds, Insects, Fishes or the like, apt to putrefie & decay with tyme," was to be drawn and colored by a skilled artist so that if, or rather when, the specimen decayed into nothingness, some document would remain. Article 8 required that "as any particular growes old & perishing, the Keeper may remove it into one of the Closets, or other repository; & some other to be substituted."[51] As a classic piece of natural history lore, article 8 was unfortunately followed too precisely in 1755, when the curator purged the museum's moldering contents and tossed them on a bonfire. Among the "useless" items was a stuffed dodo, thought to be the last surviving taxidermied specimen in the world. Only the charred head and a foot were salvaged. They are still on display at the Oxford University Museum of Natural History.

The wizened creatures left a lot to the imagination, which was in a sense precisely their power. Sometimes they would be accompanied by notes of an observer who described the actions and behaviors of the living animal. Sometimes fragments of exotic creatures inspired fabulous tales. For example, birds of paradise, native to the Aru Islands southwest of New Guinea, were long thought to exist without legs. From the late sixteenth century, traders in search of cloves and nutmeg were awed by the birds' bizarre tail feathers. Since Europeans seemed interested only in the birds' plumage, indigenous traders removed the "superfluous" legs when preparing skins for trade. And since no European had seen the birds alive, it was believed that the birds were in fact legless.[52] A romantic mythology spread that the birds—variously known as God's birds, birds of the sun, or birds of paradise—remained in perpetual flight throughout their entire lives. The ethereal creatures touched the earth only at death. The great Swedish naturalist Carolus Linnaeus perpetuated the myth by christening the largest species *Paradisaea apoda*, or footless bird of paradise. Even by the late eighteenth century, Thomas Pennant lamented that the genus was still barely known to ornithologists: "few of them are imported into *Europe*, and those, too mutilated in their feet, wings, and other parts, or distorted by having a stick thrust within their skins, and thus too much distended."[53]

Creatures in early cabinets were not universally dreadful, but well-prepared creatures deserved special mention. For example, in his travels through England in 1710, Zacharias Conrad von Uffenbach noted "a very beautiful stuffed reindeer" in the Ashmolean Museum.[54] The Swedish naturalist Peter Kalm was similarly impressed with the birds in Hans Sloane's collection during his visit in 1748, noting several stuffed birds that "stood fast on bits of board as naturally as if they had still lived" and hummingbirds "set in their nests under glass as though they had been living."[55] Typically, however, visitors' descriptions of collections list creatures, without any mention of their appearance, in one breathless stream of rapture, piling animals and birds and serpents one on top of the other, mimicking the boisterous organizational stratagem of the collections themselves.

Without some form of preservation, exotic specimens would not have been known at all, but the general inability to maintain the physical condition of wonders from distant lands only increased their tantalizing strangeness. The raw aesthetics of rudimentary taxidermy opened vistas of questions and possibilities. In other words, these things were twofold wonders, wonderful both because the creatures were barely known and because their material forms were obscure and evanescent. In short, bad taxidermy bred wonder.

GLIMPSES OF NATURE

Wonder is the foundation of all philosophy, inquiry its progress, ignorance its end.

—MICHEL DE MONTAIGNE, "Of Cripples," in *Essays* (1580)

While increasingly based on meticulously recorded observations of "facts," speculations about the natural world throughout the seventeenth century remained tied to mythology, poetics and metaphysics, celestial influences, and the raw power of the human imagination. The trajectory of intellectual thought is rarely linear, and poetic explanations of phenomena were not necessarily incompatible with empirical investigation. Take Giovanni Battista Ferrari's 1646 treatise on citrus fruits, *Hesperides, sive, de malorum aureorum cultura et usu* (Hesperides, or Concerning the cultivation and uses of the golden apple). No more exhaustive work on a single family of plants had yet appeared. In fact, Ferrari's work stands as one of the most noteworthy endeavors of classification on any single genus of fruit before the eighteenth century. Yet when baffled by strange forms that seemed to defy all of nature's known laws (such as corniculated or horned fruits), Ferrari invented stories to explain them. For example, one digitated fruit is enlightened with the myth of the beautiful-voiced Hermonillus. Tricked into tragedy, Hermonillus, in Ovidian style, metamorphoses into a citrus tree. His feet become roots; his arms are transformed into branches, and his hands—most remarkably of all—change into the digitated fruits that Ferrari seeks to explain and classify.[56]

Not all seventeenth-century naturalists were keen to perpetuate fabulous tales and mythological explanations, and none less keen than the English philosopher, essayist, and statesman Francis Bacon. Attempting to overthrow myths, ancient lore, and deductive reasoning, Bacon's inductive philosophy was based on the accumulation of facts through observation, investigation, and experimentation. The new natural philosopher accumulated knowledge slowly and carefully, without preconceptions and without rushing to generalizations.

No one, however, not even Bacon himself, could be sure which observations would ultimately prove useful, and Bacon determined that all entities and occurrences, whether mundane or rare, were worthy of study, from celestial winds and rainbows to kidney stones and snails. No subject was too lowly to be carefully observed and marked down in what Bacon termed a table of discovery, since the importance of things was "not to be measured by what they are worth in themselves, but according to their indirect bearing upon other things and the influence they may have upon philosophy."[57] Bacon's empirical method erected a utopian dream of comprehensive knowledge on a foundation of curious crumbs and isolated particulars: knowledge did not emerge from nature whole and complete but was reached by a piecemeal road built steadily but haphazardly with random, even strange, facts. Indeed, Bacon advocated that the study of curious things and singular instances—prodigies, errors, provocative resemblances between forms—might break open new pathways for natural philosophy.[58] As Daston and Park observe, the "strange facts of seventeenth-century natural philosophy were the Ur-facts, the prototypes of the very category of the factual. Strange facts defined many (though not all) of the traits that have been the hallmark of facticity ever since: the notorious stubbornness of facts, inert and even resistant to interpretation and theory; their angular, fragmentary quality."[59] In other words, leg bones and shriveled skins were worthy of serious philosophical observation: they were the very essence of new facts.

Bacon's writings were taken as a robust call to action by naturalists. In great part to perpetuate his philosophy of observation and experimentation, the Royal Society of London for Improving Natural Knowledge was established in 1660 and soon began publishing a journal dedicated to all things worth knowing in the world. The articles published in *Philosophical Transactions* make evident the delight in isolated facts and the faith that anything might hold a clue to some greater knowledge. Article titles from the first fifty years include "Observable Touching Petrification," "Observables upon a Monstrous Head," "Observables in the Body of the Earl of Balcarres," "An Observation of Saturne," and "An Observation Concerning a Blemish in an Horses Eye." One article concerns "a Monstrous Calf, and Some Things Observable in the Anatomy of a Human Ear," another "the Luminous Appearance Observable in the Wake of Ships in the Indian Seas." The first word of travelers' reports seems almost invariably to be "Observations" or "Observables."

Soon after the Royal Society was comfortably settled at Gresham College, members began donating specimens and accumulating a natural history cabinet. By 1681, when Nehemiah Grew's catalogue of the repository was published, the collection housed an unruly swarm of animal morsels: hair balls, the heart of a sea tortoise, an otter, the "pistle" of a beaver, the leg of a dodo, a merman's rib, the skin of a monstrous calf with two heads, various strange hooves, and tails from a rhinoceros, an Indian cow, and a beaver. Of the animal and bird specimens (not including chameleons, lizards, salamanders, snakes, and aquatic mammals), Grew lists 41 whole creatures and 124 parts. It is an ironic twist in the history of natural science that a methodology based on amassing particulars and isolated facts was frequently limited to studying bits and pieces of animals. How was knowledge to be squeezed out of these enigmatic shards?

Grew was not daunted. While the specimens were in essence the same wondrously opaque bits as those that evoked awe and allegory in other collectors, Grew, emboldened by Bacon's philosophy of particulars, considered the materials "a great abundance of matter for any Man's Reason to work upon."[60] The catalogue records his scrupulous observations, documenting the length, size, shape, and any distinguishing feature of each specimen. The detail of each entry varies considerably, however, from a single line to several pages, and it is tempting to suggest that the length of the entry was dependent on the quality of specimen. The catalogue is one of the earliest clear-eyed documents of pure observation, completely eschewing myth and poetry. For example, Grew dismissed the notion that birds of paradise were legless as a "silly fancy." Two notable exceptions to his clear-eyed empiricism are a merman's rib and a bone said to be taken from a mermaid's head. Grew does, however, refer to the merman as a "Fish" and compares the head bone to that of a manatee.[61]

Yet Bacon's philosophical mandate did not consist in mere descriptions of things. Bacon encouraged naturalists to look *through* materials in order to acquire a deeper understanding of nature's processes and laws. For example, in his *Abecedarium naturae* (Alphabet book of nature), Bacon proposed to pursue nature down to her fundamental building blocks—the letters or laws of nature. While the overly hasty deductive method had drawn conclusions from one or two letters and therefore had hopelessly bungled the reading, Bacon insisted on the necessity of studying nature piece by piece, letter by letter, observing all instances of such elementary properties as density, vacuity, and whiteness. Such properties, natural laws, or, as Bacon termed them, forms were endlessly interchangeable and combinable and, like letters of the alphabet, gave rise to all the multiplicity of things and motions in the world.

Strangely enough, the material limitations on what sorts of objects naturalists were able to preserve actually generated a positive step toward comparative

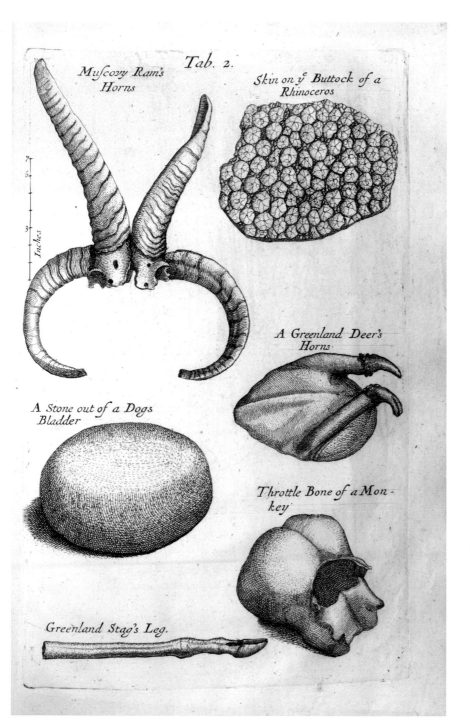

Muscovy Ram's Horns

Skin on yͤ Buttock of a Rhinoceros

7
6

3

Inches

A Greenland Deer's Horns

A Stone out of a Dogs Bladder

Throttle Bone of a Monkey

Greenland Stag's Leg.

Tab. 2.

5 An assortment of wondrous bits and pieces from Nehemiah Grew's *Musæum Regalis Societatis, or A Catalogue and Description of the Natural and Artificial Rarities Belonging to the Royal Society and preserved at Gresham Colledge* (London, 1681). Photo by Michael Mills. Courtesy of the Charles Woodward Memorial Room, University of British Columbia, Vancouver.

anatomy. Rather than attempt to decipher fragments metonymically—as pieces of obscure wholes—naturalists began to approach fragments as illuminating instances of underlying functions. For example, the tails of the rhinoceros, cow, and beaver in the Royal Society's repository gave some idea not of the animals to which they once belonged but of the principles and uses of tails. As Grew noted, a horse, "being much pester'd with Flyes . . . should have a long brush Tail to whisk them off. Whereas the Ass, which either for the hardness and dryness of his Skin, or other Cause, is less annoy'd with them, hath no need of such an one." Likewise, the naturalist who observed that "the ears of a greyhound are pricked while those of a hound hang down" would also be able to reason that the former hunts with his ears and the latter with his nose.[62] Reason was harnessed to imagination, not to invent poetic narratives but rather to see through opaque animal parts to contemplate the similarities and differences between animals' basic functions, which in turn would reveal—it was hoped—the underlying essences and deeper inner workings of nature's engine.

Although they were armed with new empirical methodologies and full of optimism, seventeenth-century naturalists nevertheless remained blocked by obscure bits and pieces of botched and decomposing creatures. Materials endlessly dictated the sort of examinations and conclusions observers were able to make. No matter how pragmatically and objectively naturalists approached certain specimens, if the animals were in bits and pieces, fragmentary, or rotting, little useful knowledge—if any—could be squeezed out. Some objects proved too opaque to decipher by purely empirical means. Well into the eighteenth century, the *potential* knowledge of specimens was always locked in by the obscurity of bad taxidermy.

From early cabinets of wonder to philosophical repositories, collections of curiosities never really displayed knowledge. Rather, they acted as warehouses of raw potentiality. Each curious fragment individually offered the possibility of some unknown, undiscovered clue about nature's laws, and together the parts of a curious collection quivered not with wisdom but its anticipation. Whether collectors were seeking allegorical or empirical truths, the objects themselves were never transparent enough, never clear enough. Like Noah's ark, that archetypal collection, afloat and swirling on an uncharted sea of thought without any sure sense of where it was heading, collections of curiosities led viewers on voyages of discovery for which reason and reality needed a little help from the imagination to fill in the bleary shapes on the horizon.

The obscurity of early preserved natural items proved increasingly troublesome throughout the eighteenth century. Eventually, collectors who delighted in wizened bits and decomposing pieces were chastised by natural philosophers working in other disciplines of natural science. Although all branches of natural history were based on the same basic principles of close observation and meticulous note keeping, natural history was invariably more unruly, haphazard, and transitory. Stars may shift across the sky; they may have appeared murky when viewed through early telescopes, but they do not decompose, or at least not at the rate of preserved fish and lizards. Interestingly, Galileo expressed one of the first derogatory opinions of the materials of natural history, snidely calling collectors "curious little men" who delighted in marshaling together things "that have something peregrine about them." For Galileo, collectors were like little children ogling petty, insignificant things: "a petrified crab, a desiccated chameleon, a fly or spider in gelatin or amber."[63] And certainly by the time of Sloane's death in 1733, the appeal of such wonders had definitely ceased for some audiences.

Sloane bequeathed the contents of his house to the nation. His art and antiquities, library, cabinets of animal parts, and folios of herbs established the British Museum, which first opened to the public on January 15, 1759, in Bloomsbury, London. However, compared to Sloane's collections of books and antiquities, or even his minerals, corals, and fossils, his fleshier items did not fare well. Of his roughly forty-five hundred natural specimens, almost all have failed the test of time. Some simply decomposed, but many were actively destroyed by the collection's subsequent curators, who either found the objects rotting or simply disliked the "Strange Things" so sought after in the previous century. Living to the advanced age of ninety-two in the early eighteenth century (something rather extraordinary in itself), Sloane had outlived his generation and the age of wonder in which his collection first began.

After Sloane's death, Horace Walpole, an appointed trustee of the new museum, wrote to his friend Horace Mann, "You will scarce guess how I employ my time; chiefly at present in the guardianship of embryos and cockle-shells. Sir Hans Sloane is dead, and has made me one of the trustees to his museum. . . . He valued it at four score thousand; and so would anybody who loves hippopotamuses, sharks with one ear and spiders as big as geese!" "You may believe that those who

Wonder does not see its objects possessively: they remain "other" and un-mastered.

—R. H. HEPBURN, "The Inaugural Address: Wonder," *Proceedings of the Aristotelian Society* (1980), supplementary vols., 4 think money the most valuable of all curiosities," Walpole added, "will not be the purchasers."[64] Although Walpole's opinion was not universally held, collections of unsorted curiosities had begun their slide toward an outdated "nicknackatory."[65] Some even considered wondrous bits and pieces downright vulgar.[66]

While keeper of the Natural History Department at the British Museum, George Shaw made yearly bonfires, beginning in 1807, of vast numbers of decomposing specimens from Sloane's original collection. He called them his "cremations." The burnings were continued by William Elford Leach, who despised the taxidermy from Sloane's era. As one contemporary remarked, "the attraction of the terraces and the fragrance of the shrubberies" surrounding the museum "were sadly lessened when a pungent odour of burning snakes was their accompaniment."[67] Natural knowledge no longer applied to such broken creaturely lumps. They were too messy, too eccentric, and, most especially, too difficult to decipher.

Such sixteenth- and seventeenth-century natural wonders—radically unknown creatures, frequently fragmented, and always on the brink of dissolution—are an extreme instance of impenetrability. But this poetics of strangeness is not exclusive to taxidermy from the early modern era. All taxidermy begs the question, what is it? Perhaps we no longer wonder *what* species the preserved creature once was, but the ontological question *what is it?* is always lurking with taxidermy.

Wonder is a discomforting term. As Descartes maintained, at best it suggests naïveté; at worst, a lazy brain. Yet for all the implications of gullibility or apathy, wonder is perhaps the primary aesthetic reaction to all taxidermy. A dead animal may be refashioned into a lively shape. It may accrue significance in various cultural and institutional contexts. It may be interpreted as an object of science, a token of affection, a symbol of human misuse of nature, or a queasy sign of psychological decay, as famously exploited by Alfred Hitchcock's classic horror film *Psycho*, whose disturbed killer, Norman Bates, broadens his passion for taxidermy to include preserving his mother. But all such analysis and inspection nevertheless rest precisely and quite simply on the animal and its startling, enigmatic aura. Even the most familiar species—cats or dogs—acquire an inexplicable strangeness when immortalized by taxidermy. It is the strangeness of encountering a once-living creature now morphed into an objectlike thing that requires periodic dusting.

Human-crafted objects are inherently endowed with meaning. They were made for particular purposes. They variously fulfill those purposes, fail, or are reimagined for other functions. In contrast, animals have no innate meaning: meaning is always a human intellectual imposition. When the obstinately unmeaningful presence of animals is purposefully manipulated through human craft, the resulting animal-thing is, predictably enough, disconcerting. All taxidermy provokes the recognition that this thing on display, at once animal and object, is neither fully animal nor fully object, or, in Patrizi's words, the vacillating experience "of believing and not believing" what the eyes are seeing.

To state the obvious, things are not ideas or mental images. Things are material entities. And because they are material, things generate encounters. As already described, wonder is both a marvelous entity and the personal experience of encountering strangeness. The duality also applies to taxidermied animals—by creating animal-things, taxidermy necessarily creates encounters. This is the strange, unsettling power of taxidermy: it offers—or forces—intimacies between you and an animal-thing that is no longer quite an animal but could not be mistaken for anything other than an animal. And how could such encounters not be provocatively intimate? Preservation allows you to get closer to an animal than you ever could in life or even on the television. It allows you to get closer than most animals would allow, if they were still alive.

This strangely queasy sense of knowing that develops during encounters with taxidermy might be called visceral knowledge: a bodily knowing that occurs in contact with physical things, a knowing that blurs emotion with materiality and may even defy reason, logic, and explanatory language. We have all experienced a powerfully visceral reaction to an unexpected or unidentified object. Within a poetics of strangeness, the thing simultaneously fascinates, looms, provokes, defies, attracts, and repels. The meaning is there; you can sense an understanding, but you cannot necessarily translate that understanding into clear thought or precise words. Taxidermied animals present an obstinately obfuscating thereness: as Steve Baker observes, "The thing seen is recognized as an animal; the nature of the experience may be less recognizable."[68]

Among the most startling genres of taxidermy are preserved examples of botched nature: two-headed, multilimbed, double-bodied anomalies of the animal world. A kitten with eight legs and two tails jars all expectations of feline form, but it affects more deeply than mere visual provocation. This kitten is not just a strange object but was once—however briefly—a living being. Like us, it breathed air into its lungs; it had yearnings, wants, and needs. At a deep

6   A kitten with eight legs and two tails preserved by Walter Potter at the end of the nineteenth century, taken from a postcard at Bramber Museum, West Sussex, England. Photo courtesy of Patrick Morris.

unconscious level, we recognize the kitten because it is like us, and the fear, revulsion, or fascination it arouses stems directly from this knowledge: it is both like and unlike us. It offers us a different version of how life could have been. The kitten offers a glimpse into a world where fantasy and reality merge into infinite possibilities and uncertainty and gives material form to Stephen Greenblatt's description of wonder as "the power of the displayed object to stop the viewer in his or her tracks, to convey an arresting sense of uniqueness, to evoke an exalted attention." Such "enchanted looking" thwarts all expectations; it is bewildering, magnetic, magically charismatic, and altogether spellbinding.[69] As we have seen, this is precisely a wonder's power: to expose the inherent, chaotic, startling potential of the natural world. But what is this animal, now that it is dead and preserved?

While all animal wonders—whether unknown, exotic, or mutant, whether in the sixteenth century or the twenty-first—evoke strange imagining, they always draw us back and bind us, so to speak, to their very real, very concrete presence. If the kitten had been made from clay or carved from wood, it might still be eerie, but it would be far less troublesome. Paradoxically, without its palpable materiality—as a genuine, unfeigned, dead creature—the kitten could hardly convey the same sense of unreality. It is *because* of and not despite this raw animal presence that reason and reality seem to waver. It is because it once lived that the kitten is able to haunt us in death.

The kitten offers an intense view into the ghoulishness that haunts all taxidermy. Because, in a sense, such a kitten should not exist, it heightens the strangeness of the very concept of an animal-thing, of animal form blurred with human-crafted liveliness. The kitten is dead yet animate, known yet unknowable. Wonder is not always a pleasant experience. Taxidermy takes visceral knowledge into a darker realm. The viewer must always acknowledge the presence of death; there can be no taxidermy without dead animals. This uneasy blurring of the recognizable (a once-living creature) and the unknowable (preserved death) casts all taxidermy in uneasy shadows.

The following chapters explore the unsettling, enigmatic quality that pervades all genres of taxidermy. In great part, the strangeness grows from the recognition that the animal-thing on display was once a sentient creature: at once lifelike yet dead, both a human-made *representation* of a species and a *presentation* of a particular animal's skin. In spite of the death, skinning, dismemberment, and refashioning, the animal form holds. The eyes may be glass, but the animal stares back. This uncanny animal-thingness is not technically verisimilitude: this *is* the actual skin of the animal being represented.

The breathless anticipation of uncovering unknown, untold natural marvels still exists. While the world's fauna has by and large been discovered, documented, classified, photographed, and captured on film, the attraction of animal idiosyncrasies hardly dissipates with acquaintance. As Edward O. Wilson writes in *Biophilia*, nature is at the very heart and source of human wonder: "Because species diversity was created prior to humanity, and because we evolved within it, we have never fathomed its limits. As a consequence, the living world is the natural domain of the most restless and paradoxical part of the human spirit. Our sense of wonder grows exponentially: the greater the knowledge, the deeper the mystery and the more we seek knowledge to create new mystery."[70] The pollen dance of an explorer bee, the anatomical confusion of a platypus, a giraffe's neck, pink flamingos, blue-footed boobies—the startling strangeness and beauty of beasts and birds surround us, if we care to look. Leaving behind the inscrutable wonders of early modern naturalists, the following chapter pursues the fascination with animal intricacies into the early nineteenth century, culminating with the petrified beauty of hummingbirds, nature's supreme creation of dainty beauty but also the frailest and most fleeting of birds.

BEAUTY

2

The Victorians were quite literally and without the least exaggeration absolutely besotted with hummingbirds. Not only did the number of known species increase dramatically in the nineteenth century (from ten in 1758 to more than three hundred by the 1850s), but each new discovery seemed to shimmer ever more brightly with all the colors of the rainbow. "There is not, it may safely be asserted, in all the varied works of nature in her zoological productions," William Bullock wrote about hummingbirds in 1824, "any family that can bear a comparison, for singularity of form, splendour of colour, or number and variety of species, with this the smallest of the feathered creation." A species native to the Americas, hummingbirds were unknown in Europe before Columbus's westward quest, and Bullock averred that "no subject of Natural History has, since the discovery of the New World, excited admiration of mankind more than this diminutive favorite of nature."[1] All the creatures of the world, all the "precious stones and metals polished by our art, cannot be compared to this jewel of nature."[2]

If I could only have seen a humming-bird fly, it would have been an epoch in my life.

—JOHN RUSKIN, "Conversation with M. H. Spielman at Brantwood" (1894)

Bullock was certainly no novice when it came to diminutive bee-birds, as they were affectionately called. In an early catalogue of his Liverpool Museum, Bullock listed nearly seventy hummingbirds, all arranged together on the spreading branches of a tree in a single display case.[3] The tiny size of the birds and their jeweled tones seemed divinely designed for such voluptuous collecting. Two years later Bullock boasted of having the finest collection in Europe, more than one hundred hummingbirds, and after his travels through Mexico in 1823, his collection had swelled to more than 170 little birds.[4]

Bullock's museum was something of an extraordinary place. The collection was first opened to the public in his hometown of Sheffield in the late 1790s. At the turn of the century, Bullock moved his museum to Liverpool and then to London in 1809. By then his collection had swelled to more than thirty-two thousand artifacts of natural history, art, and exotic curiosities, including a large number of ethnographic items acquired during James Cook's expeditions to the South Seas. More than eighty thousand visitors passed through the museum during its first year in London. In 1810 Bullock built the Egyptian Hall (named for its exotic façade) to house his ever-increasing collection and to entertain his ever-growing audience.

Bullock was among the first curators to present his creatures in theatrical, almost atmospheric displays, with an eye to both the scientific interest and the spectacular entertainment value of exotic specimens. Ever the entrepreneur, Bullock was hardly immune to the dramatic fascination that rarely seen animals held for visitors. Down the center of his museum, he arranged his large exotics, including a giraffe, an elephant, a lion, and a rhinoceros surrounded by models of tropical plants, in order to produce a "panoramic effect of distance . . . affording a beautiful illustration of the luxuriance of a torrid clime." As we will see in the next chapter, Victorians were particularly exhilarated by exotic, dangerous, and savage beasts, even in a taxidermied state. One of Bullock's display cabinets featured a Bengal tiger locked in a deadly battle with a boa constrictor, two creatures of near mythical menace. In the museum's catalogue, Bullock made sure to describe the combat as luridly as possible: "The Royal Tiger (F. Tigrina). This is represented expiring in one of those dreadful combats which take place betwixt this powerful and sanguinary destroyer of the human species, and the immense serpent of India, called the Boa Constrictor, in whose enormous folds its unavailing strength is nearly exhausted, and its bones crushed and broken by the strength and weight of its tremendous adversary."[5]

Giraffes, elephants, big cats, and bigger snakes obviously thrilled and entranced visitors, but the little hummingbirds were not outshone. In fact, of all his creatures, Bullock paid special attention to his hummingbirds, describing them at length in his museum catalogues and taking special care to express the species' most cherished physical traits: their diminutive size and shimmering plumage. Referring to a male and female *Trochilus minimus*, "little larger than the Humble Bee," Bullock described the species as exhibiting an impossible daintiness: "its bill is about as thick and as long as a small pin; and the feet are almost imperceptible to the naked eye." The *Trochilus moschitus*, or ruby topaz hummingbird, was "the most beautiful of the genus: the head and crest have the sparkling fire of the ruby, while the neck and breast dazzle like the aurora topaz of Brazil."[6] Around such exquisite frailty, no description of fairylike perfection was too saccharine. Hummingbirds lived—however fleetingly—in a world of blossoms, sweet nectar, and the untainted freshness of everlasting spring:

> It is easy to lay hold of the little creature while it hums at the blossom. It dies soon after it is caught, and serves to decorate the Indian girls, who wear two of these charming birds, as pendants from their ears. The Indians, indeed, are so struck and dazzled with the brilliancy of their various hues, that they have named them the Beams or Locks of the Sun. Such is the history of this little being, who flutters from flower to flower, breathes their freshness, wantons on the wings of the cooling zephyrs, sips the nectar of a thousand sweets, and resides in climes where reigns the beauty of eternal spring.[7]

Strangely or not, when Bullock penned his romantic vision he had yet to see a living hummingbird. It was not until his stop in Kingston, Jamaica, in early 1823 on his way to Mexico that Bullock at last saw a living hummingbird. His first hummingbird perched nonchalantly for most of the day on a twig of a large tamarind tree. He did not seem to mind Bullock coming up close, even within a few feet. "I could easily have caught him," Bullock wrote, "but was unwilling to destroy so interesting a little visitant, who has afforded me so much pleasure." Such veneration did not stop Bullock from collecting more than two hundred hummingbirds—unprotected by being Bullock's "first"—over the course of his travels through Mexico.[8]

While touring the country, Bullock kept a large aviary of nearly seventy hummingbirds. He succeeded in keeping the fragile captives alive for some weeks by feeding them sugar water, and, he wrote, "could I have devoted my whole attention to them, I have no doubt of the possibility of bringing them alive to Europe."[9] Likely as not, he would have failed. This was the eternal struggle for European collectors: the birds never survived the transatlantic voyage. In other words, for Victorian audiences, seeing a hummingbird necessarily meant seeing a taxidermied rendition of the bird.

Back in England, Bullock sought out a professional taxidermist in the hope of conveying at least something of the hummingbirds' spirit and charm in his collected skins.[10] But despite the efforts, even Bullock had to admit that his specimens were poor copies of the living creatures: "Europeans who have seen only the stuffed remains of these little feathered gems in museums have been charmed with their beautiful appearance; but those who have examined them whilst living, displaying their moving crests, throats, and tails, like the peacock in the sun, can never look with pleasure on their mutilated forms."[11] Of course Bullock was biased: he was one of the few privileged men and women living in England who had seen a living hummingbird. Although the beauty of hummingbirds is quite literally brought to life by their rapid movements, Bullock's denouncing his own specimens as mutilated forms was partly the banter of a showman. Heightening his audience's yearning for the full sparkling vivacity of the stuffed birds before them, Bullock wrote,

> I have carefully preserved about two hundred specimens, in the best possible manner, yet they are still but the shadow of what they were in life. The reason is obvious; for the sides of the laminæ, or fibres of each feather, being of a different colour from the surface, will change when seen in a front or oblique direction; and as each lamina or fibre turns upon the axis of the quill, the least motion, when living, causes the feathers to change suddenly to the most opposite hues. Thus the one from Nootka Sound changes its expanded throat from the most vivid fire-colour to light green; the Topaz-throated does the same; and the Mexican Star changes from bright crimson to blue.[12]

The stuffed birds could only display the absence of life in a creature whose beauty was defined by its ceaseless, shimmering movements. Standing in front of a glass case packed with nearly a hundred dead birds, visitors had to envision them reanimated, to imagine the flashing colors and humming velocity of their wings as the birds darted between flowers, hovering almost motionless, as if suspended in air. Simply put, Bullock's desire to capture the creatures' intrinsic beauty was impossible to fulfill: death eradicated the very source of the birds' loveliness. Stuffed hummingbirds embodied an impossible longing for animal beauty.

Almost three decades after Bullock's return from Mexico, another British entrepreneur naturalist set up his own, even grander exhibition of hummingbirds. John Gould was a renowned ornithologist, taxidermist to the royal family, and illustrator of some of the nineteenth century's most comprehensive and beautiful ornithological folios.[13] Gould produced works on the birds of Australia, the birds of Asia, toucans, partridges, and the birds of Great Britain. But it was his five-volume *Monograph of the Trochilidae, or Family of the Humming-birds* (1849–61) that is considered the naturalist's greatest achievement. Indeed, hummingbirds became Gould's lifelong passion.

Gould was obsessed with the tiny birds. If his interest in other birds waned as the book project drew to a close, his desire for hummingbirds only increased with contact. "That our enthusiasm and excitement with regard to most things become lessened, if not deadened, by time, particularly when we have acquired what we vainly consider a complete knowledge of the subject, is, I fear, too often the case with most of us," Gould wrote. Not so with the hummingbird family: "the pleasure which I experience on seeing a Humming Bird is as great at the present moment as when I first saw one. During the first 20 years of my acquaintance with these wonderful works of creation my thoughts were often directed to them in the day, and my night dreams have not infrequently carried me to their native forests in the distant country of America." Paired with the naturalist's passion to discover yet another species among the tiny family, Gould's adoration of the birds propelled his desire to know, and knowing meant possession. Gould amassed an extraordinary collection of hummingbirds totaling more than fifteen hundred mounted specimens and nearly four thousand skins.

During the Great Exhibition of the Works of Industry of All Nations, held in London in 1851, Gould, being of a commercial mind, set up his own display in the Zoological Gardens at Regent's Park, three miles away from the exhibition proper. With the approval of the Zoological Society of London, Gould financed and built a large wooden building to house a display of 320 species of hummingbird. The birds were arranged by genus and delicately posed on branches or resting in nests in twenty-four display cases, each approximately two feet high and two feet wide. Gould's venture proved to be an enormous success. More than seventy-five thousand people visited Gould's hummingbird pavilion, and each was charged sixpence for entry. And when Gould's illustrated work was finally completed a decade later, it confirmed the frenzy for the birds, a passion that increased over the following decades. During a single week in 1888, four hundred thousand hummingbird skins were sold at auction.[14] To put it mildly, the tiny beauties had enraptured the Victorian imagination.

Of course, the paradox for contemporary viewers is that the adoration of hummingbirds led to their destruction. For most nineteenth-century nature enthusiasts, killing and stuffing a bird hardly destroyed its intrinsic beauty. Rather, taxidermy distilled a bird's aesthetic charms.[15] If the sheen and shimmer of specimens faded with death, the birds were nevertheless caught up in an aesthetic culture of romanticized nature that could only see them as beautiful.

Although the vast majority of Europeans had not seen living hummingbirds, the creatures became a standard for natural beauty. The aesthetic philosopher Edmund Burke, in his *Philosophical Enquiry into the Origin of Our Ideas of the Sublime and Beautiful*, first published in 1757, singled out the family for its exceptional beauty: "hummingbird both in shape and colouring yields to none of the winged species, of which it is the least; and perhaps his beauty is enhanced by his smallness."[16] Beautiful and diminutive but also delicate, sensitive, and fleeting, the species embodied an ideal grouping of romantic characteristics.[17] As John Ruskin said, "Had I devoted myself to birds, their life and plumage, I might have produced something myself worth doing. If I could only have seen a humming-bird fly, it would have been an epoch in my life."[18] The impossibility of witnessing life in a creature that was so profoundly lively intensified Victorians' infatuation with the little birds to a near-ecstatic romantic high.

Encouraged in great part by the poetry of William Wordsworth and Percy Bysshe Shelley, a romantic branch of natural history was well in swing by the 1820s. It viewed nature not so much as a passive object of contemplation but as a vehicle for self-consciousness and an educator of senses, and indeed, only a sensitive soul could properly appreciate the beauty of nature. If the strangeness of exotic animals had disrupted expectations and startled the mind, nature's beauties were now appreciated as vehicles for inward-looking emotional exploration.

Although a more positivistic appreciation of nature developed over the course of the nineteenth century, it remained almost obligatory to preface any work on nature—even scientific books—with a few lines from Wordsworth, or at least with some poetic expression of nature's heady emotional charge.[19] As one nineteenth-century naturalist wrote, the proper way to study nature was "the poet's way," which dealt not with dry statistics but sought a poetic communion with nature's diverse beauty. Close observation could reveal the lives of starfish, beetles, and songbirds, but, more important, such contemplation aroused a poetic sensibility.[20] Nature was alive with significance: only the spiritually dull failed to appreciate nature's beauty.

In a sense, the perception of nature was inseparable from its aesthetic appreciation. The ability to appreciate birds and bees and flowers and mountains was the ability to fibrillate in tune with the natural world, although—of course—that tune was a human composition filled with lyrical melodies of beauty, sentiment, and transience. "The accepted approach to nature had become no longer to set down what one saw plainly and accurately," David Elliston Allen writes in *The Naturalist in Britain*; "the aim now was to record one's reactions—and the livelier these reactions appeared, the more beneficial, the more exalting, the more 'tasteful' the contact with nature was assumed to be."[21] Romantic nature was nature extruded through the poet's imagination, and aesthetic appreciation was an index of personal refinement. More than just displaying hummingbirds, Bullock and Gould were showcasing their era's aching appreciation for nature's favorite beauty: dead, stuffed, somewhat lumpish, yet all the more beguiling for its ephemerality.

ANIMAL BEAUTY

There is a large glass-fronted cabinet of hummingbirds on display in the Natural History Museum in London, which is believed to be Bullock's famous treasure (see fig. 7). If the Victorians swooned over the sheer number of little birds packed together in a single case, if they were downright enchanted by the shimmering colors displayed before their eager eyes, few viewers today experience that same crescendo of visual delight when faced with nearly a hundred dead birds. The cabinet might still entrance viewers with its spectacular content, but "beautiful" is hardly the typical exclamation from visitors. Encounters with taxidermy are necessarily encounters with death, but the Victorians chose to see through the

It is evident, that one considerable source of *beauty* in all animals is the advantage which they reap from the particular structure of their limbs and members, suitably to the particular manner of life, to which they are by nature destined.

—DAVID HUME, *An Enquiry Concerning the Principles of Morals* (1751)

muted coloring and less than lively poses, to sidestep death, to look beyond, in order to catch a glimpse of the birds' former beauty. This ability to look through a superfluity of death might be explained (or excused) by the fact that without taxidermy, early nineteenth-century European audiences would never have seen these creatures. Still photography was several decades away, and even then, a death would be required to capture even just a black-and-white still life of a little bird that personified motion and Technicolor dreams.

How can we, living in a Discovery Channel age, when wildlife videos can bring living, breathing, fighting, mating creatures into everyone's home, no shooting or stuffing required, criticize a longing, now almost two centuries old, to document and showcase the unique beauty of the hummingbird family? On the other hand, how can we condone, let alone appreciate, the display? Is there any beauty left here, or have our current sensitivities to the human uses and abuses—both past and present—of the natural world and its inhabitants obliterated the possibility of seeing anything other than musty, regrettable relics from a less enlightened era? By offering an encounter with nature that no longer resonates in the twenty-first century, Bullock's hummingbird cabinet forces each viewer to confront the troubled relationship between the aesthetics and ethics of taxidermy: the compelling urge to look and the worry about what made that looking possible.

The previous chapter proposed that taxidermy embraces viewers within an aura of wonder. This atmosphere of compelling strangeness arises in large part from the contradiction between the *perception* of this object on display—mute and manufactured—and the *recognition* that this is no mute and manufactured object. Viewers can never escape the startling realization that this static thing in a very real sense is an animal still: again, the eyes may be glass, but the animal stares back. It is this recognition of a captured liveliness, or rather a captured stillness, that lies at the heart of taxidermy's strange visual power. I would argue that this recognition is an aesthetic encounter with animal form. And more, whether audiences respond with delight or horror, with poetic pleasure or ecological concern, encounters with taxidermy are inexorably encounters with a ravishing and ravished animal beauty. If taxidermy raises the specter of death, that specter is nevertheless painfully, powerfully beautiful.

Beauty is an awkward word with a long and problematic history in philosophical aesthetics, so problematic that for most of the twentieth century beauty was

7   Nineteenth-century hummingbird case on
display in the Birds Gallery of the Natural
History Museum, London. Photo © Natural History Museum, London.

Dillard's short essay captures a yearning to be at one with nature, a longing to learn from nature's simplicities. Surrounded by nature, unhindered by the pressures, ills, and confusions of modern life, Dillard soaks in animal beauty. Such an encounter with nature might be defined by everything that it is not: not contrived, not materialistically driven, not polluting or wasteful. Out There, beyond the city and its heavy influences, Dillard communes softly with the simplicity and elegance of creaturely life. This appreciation of animal beauty (to experience but not to capture) probably resonates with modern viewers more deeply than the avian gluttony of Bullock's hummingbird cabinet does, but it is no less historically contingent. It is a product of a modern, increasingly disenchanted urban society for which nature is no longer a threat or a foe but an escape and a salve. Which is to say, the way a culture explains its animal encounters reveals a great deal of its broader sense of being in (or against) the natural world.[26] Or, to put it more simply, the meaning of animal encounters depends on their cultural moment. To a farmer, a weasel is a verminous chicken killer. To a poet, a weasel is a lesson in pure, wild, beautiful instinct.

But what does Dillard's weasel have to do with taxidermy? Dillard did not hunt down, kill, and stuff the weasel. It is one thing to look into the small black eyes of a living weasel; it is quite another to confront the glass eyes of a weasel posed behind museum glass. Meetings with wild liveliness are fleeting, unpredictable, precious, and perhaps even dangerous. In contrast, taxidermy offers the flat, glassy, perpetual gaze of a manhandled beast. It is the difference between a living evanescence and a dead eternity. It is hardly possible that a stuffed animal could captivate like Dillard's warm-blooded weasel. But consider Bullock's hummingbirds. Disgust, horror, fascination, admiration, wonder—no viewer is neutral toward a mass of stuffed creatures. Taxidermied animals are not indistinguishable from any sort of human-made object: no visitor can just walk by the cabinet of a hundred little birds without taking notice of what is on display. Bloodless, immortal, and eternally immobile, yes. But animals retain the power to elicit emotional reactions, whether dead or alive. We know instinctively that preserved bits or whole creatures were once pulsating with life, and we cannot help but respond. Dillard's wild weasel and Bullock's stuffed hummingbirds offer two fundamentally different encounters with animals. Both are distinctly shaped by their cultural moment's definition of animal beauty, but underlying both encounters is a palpable yearning, a longing to access animals, to experience something of their enigma, beauty, and necessity. Death and preservation may offend, disgust, and mar our ability to appreciate *ethically* the animal beauty on display. But, as this book argues, death does not obliterate animal aesthetics.

Aesthetic appreciation can be defined as the admiration of an object's intrinsic properties that have been considered worthy of attention by a particular community. The diminutive beauty of hummingbirds or, as the following chapters examine, the ferocity of lions, the enigma of zebra stripes, or the majesty of stags are all such intrinsic properties that compel the longing to capture animal beauty through taxidermy. But appreciation of our natural surroundings is rooted in attempts to *understand* our experiences with nature and, as such, can never be purely physical sensations and is hardly timeless.[27] Aesthetic experiences of hummingbirds or weasels are always contextual, always mediated by the variety of conditions, influences, beliefs, and imaginings that shape all our experiences, and aesthetic perception and judgment of nature are inevitably cultural. The same holds true for definitions of animal beauty. Any description of animal aesthetics is rooted in a network of cultural, social, poetic, and scientific associations. Early nineteenth-century exclamations over the beauty of Bullock's stuffed hummingbirds, for example, captured a romantic appreciation of the birds' ethereality. Within today's environmental ethics, declarations of animal beauty signify the importance of safeguarding animals from precisely the sort of mass collecting that Bullock's cabinet epitomizes. If Victorian taxidermy clashes with current sensibilities, in great part it is because the meaning of animal beauty has been redefined. Killing an animal in order to admire it longer is now almost a contradiction in terms. In other words, just as a romantic, spiritualized sensibility marked the nineteenth century's natural aesthetic, ecological concerns about species loss have come to characterize our evaluations of animal beauty today. Of course, in contrast to nature photography or even zoos, taxidermy is an extreme, deathly encounter with animals. But taxidermy is not motivated to destroy or mar animal form but to preserve it.

The lacing and unlacing of death, longing, and animal beauty lie at the heart of this book and will be considered and reconsidered throughout the following chapters. But here, a detour is needed. Obviously something has happened, taxidermically speaking, between the withered animal morsels composing the Royal Society's repository, described in the previous chapter, and Bullock's hummingbirds: beauty has replaced wonder as a driving force of taxidermy collections.

There is a reason why collecting birds both alive and dead became wildly popular during the eighteenth and nineteenth centuries. Birds were beautiful, one of the most beautiful parts of creation. As the illustrious French naturalist George-Louis Leclerc de Buffon described them in his highly popular *Histoire naturelle des oiseaux (Natural History of Birds)*, published in nine volumes between 1770 and 1786, the beauty of birds defied expression. Whereas a black-and-white etching and a good description of any particular beast was generally sufficient to distinguish it from its close relatives, color was far more important than shape for identifying birds, and oh, the colors! One would need "an immensity of words . . . for the description of the colors in birds; there are not even the terms in any language to express the nuances, the tints, the reflections, and the mixtures."[28] In fact, the difficulty of replicating the lustrous, shimmering colors of hummingbirds limited the number of illustrations Buffon included in his work: their colors were too beautiful, too changeable to be captured with ink.[29]

As keeper of the Parisian Jardin du Roi (renamed the Muséum national d'histoire naturelle after the French Revolution), Buffon was a vocal leader in the polite culture of nature appreciation. Although Buffon laid particular stress on the utility of natural knowledge, he also highlighted nature's innate charms and emotive appeal. Buffon's description of hummingbirds became the definitive description from which all naturalist history writers drew inspiration—and usually more than a few passages. Bullock certainly quoted extensively from Buffon, while the eccentric English naturalist Charles Waterton, whom we will meet later in this chapter, declared that "it would be arrogant to pretend to describe this winged gem of nature after Buffon's elegant description of it."[30] By describing hummingbirds as nature's gems, Buffon conferred a cultural value on the little birds, absorbing them into a world of polite curiosity and cultural polish. As Buffon describes them, some were "blackish-blue with flashes of burnished steel," while others captured "the brilliance and fire of rubies and amethysts." Another was "hardly bigger than a ruby," with a crest "like an emerald of the greatest brilliance" and tail feathers of a "blackish and shiny polished steel."[31] Assuredly, undeniably, naturally beautiful, hummingbirds were nevertheless entrenched in the cultural mores of aesthetic appreciation.

The bits and pieces and animal fragments prized in early cabinets of curiosity hardly captured the beauty and charisma of animals. Simply having a feather or pelt was no longer enough: collectors wanted to be charmed by nature. They wanted nature's beauty on display. And indeed, the shift from wonder to beauty as the motivating force behind taxidermy can be traced to early eighteenth-century France, where the polite appreciation of natural specimens matured into a sign of gentility and cultivation.

PRESERVING BEAUTY

In the early decades of the eighteenth century, natural history cabinets proliferated in polite Parisian society. More than two hundred natural history collections were established in the city by France's social elite, while more than double that number were dotted across the countryside.[32] In contrast to the previous century's delight in strangeness, the cabinets of the next generation of increasingly cultured collectors strove for elegance and beauty. As provocative departures from the regular course of things, wonders had tantalized collectors with the *possibility* of knowledge, the anticipation of revelation. In contrast, the genteel collections so popular in the eighteenth century exhibited refinement of taste. Specimens were arranged into harmonious, decorative visions in which the eye luxuriated. Objects were selected for their ability to convey visual pleasure by conforming to the aesthetic principles of the era: the pleasing, the rare, the valuable, and, above all, the beautiful.[33]

Natural history was not yet a specialized discipline in the eighteenth century. Even by the later decades of the century, few professional positions were available to nature lovers, and few individuals made their living exclusively from natural history. Rather, natural knowledge was largely dependent on a wealthy leisure class that could afford the longing to amass and display spectacular collections, and natural science was cultivated as a polite occupation.[34]

At least until the mid-eighteenth century, scientific inquiry was not distinct from aesthetic appreciation. Beauty and science, taste and taxonomy were not necessarily at odds. After all, it was the age both of Jean-Jacques Rousseau's romantic philosophy of living simply in nature and of Carolus Linnaeus, who constructed a rigorous methodology for naming and classifying nature's diversity. In short, it was an age of dilettantism and science, sensibility and reason, and, of course, of privilege. While many naturalists from the midcentury onward increasingly promoted a new natural history for which visual delight became irrelevant to the workings of science, popular appreciation of natural specimens remained tied to connoisseurs'

The collection of Madame la Présidente de Bandeville reveals her good taste for nature's beautiful creations. In it we find a very pretty series of exotic and French birds, among which are some very rare.

—ANTOINE-JOSEPH DÉZALLIER D'ARGENVILLE, *La conchyliologie, ou Histoire naturelle des cocquilles de mer, d'eau douce, terrestres et fossiles* (1753) tasteful pleasure in nature's most beautiful productions.[35] As one eighteenth-century naturalist proclaimed, "France is second to no other nation with respect to taste and curiosity: we admire the beautiful things, above all the productions of nature, as the real source of the sciences."[36]

This aesthetic passion for natural history reflected a shift in the appreciation of nature itself. In part, knowing nature was a polite exercise in social values. Nature was fashionable; nature could cultivate the sensibilities. Certainly, strange exotics continued to fascinate, but the nature that amateurs collected and displayed so passionately was above all a nature to be admired, even adored, and spoken about in rapturous language. In addition, properly admiring nature established collectors as worthy of admiration themselves. The proliferation of natural history manuals written for the social elite were also conduct guides, advising readers as to the proper attitudes, tastes, and sensibilities for members of polite society. "Natural historical knowledge," as Emma C. Spary writes, "was considered a valuable means of self-improvement because its very acquisition repeated the steps of self-development judged necessary for the enlightened individual."[37] In other words, natural beauty hardly existed beyond society. The selection of beautiful things formed a foundation for social interactions and aesthetic standards.

With the new emphasis on beauty, the most notable display innovations were lively, almost theatrical arrangements. Birds picturesquely arranged on branches (such as Bullock's famous hummingbird tree) became central showpieces of eighteenth-century collections. Taxidermy flourished as a technology of visual delight. Antoine-Joseph Dézallier d'Argenville, author of the enormously influential *La conchyliologie, ou Histoire naturelle des coquilles de mer* (Conchology, or A natural history of seashells), first published in 1757 and republished posthumously in 1780, suggested that collectors with "a considerable number of birds can display them in an enchanting manner by arranging them on the branches of an artificial tree, painted green." D'Argenville described a cabinet that he had recently arranged for a prince. The three kingdoms of nature—animal, mineral, and vegetable—were organized into three separate cabinets. For the animal kingdom, each creature was arranged according to its "proper" element: birds perching on trees, butterflies in the air, and quadrupeds and reptiles on the ground. The centerpiece of the collection consisted of two large (real) trees covered with oak leaves made out of tin. "Among the birds which we picturesquely placed, we can distinguish a blackbird, an oriole, a white pheasant, a buzzard, a kingfisher, and a multitude of others." Scientifically speaking, the birds in no way belong together, but that was not the point. The ensemble was beautiful. A scenic background was painted, with an enchanting sky dotted by butterflies and several large exotic insects.[38]

Ideally, visitors were not passive observers of nature's productions but were actively engaged in the cultivation of aesthetic and scientific discrimination. Although collectors did seek out the names and habits of their displayed birds, the emphasis was not on zoological order. Rather than laying the birds out in rows, each isolated with its own label, the conglomeration accentuated their combined shimmer and spectacle. But more, hoarding accentuated looking, and looking closely—and such attentive, engaged study could not help but highlight the aesthetic appeal of the display.

Considering the popularity of d'Argenville's *Conchyliologie*, perhaps Bullock was influenced by his visions of avian wonder when he created his hummingbird tree. But whether or not Bullock was inspired by the Frenchman, for both men arrangement was motivated by what was pleasing to the eye. As d'Argenville says of M. Bonnier de La Mosson's collection (fig. 8), it was "one of the prettiest Cabinets to be seen in Paris, as much for its arrangement as for the beautiful things it contained."[39] This appraisal was often repeated: tasteful groupings augmented nature's inherent charm. Even nature could be made more beautiful by making it conform to the principles of elegant groupings.

Interestingly, d'Argenville makes a distinction between the arrangement of shells and that of birds. Birds were displayed "picturesquely," but shells were to be classified taxonomically by their class and family, genus and species. Such ordering was not the most aesthetically pleasing, nor did it necessarily accentuate the forms and symmetries of the shells, but what appealed to the eye should not "hinder in any way the spirit of the order."[40] Of course, d'Argenville's work was focused on conchology—shells were his main subject, not birds. But his insistence that shells be arranged methodologically while birds could be displayed in pretty groupings is significant, and his reasoning has little to do with the rigors of conchology versus ornithology. Shells do not require preservation. Collections could expand over time without specimens festering or needing replacement. It was a different story with birds. Throughout the century, specimens of birds and other taxidermied creatures remained at the mercy of insects. The most beautiful collections slowly faded, wilted, and died away. In the words of Louis-Jean-Marie Daubenton, whom Buffon appointed curator of the Jardin du Roi in Paris in 1745, "There are

worms, beetles, moths, butterflies, mites, &c. which each establish themselves in the things which are most agreeable to them: they eat up flesh, cartilage, skins, fur, and feathers; they attack plants, no matter how much care was taken in drying them."[41] Even with the most beautiful birds, nature's processes invariably triumphed.

While an effective insecticide was crucial to maintaining the quality of a collection, it was only an aftereffect; that is, specimens had to be worth defending from attack. The animals that have survived from the eighteenth century are typically wooden, taut, and pitiful. But time is never kind to skin, whether dead or alive, and time is particularly unkind to centuries-old skins. What did eighteenth-century taxidermy look like to eighteenth-century collectors? It is hard to say, exactly. On the one hand, collectors might have thought these preparations were exquisite. Without seeing any better preparations, and perhaps never having seen the living animal, how could they know how poor the taxidermy really was? On the other hand, eighteenth-century naturalists deplored the crusty state of most specimens.

In truth, most eighteenth-century taxidermy was hardly elegant; early specimens were really no more than stiff, overstuffed skins with brittle legs and discolored beaks. Take René-Antoine Ferchault de Réaumur's collection. With more than six hundred birds, it was widely considered one of the best in Europe in the mid-eighteenth century. Open to the public, the collection inflamed the popular passion for birds and cultivated a new age of bird connoisseurship in France. But according to an early nineteenth-century treatise on the art of preparing specimens, the birds were hardly lifelike: "Reaumur received birds from all parts, in spirit of wine, according to the instructions he has given; he contented himself by taking them from this liquor, and introducing two ends of a wire into the body behind the thighs; he then fastened the wire to the claws, the ends, which passed below, serving to fix them to a small board; he put two black glass beads in the place of eyes, and called it a stuffed bird."[42] This vision of shrunken, wizened animals was conjured up by most naturalists. Two ocelots in the Museum für Naturkunde in Berlin offer a dramatic comparison between good and bad taxidermy (fig. 9). One of the animals was mounted in 1818 by a taxidermist who had never seen a living ocelot. With an unnaturally broad face, torn ears, glazed eyes, and shrunken gums, the creature lacks even a hint of its former liveliness. The other ocelot, however, could very well be a living creature, captured in stillness by the photograph.

It was prepared in 1934 by Gerhard Schröder, who modeled the animal on studies of ocelots living in the Berlin Zoo.

In a series of four letters to the Royal Society in 1770, the English naturalist Tesser Samuel Kuckahn proclaimed the typical specimen "a poor shrivelled-up carcase of a bird, in which neither the natural shape, dimensions, or colours, are preserved, and which continually excites the disagreeable idea of the poor thing's having been starved to death on purpose."[43] Likewise, in his *General History of Quadrupeds*, first published in 1790, Thomas Bewick noted that a great number of his apes and monkeys were "wholly impossible to trace from a stuffed skin, void of every kind of expression; the muscular parts, which should convey the idea of action, being generally ill supplied, or entirely wanting," so that the greater part of his monkey tribe was without illustration.[44] While the colors and plumage of birds were always beautiful, most taxidermy was simply too rudimentary to capture the charisma of animal form.

And yet, such mediocre taxidermy was vastly appreciated by the opulent world of eighteenth-century collectors. How did badly stuffed birds become a marker of cultivated tastes and a well-padded purse? Within a world of luxury and affluence, why did collections of natural beauty prevail as the epitome of refinement? That expensive gemstones, antiquities, and exotic imports should be highly sought after is understandable, but dead, stiff birds?

Birds belonged to the larger cultural taste for rustic nature that flourished throughout the eighteenth century and was emboldened in no small part by the nature writings of Rousseau and the sense of preeminence aroused by the great luminaries of the Enlightenment.[45] Nature's energies were increasingly harnessed, its mysteries explored and delineated, yet its glories were not in any way diminished. Confident in reason's ability to triumph over unruly forces, nature could be admired—wildly admired—as a delightful, containable object of contemplation. It seems that an appreciation of nature and rustic simplicities arises precisely when human endeavor—in philosophy, science, or technology—has accomplished the extraordinary. When nature is no longer menacing, when knowledge has achieved new heights of understanding, when the wild beasts have been eradicated, nature is resought, reevaluated, and appreciated with new eyes.[46]

The eighteenth century was precisely such a historical point. Confident in the new knowledge of the Enlightenment and yet uneasy about the corrupting influences of modern life, polite society became enraptured by an idealized vision

9   Two ocelots in the Museum für
     Naturkunde. Photo courtesy of Museum
     für Naturkunde, Berlin.

of nature. The educated classes cultivated a pastoral nostalgia for the rustic, the simple, and the pure, perhaps to steady themselves, perhaps to find solid meaning in a world of uncertain possibilities. The farcical epitome of such stylized nostalgia is perhaps Marie Antoinette's rustic country escape from Versailles: the little château known as Petit Trianon, a gift from Louis XVI. Known for her fashion extravagances, her elaborate hairstyles and excessive gowns, at Petit Trianon Marie Antoinette cultivated an informal bucolic simplicity. The queen and her attendants frolicked in muslin shifts and straw hats, played the part of shepherdesses, and milked well-scrubbed cows. The appreciation of nature's intrinsic beauty is always tied up with cultural mores and philosophical projections.

The bits and pieces of creatures in sixteenth- and seventeenth-century collections—bones, a bundle of feathers, a pelt—were not only intrinsically disorderly. Above all, they lacked the organic integrity and grace of the beasts and birds they had once been. If Parisian cabinets strove to accentuate nature's beauty, something had to be done about the quality of taxidermy. There were two problems to consider. As we have already seen, eighteenth-century naturalists constantly lamented the poor quality of taxidermy and endlessly sought better techniques for capturing the lively beauty and charisma of animals. But this problem was secondary. Beauty hardly mattered if the specimen was rotting or dropping feathers. The first and more vital problem was basic preservation: how to prevent the insects and rot from destroying collections. If Kuckahn dismissed the typical specimen as "a poor shrivelled-up carcase of a bird," he likewise had nothing good to say about eighteenth-century preservatives:

> Considering the number of vertuosi [sic], who apply themselves to the collecting [sic] natural curiosities of the insect, bird, and beast kinds, it is surprizing that so few have endeavoured to discover effectual means of preserving their curiosities, when collected; one would imagine that those Gentlemen, in particular, who write on natural history, would be exceedingly desirous of such effectual methods, which, if once discovered and communicated to the public, would be the means of their receiving many rare subjects, and even non-descripts from different parts of Asia, Africa, and America, which would afford infinite pleasure to naturalists, and greatly encourage the study of natural history. But instead of this,

it is too common to see people, for want of knowing better methods, persevering in those which their own experience, and that of their acquaintance, daily convinces them are ineffectual: although they have the mortification of seeing their collections, which have been made with great trouble and expence, continually dropping in decay.[47]

Kuckahn offered some advice on the matter, suggesting two concoctions. The first was a liquid varnish of raw turpentine, camphor, and spirit of turpentine, the second, a dry compound composed of corrosive sublimate, saltpeter, alum, flowers of sulfur, musk, black pepper, and ground tobacco. Once these preservatives were prepared, the bird was to be skinned, as much flesh as possible removed, and all exposed parts varnished and sprinkled with the dry compound. The wings were held in place with wires, the tail supported by another wire run through the rump and up the backbone. With this rudimentary armature in place, the body and head cavities were stuffed with a mixture of equal parts tansy, wormwood, hops, and tobacco. For the breast bone, Kuckahn suggested cutting an artificial model from a soft wood. By pushing wires in through the feet (attached to a board beneath) and fixing them to the wooden breast plate, an upright position could be achieved. At every state of the process, all parts—skin, thread, wood, and wires—were to be painted with the toxic varnish. He recommended keeping the birds from direct light, as the sun "will certainly discharge the finer colours of the plumage."[48]

With specimens prepared, the naturalist's job was hardly over. Unremitting attention was required to keep insects at bay. Although Kuckahn claimed that his chemicals perfectly preserved specimens, he advised keeping birds in individual airtight cases (the use of individual cases contained a potential infestation to one case), which were to be washed with a mixture of boiled turpentine and camphor. He also admitted that the only dependable insecticide was an oven and strongly recommended baking freshly prepared mounts in order to set the preservative. Specimens were also to be baked every two to three years to destroy eggs, if "the bird has been dead some time and has any disagreeable smell."[49] Yet constant baking did nothing to preserve the delicacy of skin around the eyes and mouth, the vibrancy of feathers, or the overall freshness of the specimen.

Although many naturalists worried that an effective insecticide would never be found, taxidermy got its great leap forward with the innovative chemical experiments of Jean-Baptiste Bécoeur, from the town of Metz in northeastern France.[50]

In 1738 Bécoeur began experimenting with fifty chemicals to determine which were most effective against insects. He tested one chemical on fifty different specimens, leaving the birds exposed to any type of hungry worm or mite or fly that might be passing by. After four years, only four specimens were free from insect attacks. He decided to mix the four chemicals used on these specimens—ground arsenic, camphor, potassium carbonate, and powdered calcium hydroxide—with soap in a preparation that has become known as arsenical paste.

After years of trials, failures, and eventual unparalleled success, Bécoeur was keen to trumpet his success but loath to divulge the secret ingredients of his near-magical preparation. He resolved to send his specimens to the renowned Buffon at the Cabinet du Roi. Bécoeur hoped that the excellent quality of his birds would publicize his remarkable achievement without forcing him to divulge his secret formula. His decision was inspired. Buffon was more than impressed with the birds. Where most specimens only survived several years and then only if sealed airtight behind glass, Bécoeur's birds remained free from attack even when left exposed in the open air. Buffon wrote to Bécoeur in 1758, informing him that all the birds were still "in excellent condition" and requesting more specimens. Despite the popularity of his methods, Bécoeur was unwilling to publish the recipe for commercial reasons and succeeded in keeping his recipe secret during his lifetime. The formula was eventually discovered, published, and popularized by one of France's most famous taxidermists, Louis Dufresne. By the 1820s arsenic had emerged as the standard preservative against insect attack.[51] It was taxidermy's turning point.

Once naturalists could stave off insect attacks, collections of birds and beasts expanded almost as steadily as shell collections. Also, with better preservatives, naturalists had more reason to develop better artistic methods. And in this as well, Bécoeur surpassed his contemporaries. Bécoeur's collection was something of a visual marvel. Among the most comprehensive collections of European birds, it exuded equal parts enchantment and scientific vigor. As one contemporary admirer, Bernardin Pierron, wrote:

Had Bécoeur lived in ages past, he would have been accused of witchcraft and enchantment. What wonders has this excellent naturalist not been able to unite in his cabinet. These are truly immortal animals. The dog barks (or so it seems), the monkey changes posture, the hedgehog hides below its spines, the timid hare lifts its ear to listen, the sloth fears to move in search of food. . . . The birds soar or play with their feathers painted in a thousand different colours. They are marvelously assorted in the bird of paradise, which has a golden head, a green collar, a bright red back and wings equal to the rainbow in beauty; yet it is not inferior to the humming-bird whose lively brightness surpasses all masterpieces of art.[52]

POETIC TAXIDERMY

Hummingbirds were certainly the epitome of natural beauty, but the rest of nature—even the most local, mundane parts—was hardly ignored by nature admirers. In fact, collecting, studying, and admiring local nature (not everyone could afford an exotic hummingbird collection) became something of a European obsession by the mid-nineteenth century. Perhaps the discovery of arsenic and the sheer quantity of taxidermy being produced explained the new vogue. Or perhaps it was the urbanizing effects of the Industrial Revolution, the waxing of romantic rustic nostalgia, and a growing sense of dislocation from the countryside. Perhaps the growing middle class needed to fill their newfound leisure time and satisfy their love of material objects. Whatever the cause, by the mid-nineteenth century taxidermy had reached its apotheosis in western Europe, and most particularly in England. No longer the amusement of an elite few, taxidermied creatures were democratized as gorgeously ennobling for everyone.

If it is difficult to exaggerate the mass appeal of natural history in the nineteenth century, it is equally impossible to overemphasize the influence of its popularizers. The passion for nature inspired by collectors such as Bullock and Gould was matched—if not exceeded—by popular writers like the Reverend John George Wood and Philip Gosse. The impact of these two men alone is best evinced by the collecting crazes they provoked, which quite literally swept the ferns, seaweeds, shells, and birds from England's seashores and meadows into Victorian parlors. Wood's *Common Objects of the Country* (1858) sold one hundred thousand copies in one week, and his *Common Objects of the Seashore* (1857) only increased the mania for seashore collecting trips set in motion by Gosse's introduction to seashore rambling—*A Naturalist's Rambles on the Devonshire Coast*—published four years earlier, in 1853.

This setting-up of birds naturally is . . . the very poetry of the art. It must be learned direct from nature. . . . Hence it is that most London-stuffed birds, though often marvels of mechanical skill, are seldom pleasing to look upon.

—HENRY HOUSMAN, *The Story of Our Museum: Showing How We Formed It, and What It Taught Us* (1881), 45

10 John Everett Millais, *The Ornithologist* (formerly *The Ruling Passion*), 1865. Oil on canvas. Photo courtesy of Glasgow Museums, Art Gallery and Museum, Kelvingrove, Scotland.

Any Victorian household would have at least one or two stuffed birds under glass, along with some small natural history collection: pressed ferns on the parlor wall, a collection of butterflies, or at least a few shells, feathers, or minerals.[53] During his visit to Liverpool in 1826, the great American ornithologist John Audubon dined at the country estate of the Rathbones, a wealthy merchant family, in the hope of ensuring their patronage for his illustrated works. As he entered the residence, Audubon observed "a full and beautiful collection of the birds of England, well prepared and arranged." But stuffed birds were hardly limited to the entrance halls of the upper classes. Two days later, while strolling through the Liverpool market, Audubon made note of the wares for sale: "I saw here viands of all descriptions, fish, vegetables, game, fruits—both indigenous and imported from all quarters of the globe,—bird sellers, with even little collections of stuffed specimens, cheeses of enormous size, butter in great abundance, immense crates of hen's-eggs packed in layers of oats imported from Ireland."[54] Taxidermy was everywhere, from the conservatories of the wealthiest patrons to the market stalls, and everywhere in between.

While fads in collecting came and went (seaweeds were immensely popular for a period, as were anemones, anything capable of inhabiting aquariums, mosses, and ferns), taxidermy was a persistent presence in Victorian collections. As the naturalist William Swainson noted in 1840, "in nothing has the growing taste for natural history so much manifested itself, as in the prevalent fashion of placing glass cases of beautiful birds and splendid insects on the mantel piece or side-table." Such collections emphasized "the beauty and variety in Nature's form" and fed the "gratification of the eye." And more, through exposure to nature's beauty, Swainson writes, the "attention of the most indolent is attracted, the curiosity of the inquisitive awakened; and thus a first impulse may be given, particularly to youthful minds, to tastes and studies which may prove the solace and delight of after years," which is to say, a collection of stuffed birds did more than decorate a room.[55] The beauty of the birds awakened the senses and calmed the mind. Natural beauty was not irrelevant, particularly to the weekend collector.

The enthusiasm for studying and collecting nature derived in great part from the close connection between natural science, nature's aesthetic appeal, and moral edification. In accordance with natural theology, the design of nature was not seen as random or meaningless, but quite the opposite. William Paley's *Natural Theology, or Evidences of the Existence and Attributes of the Deity, Collected from the Appearances of Nature* (1802), argued that God's existence could be deduced from the wondrous and intricate design of all his little creatures. In other words, animal beauty was not merely visually satisfying but provided incontestable proof of a benevolent deity, and nature's beauties were upheld as all that was good and moral. As Shirley Hibberd put it in his wildly popular *Rustic Adornments for Homes of Taste, and Recreations for Town Folk, in the Study and Imitation of Nature*, first published in 1856, "it would be an anomaly to find a student of nature addicted to the vices that cast so many dark shadows on our social life; nor do I remember among the sad annals of criminal history, one instance of a naturalist who became a criminal, or a single gardener who has been hanged."[56]

With the publication of Charles Darwin's *On the Origin of Species* in 1859, natural theology withered, but appreciation of the beauty and fitness of nature remained solid. Darwin later wrote in his autobiography that the "old argument of design in nature, as given by Paley," had given way to the laws of natural selection. "We can no longer argue that, for instance, the beautiful hinge of a bivalve shell must have been made by an intelligent being, like the hinge of a door by man." Yet, while there was no more design in the variability of organic beings than in the direction of the wind, organisms of every kind "are beautifully adapted to their habits of life," which is to say, theories of adaptation and natural selection hardly diminished the longing for the organic elegance and fitness of life.[57]

Although the solidarity of natural theology was dismantled, popular writers maintained a revised form of natural theology, and their readers remained enthralled by the traditional moral and aesthetic qualities of the natural world. Nature could save your soul. Even if dead and stuffed, natural beauty was spiritually cleansing, which meant that natural history and taxidermy were particularly beneficial to young minds. In *The Story of Our Museum: Showing How We Formed It, and What It Taught Us* (1881), the Reverend Henry Housman reconsidered the importance of his boyhood fascination with nature. He explained that "the constant habit of looking for our recreation and pleasures to the world of nature begat within us a certain sympathy with everything we found there, and a reverence for the wonderful beauty we saw in everything we examined." Other lessons of boyhood had been forgotten, but the acquisition of "that indefinable love for all living creatures" remained. The best way to approach nature was to "observe reverently," Housman concluded. "Cultivate a feeling of reverence for the beautiful things of this most beautiful world."[58] Killing a bird was not a wanton act if its body was stuffed and neatly arranged in a collection. That even a boy's collection of taxidermy expressed an indefinable love for all living creatures gives an idea of just how resonant the social evaluation of animal beauty was in Victorian England. Displaying a stuffed bird was an act of an elevated, cultivated, pious, and pragmatic spirit.

Appreciating natural beauty in nineteenth-century England was a cultural activity of such ubiquity and importance that it can be understood as an unofficial social program. In fact, after passage of the Elementary Education Act of 1870, natural history became a compulsory school subject. William Henry Flower, the director of the Natural History Museum in London, claimed that while "easy" childhood methods of learning about nature, such as nature books and lectures, were useful, such inquiries could hardly compare to "the downright hard personal work by which all solid, lasting knowledge must be gained," that is, the hard work necessary to create one's own collection. Collecting inculcated socially useful and practical virtues such as originality, order, neatness, patience, passion, curiosity, physical vigor, taste, a desire to pursue knowledge, and a degree of national pride fostered by studying England's bounteous share of nature. In a sense, taxidermy made good citizens.[59]

But if taxidermy flourished in the nineteenth century, it is hardly a given that techniques improved. As ever, quantity does not necessarily mean quality. In fact, laments about disastrous taxidermy continued almost unabated throughout the century. Even by the very end of the century, in an address to the British Association for the Advancement of Science, Flower, the association's president, could not "refrain from saying a word upon the sadly-neglected art of taxidermy, which continues to fill the cases of most of our museums with wretched and repulsive caricatures of mammals and birds, out of all natural proportions, shrunken here and bloated there, and in attitudes absolutely impossible for the creatures to have assumed while alive." Taxidermy was an art that required "natural genius as well as great cultivation," Flower continued, and the practice would never improve until museums and collectors paid taxidermists accordingly: "the present conventional low standard and low payment for 'bird-stuffers' . . . is utterly inadequate to induce any man of capacity to devote himself" to the practice.[60]

Besides the mass of questionable taxidermy done by amateurs (encouraged by a growing number of how-to manuals), many village taxidermists' studios, unable to sustain themselves on their talents, advertised such services as hairdressing, policing, picture framing, and knife sharpening. The promiscuous list speaks volumes. Most taxidermy produced in village shops and by nature lovers was hardly well done. This is not to say that no good taxidermy was produced in the nineteenth century, only that a good percentage was distinctly amateurish.

Among the earliest and most poetic advocates of better taxidermic techniques was Charles Waterton, an English aristocrat, showman, madcap adventurer, and avid, even obsessive, student of nature. In 1828 Waterton published his highly popular *Wanderings in South America, the North-West of the United States, and the Antilles, in the Years 1812, 1816, 1820, & 1824*. In his charming style, Waterton recounted the curious sounds, delights, and dangers of his life in the South American jungle. He described his encounters with big snakes and his effort to tempt a vampire bat with his toe. He considered the arboreal life of a sloth (previously believed to live on the ground), narrated his notorious ride on a caiman, and described how, while chewing a stew of boiled toucan, he hit on an idea for preserving the colors of the bird's extraordinary beak.[61] In short, *Wanderings in South America* exhibits that raw, rambunctious enthusiasm for nature that characterizes the writing of so many Victorian naturalists.

In his brief taxidermy instructions, "On Preserving Birds for Cabinets of Natural History," appended to the end of his book, Waterton offered some advice to the would-be taxidermist. First, he advised, develop a complete understanding of ornithological anatomy. Retreat to the haunts of birds. Scrutinize each species' attitudes and expressions in life. Without a true knowledge of the creature, "ere death, and your dissecting hand, brought it to its present still and formless state," no good taxidermy could result.[62] Skins stretched. The membranes around the eyes were easily distended by a careless or inexpert hand. Limbs were unnaturally elongated. Features collapsed. The soft tissues of noses and muzzles shrank and cracked, and the colors of bird legs and bills faded or simply turned as black as death. Death in actuality begot death in simulated life:

> Were you to pay as much attention to birds, as the sculptor does to the human frame, you would immediately see, on entering a museum, that the specimens are not well done. This remark will not be thought severe, when you reflect that,—that which once was a bird, has probably been stretched, stuffed, stiffened, and wired by the hand of a common clown. Consider, likewise, how the plumage must have been disordered, by too much stretching or drying, and perhaps sullied, or at least deranged, by the pressure of a coarse and heavy hand,—plumage which, ere life had fled from it, was accustomed to be touched by nothing rougher than the dew of heaven, and the pure and gentle breath of air.[63]

But more difficult still—in fact, the real poetry of taxidermy—was imparting the suggestion of life by capturing an animal's character. Ideally, taxidermy not only protected the carcasses of birds from decay, insects, and the ravages of time but preserved the elegance of life. For Waterton, taxidermy was an act of artistry,

Plate I.

PEREGRINE FALCON ON FLIGHT.

SHOWING METHOD OF BINDING, &C.

Frontispiece—see Page 111.

11 Showing a method of binding or "setting up" a peregrine falcon with wires and cardboard braces. From Montagu Browne, *Practical Taxidermy: A Manual of Instruction to the Amateur in Collecting, Preserving, and Setting Up Natural History Specimens of All Kinds*, 2nd ed. (London: L. Upcott Gill, 1884).

requiring a delicate hand, a sensitive touch, and a deep appreciation of nature's forms.

On his travels through South America, Waterton had seen hummingbirds for himself. Typically enough, he awarded the glittering little birds first place among the birds of the Americas. To see a hummingbird in flight took one's breath away: "see it darting through the air almost as quick as thought!—now it is within a yard of your face!—in an instant gone!—now it flutters from flower to flower to sip the silver dew—it is now a ruby—now a topaz—now an emerald—now all burnished gold!"[64] And yet, of hummingbird specimens in British and European museums Waterton contended that they had, "all of them, evidently been done by the hand of man, who knew not what he was doing."[65] Any common clown could "stuff" a bird or (a frequent error of amateur taxidermists) overstuff the skin. But to craft a specimen that gave some suggestion of the proportions, musculature, and harmony of the whole form required a great deal of experience with a knife, some cotton, a needle, and, above all, the beauty of living nature itself.

Knowing nature, however, was not simply a matter of counting teeth and measuring limbs. For Waterton, knowing nature meant penetrating the physical form to capture a sensuous understanding of creatures' attitudes, moods, and physical expressions. Knowing was carnal. Calling upon his classical reading, Waterton elevated taxidermy to a poetic art, capable of exposing the aesthetic resonance—indeed, the inner "truth"—of animal beauty and thereby able to transmute a lump of skin into a revelation of essence. Waterton argued that Horace's instructions for poets, which encouraged them to access the vital core of their characters' moral fiber, were equally germane to taxidermists: "Let Medea, says he, be savage and unconquerable; let Ino be in tears; let Ixion be perfidious; let Io be vagrant; and let Orestes be in sorrow."[66] Taxidermy was no routine exercise of manual labor: "you must possess Promethean boldness, and bring down fire, and animation, as it were, into your preserved specimen." The result? You will "be in ornithology what Angelo was in sculpture."[67]

Waterton's methods were not like those of his contemporaries. He did not use arsenic, preferring corrosive sublimate. Also, he developed a method of internal modeling by which skins were not mounted on molds but rather pushed out from within. The process was extremely successful but also extremely time consuming. Neither Waterton's preservatives nor his modeling methods were taken up by his peers, although all agreed that his techniques produced outstanding specimens, which have admirably survived the passing decades and are still on display in the Waterton Gallery at Wakefield Museum in Wakefield, West Yorkshire.

Waterton was hardly a vanilla character. His lifestyle was as flamboyant as his language, and his taxidermic methods were too laborious for most naturalists. Yet he was perhaps the first writer, certainly the earliest English writer, to offer any guidance on the posture and expressions of birds:

> Then you will place your Eagle, in attitude commanding, the same as Nelson stood in, in the day of battle, on Victory's quarter deck. Your Pie will seem crafty, and just ready to take flight, as though fearful of being surprised in some mischievous plunder. Your Sparrow will retain its wanton pertness, by means of placing his tail a little elevated, and giving a moderate arch to the neck. Your Vulture will show his sluggish habits by having his body nearly parallel to the earth; his wings somewhat drooping, and their extremities under the tail instead of above it,—expressive of ignoble indolence.
>
> Your Dove will be in artless, fearless innocence, looking mildly at you, with its neck not too much stretched, as if uneasy in its situation, or drawn too close into the shoulders, like one wishing to avoid discovery; but in moderate, perpendicular lengths, supporting the head horizontally, which will set off the breast to the best advantage.[68]

A closer, more intimate, more carnal knowledge of nature coupled with an improved science of preservation meant that simply stuffing a bird was no longer enough. Collectors expected specimens to express something of the creatures' charisma and beauty, of their disposition and posture. Doves, hawks, and vultures differ not only in size, coloring, and plumage but also in mood, carriage, and attitude: Nelson's noble eagle, the mischievous pie, the wantonly pert sparrow, the innocent dove. The mummified creatures of cabinets of wonder hardly conveyed a sense of a creature's beauty. Dehydrated, brittle, lacking all animation or vibrancy, most were so rudely prepared that they hardly offered a notion of a creature's typical poses or expressions. But with improved techniques in the nineteenth century, admiration for the beauty of a preserved creature necessarily emerged not merely as appreciation of natural beauty but also as appreciation of a naturalist's knowledge and an artist's skill. And with this intrusion of artistry, a new question arises: is taxidermy art, nature, or something in between?

Of all the motivations for taxidermy, the longing to immortalize animal beauty is perhaps the most pervasive. It is the desire to perpetuate the looking, to look lingeringly and closely. But humans can rarely look on nature without imposing meaning, and, as we have seen, raw nature is endlessly enhanced or distorted by imaginative interpretation and cultural infatuation. The next chapter pursues that infatuation to the other extreme of animal beauty—from hummingbirds' fragility to the dangers of man-eaters—in order to explore how artistry, imagination, and nature hang together in the theatrics of display.

SPECTACLE

3

The self-taught French artist Henri Rousseau was well-known for his jungle paintings. In fact, his dreamlike jungles, completed in the last decade of his life and filled with exotic creatures, animal violence, and fantastically luscious vegetation, are considered the apotheosis of the artist's style. Some of his jungles are peaceful, depicting monkeys playing with oranges or peeking out from behind enormous fronds. However, arguably his most popular images (and certainly his most sensational) are those of animal attacks, mostly painted from 1904 to 1910. In one painting a lion tears an antelope; in another, a lion is eating a leopard. A tiger attacks a water buffalo; a leopard rears up against a black silhouette of a man; a jaguar brings down a white horse, all amid the excessive fertility of overblown flowers, colossal leaves, and hanging bananas.

What makes Rousseau's paintings particularly beguiling is that the artist never traveled to those distant geographies to witness tropical nature for himself. His paintings are aggregations, imaginative constructions drawn from the

For some animals, of course, their beauty does not rest with a gentle aesthetic display, but with one of power and aggression such as the lioness running down the antelope, the pinch and grab of the crab, the sucking and entwining octopus.

—ALAN BLEAKLEY, *The Animalizing Imagination: Totemism, Textuality, and Ecocriticism* (2000), 36 popular culture of tropicality that blossomed within turn-of-the-century Paris. In addition to postcards and photographs from French colonies, books of wild and bloodthirsty beasts, adventure tales of heroic hunters, and popular scientific journals, Rousseau drew inspiration from the Paris hothouses, the animals in the zoological gardens, and the galleries of taxidermy at the Muséum national d'histoire naturelle. As the "heady mixture of the real and the imagined filed down to a popular audience," Nancy Ireson writes of Rousseau's creative process, "the jungle started to become entertainment, the dangers of the unknown a source of excitement."[1] This is the atmosphere of Rousseau's paintings. Filled with his era's desire for the bewitching dangers of the colonial frontiers and his own strange dreams of exotic animal savagery and lush abundance, Rousseau created "tropical forests for Northern imaginations."[2]

Alongside its territorial acquisition and economic advantages, imperialism asserted particular ideologies about what made Europe and Europeans so very different from various colonial geographies and their inhabitants. By the middle of the nineteenth century, an established package of themes, metaphors, images, and analogies conveyed the uniqueness and strangeness of tropical nature, its otherness and difference from home and the familiar, to European audiences. The tropics were characterized by extravagant vegetation, colossal flowers, heavily perfumed fruits and exquisite birds, excessive heat and humidity, and dangerously large snakes, spiders, and cats.[3] Geographical variation in tropical imaginings surely existed (African tropics were viewed as a dark place of disease, whereas South America offered more lyrical images of vegetal abundance), yet the chief tropes were pervasive: fertility, savagery, and superabundance, all bound together with the romance of danger.[4] Plants were more prodigious, more vast; beasts were bolder, lither, more dramatic. Life was imagined to be rawer at the edges of the world, death more vivid. Even the birds and blossoms were more brilliantly colored.

Titled Henri Rousseau: Jungles in Paris, a 2005 exhibition brought together forty-eight paintings with an extensive selection of images and ephemera from turn-of-the-century Paris, including a piece of theatrical taxidermy, crafted in 1886 by Parisian taxidermists A. Terrier and J. Quantin, called *Oryx algazelle et lionne*, depicting a lioness attacking a white oryx.[5] The scene is vicious: a lioness sinks her teeth into the neck of an antelope, a massive clawed paw ripping the dying creature's face and dragging the beast to the ground. The dramatic scene sufficiently exhilarated Rousseau's imagination for him to replicate the terror in precise detail.

The Hungry Lion Throws Itself on the Antelope (1905) reproduces the exact angle of the attack, the thrust of the lion's heavy paw, and the anguished upturned tilt of the antelope's head as the creature is brought to its knees (fig. 12).

Certainly Rousseau enhanced the sensationalism by envisioning a looming panorama of towering vegetal fertility and deep bloody gashes on the antelope's haunches. A leopard and two birds lurk in the trees above, hoping to get a piece of the kill. Rousseau even transfigured the female lioness into the more potent symbol of a male lion with full mane. In short, the painting is a typical scene of the "savage exotic," teeming with terror, fascination, and more than a dash of raw primal energy. When Rousseau exhibited the painting at the 1905 Salon d'Automne, it was accompanied by the following caption: "The hungry lion throws itself upon the antelope, devours him; anxiously the panther awaits the moment that he too can claim his share. Birds of prey have torn a strip of flesh from the poor animal that is shedding a tear! The sun sets."[6]

If Rousseau's image was inspired by the taxidermic rendition of animal savagery, so was the taxidermy shaped by its cultural moment. Despite Rousseau's exuberant visions, the actual battle in taxidermy has no lush tropical backdrop, just a hint of desert sand on the mount's small rectangular base. The scene suggests an arid climate, a vision more North African in leaning than tropical. And, certainly, flanking European tropical imaginings was a network of interests informing how the Orient was portrayed and experienced in western Europe. Orientalism, as Edward Said classically described it, was mainly a British and French colonial and cultural enterprise, encompassing territories vaguely located in northern Africa and the Near East. Darkly romantic, dangerous, and seductive, the Orient embodied Western longings for exotic otherness. The Orientalist images and texts circulating within western European culture, as Said explained, were not truths but representations framed by political and cultural imperialism, and the meaning of such representations—as with tropical imaginings—held a special place in western European formation. In other words, "that Orientalism makes sense at all depends more on the West than on the Orient, and this sense is directly indebted to various Western techniques of representation that make the Orient visible, clear, 'there' in discourse about it."[7] And one of those techniques for crafting spectacles was taxidermy.

Whether Orientalist or tropical in leaning, whether in paint or in fur, both Rousseau's paintings and theatrical taxidermy aimed to construct a spectacle of

12 Henri Rousseau, *Le lion, ayant faim, se jette sur l'antilope,*
1898/1905. Oil on canvas. Photo
by Robert Bayer. Courtesy of
Fondation Beyeler, Riehen/Basel.

nature that resonated with their cultural moment. For such scenes of theatrical drama, the animals were not posed primarily to highlight their coloring and
shapes, genus and species, lion and antelope. But neither was the point simply to
indulge in a thrilling scene of dangerous nature. The point rested quite precisely
in what such spectacles of nature meant, on who was doing the looking, and why.

Imaginings of colonial landscapes were part of a system of collecting the
world, exotic object by exotic object, fantasy by fantasy. All collections are composed of things that have been particularly selected and isolated from the heterogeneous clutter of the world, which means that collections are always shaped
by daydreams about how the world and its contents relate to us. Why have these
particular things been selected and not others? What sort of spectacle do they
create together? In a sense, collections are choreographed performances, and each

collected item emboldens the fantasy.[8] For example, early modern collections of exotica, with wonders piled on top of wonders, painted precisely the world that was desired: a world teeming with visual delight and unending marvels. Similarly, the images of colonial regions, the imported animals and plants, the hunting narratives and animal trophies brought home by adventurers and big-game hunters did not merely reflect colonial places but actively created their identity for Europeans. And, not surprisingly, the most desired beasts for European audiences were the hardest, most dangerous, most thrilling beasts to kill. After all, the majority of savage animals had long since been eradicated from western Europe.

Over the course of the nineteenth century, large animal scenes, especially sensational scenes of animal combat between predator and prey, emerged as the zenith of artistic taxidermic skill and as an awe-inspiring precinematic technology for revealing dramatic animal action. In our twenty-first-century world of image saturation, when living, breathing, fighting, mating, attacking animals from all parts of the globe enter our living rooms via the television in big, bold full color, we easily become blasé about the imagery. Yet in an era before animal documentaries and moving color images of animals, such dramatic spectacles of animals in action were limited to an elite class of travelers. Paintings could portray animal attacks. Photography captured static postures of exotic beasts—usually after they had been vanquished by hunters, and only in black and white.[9] The enormous popularity of zoos and menageries suggests just how exciting exotic animals were in the nineteenth century. To see animals in motion, even if only frozen in motion, even if only dead and stuffed, was something marvelous to audiences.

The taxidermy discussed in the first two chapters of this volume could never have inspired Rousseau's sensational reinterpretation in paint. This was not mere preservation but a new, bolder genre of taxidermy. It spoke to the imaginative potency and potential of taxidermy, but it also raised more general questions about the blurring of reality and representations, the fusion of nature and culture, animal and imagination, that defines all taxidermy.

Animals seem to offer themselves as direct access to truth, to a reality that exists above, beyond, prior to representation. Animals literally are animals, obviously. But our perception of animals is tied up with our relation to them. Is the animal a wild lion or a domestic cat? Does it live on a farm, in a forest, in a jungle, or in a zoo? Is it endangered? Is it beautiful? Is it an urban "pest"? Is it invasive? Any animal catalogue engages spatial, emotional, symbolic, and ecological relationships, which are in turn shaped by their cultural, historical, and political moment. This is not to say that there is no animal reality outside representation, no nature beyond culture. Nor is the issue a matter of exploring how independent entities—nature/culture, reality/representation—*become* mixed in particular scenarios. Rather, nature and culture are always mixed within the human imagination.[10] Animal phenomena and human meaning are inseparable. And this is particularly true of taxidermy. As an intentional, desiring act, taxidermy necessarily endows animal form with human significance. There is no taxidermy without human longing to perpetuate the ability to look at animals. And in looking at taxidermy, viewers must always ask themselves why and for whom this particular creature has been preserved; what desire, ideology, or aesthetic craving it satisfies. That is, despite the raw materiality of a genuine animal skin, all taxidermy is simultaneously a *representation* of raw animal materiality. In looking at taxidermy, the point is not to untangle the untangleable (what parts are nature, what parts artifice) but to explore the resonance and motives of such promiscuous mixing. In this case, what are the qualities of the spectacle? What is being portrayed? How, and for whom?

This chapter examines two different sorts of animal spectacles: scenes of animal savagery popular in the late nineteenth century and dioramas of ecological peace crafted in the early decades of the twentieth century. Despite their difference in emotion and purpose, displays of animal violence were the conceptual forerunners of the more demure habitat dioramas. Both exude a longing for spectacle, a longing for a privileged look into the private lives of animals and a desire to experience them "firsthand." Both used taxidermy as a technology for making nature visible for particular audiences in order to elicit particular emotional responses. Just as taxidermy is inherently laden with human significance, meticulously crafted spectacles of nature can never be free of cultural meaning.

There was a catch to all such mythmaking. Bad taxidermy, lacking any sense of musculature or physical intensity, is rarely able to cast a spell of "living nature." Bad taxidermy makes the craft of preservation too blatantly visible to inspire an emotive spectacle. Certainly anatomical correctness is important for all taxidermy, but correctness is perhaps more important in taxidermy designed to *affect* its audience. The more skill a taxidermist possesses, the more able he or she is to impose an artistic vision on the animal, to craft a mood, to fashion a disposition, a feeling, an aura, a spectacle. The power of theatrical taxidermy rests precisely in taxidermy's artful artlessness. The same can be said of contemporary animal documentaries. Viewers do not want to see filmmakers at work. They want to experience the fantasy of a private view into nature's most intimate moments, as if they were unedited and unchoreographed. As with taxidermy, when too much labor is visible, the fantasy of transparency is ruined. So how were the animals made?

MAKING LIONS

Both the quantity and the proficiency of mammal taxidermy lagged far behind avian mounts well into the nineteenth century: beasts—particularly murderous, snarling, dying beasts—were vastly more difficult to prepare than birds daintily placed on branches. Bigger, more articulated bodies meant that more things could go wrong, anatomically speaking. Feathers hide a multitude of defects. Shaggy hair likewise conceals structurally specious bodies. But with short-haired animals like lions and tigers, with no thick fur or feathers to hide errors, every bulging, sagging blunder showed. Animals in tight action were even more challenging, since every detail was crucial to capturing the truth of the action—the musculature in the animal's legs, the tension across the back, the folds of skin at the neck, not to mention the facial expression, the snarling lips and hooded eyes. To achieve a true sense of anatomical correctness and vigor, taxidermy required a high level of zoological knowledge, technical skill, and delicacy of touch, and this combination of science and art was hardly the norm among mid-nineteenth-century taxidermists.

Early mammal taxidermy involved building animals up from the barest internal armature by stuffing skins with straw, paper, tow, or some other soft material. (The skins of early taxidermied beasts still on display in some museums are often cracked and split, revealing the creatures' straw underpinnings.) Certainly skins were bulked up, but the method only allowed the most rudimentary suggestion of muscles and tension. More problematic still was the way skins shrank as they dried. Taxidermists might strive to create naturalistic undulations by molding supple, dampened skins. But as skins dried, such folds and wrinkles usually flattened out. Skins became as taut as a drum, eliminating any sense of musculature or natural form.

A new method of preparing large animal mounts developed in the last decades of the nineteenth century: internal sculpture. This method, with various idiosyncratic variations, arose almost simultaneously across Europe and North

Now, should I call upon any one . . . to step forward and show me how to restore majesty to the face of a lion's skin, ferocity to the tiger's countenance, innocence to that of the lamb, or sulkiness to that of the bull, he would not know which way to set to work. . . . He could produce nothing beyond a mere dried specimen, shrunk too much in this part, or too bloated in that; a mummy, a distortion, a hideous spectacle, a failure in every sense of the word.

—CHARLES WATERTON, *Essays on Natural History, Chiefly Ornithology*, 2nd ed. (1838), 300–301

America, each taxidermist who practiced it declaring himself its inventor.[11] The new process began in the same way as traditional stuffing: four leg wires, bent to proper shape, were attached to a vertical centerboard of wood. Two additional rods supported the skull, and another, if required, the tail. This armature or "manikin" was wrapped tightly with thinly shaved strands of wood, known as excelsior, and bound with twine until it perfectly resembled the creature in every possible undulation and bulge, creating a perfect animal sculpture (fig. 13).

To make up thick muscles in the legs, a bunch of excelsior was bound in place with twine. Smaller protuberances and muscles were made with soft, long-fiber tow. The process was slow and meticulous, and it required the constant critical assessment of a naturalist's eye and comparison with the skin. Attention to the most minute details was imperative. For example, to bring out the prominent muscles in the leg, William Hornaday, one of America's greatest taxidermists, recommended sewing through the leg along a vertical line "to produce certain depressions that exist between the larger muscles."[12] Achilles tendons were made with a twisted wire attached at the heel and wrapped with tow. The key was never to make the manikin too big—it could always be built up, but removing layers of twine and excelsior involved painstaking labor.

Absolute anatomical accuracy was crucial, and the overall success of a mount was often dependent on the measurements taken before the animal's skin was removed. Vague notions of animal form could hardly produce anatomical correctness. Polished taxidermy on the outside depends on exacting, meticulous reproduction of an animal's internal form. Taxidermists usually also drew an outline of the animal on paper and sometimes, when possible, took casts of its face, feet, and other features.

The real secret to an anatomically correct taxidermy mount rested in the next step: adhering a skin to the manikin. And on this subject, Hornaday was the self-proclaimed inventor of the manikin covered in clay, rather than materials used by other taxidermists such as papier-mâché or plaster. Hornaday instructed his readers to mix up enough clay—soft enough to smear—to cover the entire twine sculpture with a quarter-inch-thick coat of clay. When the manikin was completely covered from nose to tail—"a complete clay statue of the animal"—the skin was pressed into the clay, leaving no air bubbles or looseness. Next, the skin was sewn up. "You can actually model the skin down upon the body," Hornaday wrote, "and it will not only take the exact form of the manikin—every depression and every

Plate IV.

LION MOUNTED FROM THE "FLAT."

SHOWING POSITION OF "BODY BOARD" AND LEG IRONS, &C., BUT WITHOUT FALSE RIBS.

13 Showing the positioning of a flat "body board" and rods for setting up a lion skin. From Montagu Browne, *Practical Taxidermy: A Manual of Instruction to the Amateur in Collecting, Preserving, and Setting Up Natural History Specimens of All Kinds,* 2nd ed. (London: L. Upcott Gill, 1884).

elevation—but it will also *keep* it." The taxidermist had to work quickly, while the skin and clay were still wet (Hornaday recommended that two taxidermists work together on a large mount, keeping the skin damp with towels). The efforts were enormous, but the result was a perfectly molded skin, perfectly forming every undulation and muscle. "There is a supreme pleasure in crowning a well-made manikin with a handsome skin, and seeing a specimen take on perfect form and permanent beauty as if by magic. It is then that you begin to be proud of your work; and finally you revel in it. You say to yourself, '*This* is art!'—and so it is."[13]

The next stage—and perhaps the most difficult—was the face and mouth, particularly if the mouth was open in a snarl, exposing teeth, gums, and tongue. Unless represented in the act of seizing something, jaws should not be opened too widely, or the animal would seem to be laughing or, worse, yawning. "The large *Felidæ* (tiger, lion, leopard, etc.)," Hornaday wrote, "are the finest subjects for the taxidermist that the whole animal kingdom can produce. They offer the finest opportunities for the development of muscular anatomy, and the expression of higher passions." As always, Hornaday was adamant: "In the first place, *strive to capture the spirit of your subject*." The expressive spirit of the beast was captured in the smallest touches. When snarling, the fleshy skin around a lion's nose bunches together, and the upper lips contracts toward the nose, while the lower lip falls away from the incisors. The eyelids are drawn over the eyes, and the eyebrows pull together "until the scowl becomes frightful." The ears should be flattened to the neck, and the tongue "also pulls itself together, contracts in the middle, curves up at the edges, and makes ready to retire farther back between the jaws at the instant of seizure."[14] But fleshy parts of the mouth shrank, dried, cracked, and lost all color once life had departed.

To counteract the effects of death on the lips, gums, and tongue, several ingredients were needed: clay, papier-mâché, needle and thread, a few delicate sculpting tools, wax, and oil paint. First, the inside of the lips against the jaw bone were filled with clay to pad out the mouth area. With the desired expression achieved, a few stitches would hold the lips in place while they dried. Papier-mâché was pressed into shape to replace the fleshy gums, filling up the edges of the lips so that they seemed attached to the teeth, like gums. If the mouth was wide open, the roof would be visible and the surface would need to be molded into the "same peculiar corrugations that you saw in the mouth immediately after death. This is slow work. It requires a good eye, a skilful, artistic touch, and unlimited patience. If you are an artist, prove it now by the fidelity with which you copy nature in this really difficult work." To finish the gums, two or three coats of oil paint were needed—better still, a thin coat of tinted hot wax—to properly imitate their color. The technique required a dexterous touch, but it was a skill worth acquiring: "the beauty of the results will amply repay your labor." If the mouth was open, the roof of the mouth also had to be waxed—but in black. For this the animal was turned upside down. When dealing with the joint between the black mouth wax and the pink gum wax, Hornaday offered a handy tip: "the two colors can be nicely blended by letting the last layers of pink wax lap over a trifle, upon the black, so that the latter will show through the former here and there, and give the line of demarcation a mottled appearance, with the two colors blended together."[15] No detail was too small or irrelevant.

And finally came the tongue. For Hornaday, the only perfect tongue was a real tongue. Otherwise, all the delicate papillae would be lost. To mount a tongue, Hornaday told his readers, you first cut a piece of lead sheet into the right size and shape. Cover the metal with clay (to replace the flesh of the tongue) and then press the skinned tongue into the clay. Like all fleshy parts, tongues lost most of their color when dried. Varnish it with oil paint diluted with a little turpentine so that the surface isn't too glossy. "Vermilion and white are the best colors to use, and above all do not make the tongue or lips look too like pink candy, or red flannel, or red sealing-wax." If in doubt about color, Hornaday suggested consulting the household cat: a "patient old tabby is an invaluable ally in the mounting of feline animals of all sorts."[16] And throughout the whole process, the animal's expression had to match its bodily posture. A snarling face hardly sits well on an otherwise peacefully posed animal. "The attitude must match the expression of the face, or the tragedy becomes a farce," as Hornaday put it. Man-eaters had to look like man-eaters to be effective.

ELOQUENT SKINS

Animals were certainly a tantalizing ingredient in this Western fashioning of colonial otherness. Large African predators in particular—lions, tigers, leopards—were metonymic of entire geographies, concentrating in animal form what made those distant landscapes so ferociously exciting, so *exotic*. Big cats just seemed to emanate the savagery, rawness, and magnificence that characterized colonial landscapes in the Western imagination, symbolizing the psychological heart of

There is nothing like the fear that man-eaters bring. They own the night and kill so quickly.

—NARRATOR OF *The Ghost and the Darkness* (1996), directed by Stephen Hopkins the untamable exotic. Animal attacks were necessarily exotic: they were what happened *out there,* beyond the controlled environments of "civilized" European urban centers.

Writers, adventurers, and artists all indulged in the lurid mythmaking and excitement of little-known geographies, particularly those inhabited by large predators. Popular periodicals such as *La Nature, Le Petit Journal,* and *Le Journal Illustré* regularly printed stories and images of the most appalling beast attacks. Among the most famous *animaliers,* practitioners of a highly popular romanticized genre of animal art, were Emmanuel Frémiet, whose bronze sculpture of a gorilla abducting a naked woman won the medal of honor at the Paris Salon in 1887 (a similar scene still graces the entrance hall of the Galerie d'anatomie comparée at the Muséum national d'histoire naturelle), and Antoine-Louis Barye, who created works with such scintillating titles as *Tiger Devouring a Crocodile, Tiger Hunt,* and *Lion and Snake.* Exotic big-game hunting, with its underlying subplot of white man versus the dark unknown, was embedded in the imperial enterprise, and from midcentury onward, hunters pictured amid heaps of recent kills became the archetypal colonial adventurers. Bagging a lion or a tiger was the king of sports, an exercise of vigor, courage, endurance, sportsmanship, and dominion over landscapes and their inhabitants, whether human or otherwise. African trophy hunters such as the renowned Roualeyn Gordon-Cumming, Frederick Courteney Selous, and the duke of Orléans emerged as nothing short of national heroes. Readers gobbled up their adventure stories of near-death encounters, heart-pounding chases, and the triumphant, primal surge of conquest.[17]

Even natural history writers professing some degree of austerity indulged in exotic dangers. The popular writer Philip Henry Gosse could not refrain from adding a chapter titled "The Terrible" to his *Romance of Natural History* (1860). The chapter details a long list of anecdotal stories of humans being bettered by wolves, bears, elephants, rhinoceroses, buffalo, kangaroos, gorillas, sharks, crocodiles, and a variety of snakes, including a "shocking story about a very deadly snake" whose bite caused a young man to swell "to a horrible size," to bleed at the eyes, nose, and mouth, and to expire in less than half an hour. Terrible indeed for the young man, but delicious for Victorian readers. It is hardly by chance that the book's flyleaf etching depicted a gorilla assaulting two terrified natives, and the front cover featured a violent rhinoceros attack. As Gosse put it, merely imagining the "stern conflict for life, when man stands face to face with his bestial foes," produced an "excitement of the imagination, and a thrilling of the nerves" that was highly pleasing for readers. The reality of such battles, Gosse was quick to highlight luridly, was rather less pleasant: a "most horrid form of death."[18]

While such dangers oozed through most representations of exotic predators, the reality of nineteenth-century zoological gardens and traveling menageries was somewhat less exhilarating. Like many Parisians, Rousseau wandered among the living animals crammed into the zoological gardens, examining these captive symbols of imperial dominion over exotic territories. Scrawny lions, tigers, and jaguars paced their small, badly ventilated cages. The Monkey Palace was an even sadder space, apparently so filthy and barren of amusement that most of its inhabitants weakened and died.[19] The average lifespan of the big cats in the early years of London's Zoological Gardens (opened in 1828) was about two years, which meant that one lion, tiger, leopard, or puma died each month.[20] Most zoological parks offered only a whiff of the wild beyond. Yet even the dreariest scenes hardly eradicated the pleasures of spectacle. Visitors were simply required to supply their own imaginings, fed on a diet of wild animal stories. Feeding time at zoos was the most popular event of the day, and it surely helped that animals often attacked visitors through the bars or mauled their handlers. They sometimes even escaped to terrorize the surrounding district. The frequent animal deaths at zoos nevertheless provided bounteous materials for natural history museums. What could not survive reality was reborn to stiff eternity.

The new zoological galleries at the Muséum national d'histoire naturelle in Paris had opened to a delighted public in 1889. The monkeys, apes, and carnivores occupied the first-floor galleries. Displayed together in low, long glass cases, the big cats drew particular attention, and not surprisingly. The taxidermy was expertly conceived and executed. "The cases are filled with individuals admirably stuffed in postures which they had commonly assumed in life," according to the popular press of the day.[21] And tucked between a group of lions and a series of chimpanzees, all posed in neutral stances, was the lion-and-antelope scene that so enthralled Rousseau.

The galleries had been prepared for the opening of the 1889 Exposition Universelle, held in Paris as part of the centenary commemoration of the storming of the Bastille. The exhibition itself covered almost a square kilometer. The Tour Eiffel was unveiled. Hot air balloons littered the sky. It was a triumph of republican France, of industrialism, technological development, and colonialism. Along the Seine on the Esplanade des Invalides, villages were imported from a dozen or so colonial nations and populated with similarly imported indigenous inhabitants, who played instruments, danced, cooked, or simply got on with living their transported lives.

The 1889 exposition was one of several major international fairs held in Paris during Rousseau's lifetime. Between 1851 and World War I, fifty-eight international fairs were held in Europe, Britain, and North America, of which about a dozen, including the 1889 exposition, were considered major exhibitions. The first was the Great Exhibition of the Works of Industry of All Nations, held in London in 1851, which received six million visitors over its six-month run. It was followed by the 1867 Exposition Universelle in Paris, the Centennial Exposition of 1876 in Philadelphia, the Colonial and Indian Exhibition of 1886 in London, and the World's Columbian Exposition, held in Chicago in 1893 to commemorate Christopher Columbus's four-hundredth anniversary, to mention just a few. Such events literally exhibited the world and, significantly, were key instruments for showcasing the potency and sway of nation and empire. Colonial modernity, as Timothy Mitchell argues, involved creating an effect that was recognized as "reality" by choreographing pieces of the world—particularly non-European pieces—to create and endlessly repeat it. New technologies, arts and cultural merchandise, and the natural products of distant lands—whether animal, vegetable, mineral, or human—were arranged as an endless series of ever more enticing pictures for roving, pleasure-seeking spectators. Captured both materially and metaphorically by the imperial lens, the world itself became the exhibition: a panorama of visual delight.[22]

Interestingly, taxidermy was featured prominently at all the exhibitions, particularly theatrical scenes engaging two or more animals. A wide range of taxidermy was shown, and the majority was, admittedly, the emotionally neutral variety of natural history mounts—lines of ducks or trophy heads, shows of regional beasts. Yet what truly distinguished taxidermy at the world exhibitions were emotive scenes of large animal violence, the sort of spectacles that stirred the emotions and showcased the glorious struggle for life. Although prior examples existed, taxidermic scenes of exotic savagery can be said to have developed precisely for such exhibitions of nationalistic propaganda.[23]

Since the best taxidermy depended on superior knowledge of nature, chemistry, and sculptural techniques, taxidermy asserted not only an empire's rule over natural resources and its discovery of new beasts but also its innovation and scientific knowledge. After all, world exhibitions were competitive platforms for displaying each nation's supreme achievements. In the twenty-first century, taxidermy is considered a low technology for making nature visible, as compared, for example, to animal documentaries, with their ability to follow creatures into their burrows or to capture high-speed chases. At the end of the nineteenth century, however, skillfully crafted animals emerged as precisely the sort of high art and science of which an empire could be proud. Good taxidermy depended on high-quality skins and precise natural knowledge, which in turn depended on exploration, travel, discovery, and conquest.

At the 1867 Exposition Universelle in Paris, British taxidermist Edwin Ward exhibited several animal groups, including *The Struggle*, depicting a lion and a tiger, both rearing up on their hind legs, locked in combat over the dead deer between them. At the same exhibition, French taxidermist Jules Verreaux won a gold medal for excellence for his bloodthirsty work *Arab Courier Attacked by Lions* (fig. 14). The scene depicted two Barbary lions, a subspecies that once inhabited the French colonial territories of northern Africa, attacking a camel rider. One lion is dead. The camel is bellowing in fear and pain. The rider is in a desperate struggle with the remaining lion.

On the one hand, the work presents the natural history of a colonial region: a camel and a geographically circumscribed subspecies of lion. On the other, the scene is luridly exciting. The intensity of the lions' fury, the fear in the eyes of the camel, the tension and weight of bodies: this is as sensational as taxidermy gets. The label only heightened the sublime dangers of an exoticized Orient: "'The Jaws of Death' Action that cries for sound—a vibrating roar from the big cat mingled with the bellowing groans of the terror-stricken Dromadary [*sic*]. The one-ball flintstock, lying with ramrod twisted and useless across the slain lioness, has done its work. One thin blade remains to stand off the finality of the charge—a charge with the swiftness of death in it."[24]

At the Colonial and Indian Exhibition held in London in 1886, Rowland Ward, brother of Edwin and perhaps the most famous of all Victorian taxidermists, presented *The Jungle*, or *The Trophy of Cooch Behar*. The massive tableau contained around a hundred trophy animals from India, including an elephant, two tigers (one sinking its teeth into the elephant's trunk), alligators, snakes, and even a bear. The newspapers swooned over the tense drama of the construction. The *Morning Post* declared that the scene "will unquestionably be one of the

14 *Arab Courier Attacked by Lions,* created by taxidermist Jules Verreaux in 1867. Photo © Carnegie Museum of Natural History, Pittsburgh.

leading attractions of an exhibition that is already full of marvellous things," while the *Times* claimed that everything else in the exhibition "is likely to be forgotten in the presence of the wonderful jungle scene." According to the *Daily News,* the "scene is rendered with true tragic power."[25] And if such a dramatic spectacle was not enough to inflame viewers' imagination with exotic dangers, the tableau was infused with an additional dark delight: the animals had been killed by celebrated hunters. Ward had issued an appeal "to private gentlemen, sportsmen who have hunted among the game of India, and who may possess skins of animals, birds, &c., from any of the Presidencies," who might be willing to contribute specimens to the enormous tableaux.[26] Perhaps most thrillingly of all, one of the leopards was killed by a Mr. Beauchamp Downall with his knife at close range.[27] The beasts had been vanquished, but with the magical arts of theatrical taxidermy, viewers could almost imagine themselves participating in the hunt.

Humans are absent from the scenes (with the exception of Verreaux's camel rider), yet they implicitly suggest a desiring human gaze. Viewers easily transported themselves into the spectacle, into the turbulent jungle, into the hunter's boots to view the combat. The thrill of bloodlust, the agonized self-identification with the victim, the pain and fever of combat all resonate in the viewing. In a sense, such imaginative self-inclusion foreshadows contemporary wildlife films' melodramatic action sequences of animals struggling for survival. In an age before color photography and moving images, taxidermy was the technology for making animal action visible, replayable, endlessly available for repeated viewing. But, as always, the success of the emotive spectacle depended on the erasure of human manipulation. As with taxidermic scenes, animal documentaries offer themselves as windows onto nature, often veiling the presence of the cinematic team in order to make viewers feel as if they are the adventurous photographer: you are implicitly in the scene; you are watching the drama close up from your sofa; your eye is the lens of the camera.

As animal historian Jonathan Burt observes in *Animals in Film*, "when it comes to animals, the line between art and 'propaganda' can be very fine indeed," which is to say that animals have an uncanny ability to sustain and bolster any number of human fantasies and longings.[28] The symbolic potential of animals is extraordinarily rich. The potency of that symbolism rests on the intrinsic material fact of animal authenticity. Moreover, animal imagery is not seen in the same way that other forms of animal representation are. Audiences respond to animals in film as if the imagery were not manufactured, not edited and framed by musical overlay. The material truth of animal form obscures or neutralizes any propaganda motivating the image. However, there is a visceral, experiential difference between taxidermy and animal documentaries. With film, the animal is virtual—a play of colorful light projected in viewers' living rooms. With taxidermy, the animal is palpably present in the viewers' physical space. Spectators can approach within inches of a lion and compare themselves physically. They can see the vast size of its jaws and the sharpness of its claws. Here is the actual skin of a lion. With taxidermy, viewers must confront the physical reality of animal presence and animal death.

Neither animal proximity nor animal death is ever irrelevant, physically or emotionally. And together they engender an unsettling intimacy, allowing audiences to see animals more closely than they ever could in life.

A new term had arisen by midcentury: *artistic taxidermy*. Artistic taxidermy expressed animals in the act of living, which in the nineteenth century more often than not meant animals struggling for survival. Artistic taxidermy was still considered scientific—it still faithfully presented beasts—but the science of natural history was blurred with emotion. The goal was expressiveness, in a word, emotive artistry.

Toward the end of the nineteenth century, Montagu Browne, a prolific writer of taxidermy manuals, made a point of underscoring the shift in taxidermic expectations: it was animated animal groupings, not solitary creatures, that "most exercise[d] the skill and judgement of the taxidermic artist."[29] Any weekend taxidermist with a few basic skills could mount a bird. But artistic taxidermy infused drama, liveliness, and emotion into the postures of the beasts. The artistic taxidermist sought not merely to present basic anatomical facts but to entrance viewers with the spectacle's emotional charge, to transport them into the melodramatic scene. Interestingly, for Browne, the best source of emotional inspiration was not nature itself or even natural history illustrations but emotive animal paintings, particularly those depicting groups of animals caught in combat. The assertion is extraordinary: taxidermic inspiration could be drawn from artists whose aim was not austere scientific representation of bodily forms but spectacles of pathos. The best scenes suggested a narrative, often a narrative of struggle, and—crucially— the viewer emotionally completed the scene.

Browne advised "reproducing large groups of some of Landseer's pictures," perhaps the best tutorial available to a taxidermist. The famous British artist Sir Edwin Landseer is best known for depictions of hunting in the Scottish highlands for England's royalty and aristocratic elite. Endowed with titles such as *The Death of the Stag at Glen Tilt* and *The Monarch of the Glen*, Landseer's most lauded scenes depicted noble stags in the throes of death, mouths open, panic stricken, often surrounded by snapping hunting dogs, sometimes after death, alone. The extreme naturalism of the paintings, combined with the extreme emotional charge of the subjects, augmented audiences' sense of engagement with the hunted animal. The raw passion aroused an agonized sympathy or a vicarious participation in the killing, or both.[30] The same is true of taxidermied combat scenes. They are spectacles of human desire wrapped in animal form. The animal becomes a vehicle for the imagination.

Representations always involve a staging, a framing of the world. They require deciphering, and deciphering depends on culturally agreed-upon codes for understanding their intended meaning. How animals are represented at particular historical moments, especially animals from distant geographies, is never irrelevant. Although lions are vicious and do indeed eat antelopes and even humans on occasion, fabricating such melodrama in fur is hardly innocent, hardly unmotivated: this is taxidermy emboldened by ideology. All taxidermy is a choreographed spectacle of what nature means to particular audiences at particular historical moments. The longing to capture an animal's aesthetic presence with taxidermy invariably exhibits not just beasts but particular ways of thinking about the natural world.

Spectacles are staged events that involve audiences and actors. A successful theatrical performance engages its actors to blur the line between truth and fantasy, allowing viewers to transport themselves into the drama, just for a moment. Just for a moment, actors and fantasy fuse. Spectacles—at least successful spectacles—demand their audiences' emotional participation. The same holds true for taxidermied spectacles. It is impossible to pull the animal from the artistry, to detach desire from organic form. Daydreams and animal skins blur together to create a spectacle that erases its own artificiality.

The power of any dramatic taxidermy rests on the liveliness and finesse of the beasts exhibited. In such sensational works, the admiration of nature and the admiration of the artistry were not ends in themselves: they were designed to arouse lurid visions of more violence, more terror, more danger lurking in colonial landscapes. The taxidermied beasts posed in vicious combat did not merely represent distant dangers. They embodied them, literally. They materialized "truths" by being authentic animal skins, and, by doing so, they accelerated cultural longings to exaggerate the fierceness of distant places and to tremble indulgently. Lion skins were powerful cultural agents because they eliminated the divide between truth and desire, artifice and animal. Invested with a dramatic symbolic significance, ferocious beasts embodied imperial desires, purposes, and experiences, whether lived or imagined.

In a sense, the raw animals were literally shot through with a violent emotional charge. Animal violence fed a self-fulfilling mythology that naturalized colonial assertions of power, and animal combat was a symbolic celebration of conquest, expansion, and dominion. Representing an empire's geographic reach and symbolizing its power to tame unruly lands, exotic animal skins were transformed into colonial propaganda. Savage animals savagely posed offered "natural" proof of the turbulence of exotic landscapes and, more obliquely, stood as testimony to the validity of European colonial management. The taxidermied beasts were celebrations of all that empire stood for: dominion, courage, vigor, undaunted determination, triumph over the "untamed," and eventual victory.

It is perhaps more challenging to appreciate taxidermy as a historical and cultural artifact than to view art as a reflection of its times. Rousseau's paintings are unquestionably of their historical moment. The painterly dreams of exotic savagery mesh with his culture's imaginings and desires surrounding colonial geographies. What makes taxidermy a more complicated cultural artifact is the simple material fact of the animal. Although the postures of taxidermied animals might shift according to shifting sensibilities, at root the potency of all taxidermy rests precisely on a genuine organicism of the beast itself.

A WINDOW INTO NATURE

Although hunting and hunting trophies are discussed more fully in chapter 5, hunting—often euphemistically termed "collecting"—underscores most taxidermic displays. Well into the early twentieth century, many museum labels listed the species' common and Latin name, the sex and geographic location of the specimen exhibited, and the "collector." Museums cultivated the relationship: if hunters could wash their bloodlust in the nobility of knowledge, museums acquired valuable specimens from hunters, including, perhaps, new species from remote locations. In fact, the naturalist and the hunter were often the same figure.[31] Even the most ardent, scientifically minded naturalist was hardly immune to the fever of the chase. As Daniel Herman puts it in his *Hunting and the American Imagination*, "To know natural history was to claim dominion over the earth; that is what made natural history so attractive to hunters." Indeed, Herman continues, "the so-called Great Reconnaissance of nineteenth-century naturalists might be called the Great Hunt. Hunters and naturalists together entered nature to take command of it."[32] Museums did not try to obscure the hunter behind the scientist, but neither were the sensationalistic struggles of life and death considered wholly appropriate for a sober scientific institution, particularly toward the end of the nineteenth century. The animal violence and aggressive displays of imperial conquest of the natural world had meshed perfectly with the political and cultural agendas of the world exhibitions. However, increasingly throughout the late nineteenth and twentieth centuries, natural history museums shifted their taxidermic spectacles to offer more thoughtful, more respectful attitudes toward the natural world.

For example, take Verreaux's *Arab Courier Attacked by Lions.* It almost did not survive its transition from gold medal winner into the more poised world of science education. The piece was purchased, along with the entire Verreaux collection, by the American Museum of Natural History in 1869. It was subsequently exhibited at the Philadelphia Centennial Exposition in 1876 to wide acclaim. And yet, despite its public appeal, the museum's directors decided to dispose of *Arab Courier.* The taxidermic skill of the piece was incontestable, but its overt and deadly theatricality was too emotional and distracting for educational purposes. However, the scene was eventually purchased by the Carnegie Museum of Natural History in Pittsburgh in 1899, where it remains on display to this day, not so much for its nature as for its historical import; that is, the work has been reinterpreted as a cultural document showcasing a now outdated view of exoticized, perhaps even eroticized, nature. In addition, the work exhibits two individuals of a subspecies of lion that became extinct in the wild around 1942. As the significance of nature and animals changes, so too does the meaning of the spectacle.

It is somewhat ironic that the American Museum of Natural History discarded the tableau. It was the first diorama exhibited at the museum, which subsequently became famous for its own dioramas, built in the early decades of the twentieth century. Of course, these later animal scenes formed a different sort of spectacle. Instead of action scenes of animal violence, habitat dioramas positioned animals in natural postures, as if caught unawares, as if unposed, at peace. While earlier theatrical scenes offered minimal if any sense of surrounding environmental features, later dioramas placed taxidermied animals in meticulously created environments to mimic in every way possible the ecological habitat of the creatures. Artificial rocks, trees, and grasses blended imperceptibly into painted panoramic backdrops, giving an impression of space and distance. A total environment was created, a window onto nature offering an illusion of wilderness untouched by human artifice.

For example, no detail of the African lion diorama in Akeley Hall of African Mammals at the American Museum of Natural History (fig. 15) was vague or invented. In 1928 the museum's director of arts and preparation, James Clark, along with William Leigh, a master background painter, and a team of naturalists traveled to the Serengeti Plain in Tanzania. Upon arriving, Clark and Leigh chose a particular site and crafted a small-scale model of the final diorama. This model helped the team determine the exact sketches that would be required for the painted background and the exact plants and vegetation to be collected and preserved. Clark photographed and measured each of the lions killed for the diorama, made plaster impressions of their bodies to capture their distinctive anatomical details, and prepared their skins and skeletons for transport back to New York.[33] The end result was a scene so realistic that viewers can almost smell the creatures on view. Although museum dioramas were in no way untouched by animal killing, their serene aura is meant to neutralize all the violence and lurid drama of earlier animal spectacles. And surely one of the most lurid narratives of all times centers on two lions displayed at the Field Museum of Natural History in Chicago.

Perhaps you already know the story of the Tsavo lions. The events were commemorated a century later in the 1996 film *The Ghost and the Darkness*, directed by Stephen Hopkins and starring Val Kilmer and Michael Douglas. Animal attack movies are a cinematic staple, a well-worn genre that requires only the most basic of storylines to raise heartbeats: the primal terror of man-eaters does the rest. But unlike *Jaws, Anaconda, Lake Placid, Grizzly,* or even the Hitchcock classic *The Birds, The Ghost and the Darkness* was based on a series of real and very deadly lion attacks during the building of the Kenya-Uganda Railway in early 1898. The details were recounted by chief engineer Lieutenant Colonel John Henry Patterson, employed to build a bridge in 1924.

> I fully expected to encounter many trials and hardships while engaged in building the railway through an inhospitable and savage territory. I anticipated engineering difficulties, perils from sunstroke and fevers, a possible scarcity of food and water,—but never for a moment did I realize that the African wilderness held in its mysterious recesses two prowling demons who looked upon myself and my workmen as a sort of manna sent down from Heaven for their special delectation. All other difficulties were as nothing compared to the terrible toll of human sacrifice exacted

nightly by these savage monsters who made Tsavo their headquarters and gave to that district an evil repute which lasts to this day.[34]

In early 1898 the railhead had reached the Tsavo River, located about 130 miles west of Mombasa on the Kenyan coast. Patterson had only just arrived to start work on the bridge when workmen began disappearing. At first Patterson dismissed the workmen's stories of devouring lions. But then he had the grisly opportunity to witness the carnage: Ungan Singh had been seized during the night, dragged away by the neck, and eaten. Patterson tracked the lion from the

15 The African lion diorama in Akeley Hall of African Mammals, American Museum of Natural History, New York. The scene depicts the Serengeti Plain, east of Lake Victoria, Tanzania. Photo courtesy of Asterio Tecson.

16　The Tsavo lions at the Field Museum of Natural History, Chicago. Photo courtesy of Devon Morgan.

furrows made from the victim's heels to the spot where the lions had devoured Singh: "Here a dreadful spectacle presented itself. The ground all about was covered in blood, morsels of flesh, and the larger bones, but the head was left intact, save for a couple of holes made by the lion's teeth. It was the most gruesome sight I had ever seen."[35]

Over the next nine months, the death toll continued to rise. Early estimates numbered more than a hundred victims, although a recent study suggests that the number was closer to thirty-five.[36] The lions attacked at night, dragging their victims from their tents and hauling them through the fences of thorns erected to protect the camp. The lions' methods, Patterson writes, "became so uncanny and their man-stalking so well-timed and so certain of success that the workmen firmly believed that they were not real animals at all, but devils in lions' shape."[37] After months of unsuccessful stakeouts and endless sleepless nights, Patterson finally shot and killed both lions. The first was shot as it stalked Patterson in the near-pitch darkness of the African night. The second only succumbed after six shots.

Patterson had both lions skinned for floor rugs. Two decades later, in 1924, the skins were purchased by the Field Museum in Chicago for the large sum of $5,000. The way the animals had been skinned (for floor rugs, not taxidermy displays), the bullet holes, and the general wear and tear of the passing years made the process of mounting the skins extremely difficult. As a result, the lions appear far smaller in death than they were in life. This unavoidable reduction of visceral drama was matched by a purposeful effort to downplay the emotional violence of the scene. The lions seem playful rather than aggressive. The potential lurid enjoyment of man-eaters has been almost eradicated. There is no papier-mâché dead human to ogle, no struggle of life and death. The animals are inserted into a fastidiously constructed vision of their native habitat to create an aura of nature untouched. Here are the thorns, the red dirt, the particular shape of the area's sedimentary rocks. Most notably, all hint of narrative is absent: there is no suggestion of action before or after the captured moment. This is not nature agitated but nature stilled for contemplation (fig. 16).

It could be said that earlier displays of theatrical violence exaggerated or even falsified the animals, while dioramas present more truthful (because more emotionally neutral) lions. But what is a lion's typical pose? What is any animal's typical pose? For that matter, what is a human's typical pose? Violent attacks on antelopes are just as much part of a lion's routine as sleeping. Habitat dioramas presented scenes of tranquil nature, but they are still staged spectacles, still infused with propaganda about what nature is, and for whom. The actors are the same, but both audience and performance have changed. Whether particular landscapes and their nonhuman inhabitants are interpreted as unlimited resources for conquest and exploitation or as fragile ecosystems in need of protection, taxidermic spectacles command and bolster their audiences' beliefs, desires, and emotions.

Debate surrounds the question of who built the first habitat diorama, but certainly Carl Akeley and William Temple Hornaday stand as North America's greatest creators. Both men were trained at Ward's Natural History Establishment, which was founded in 1862 by the merchant and naturalist Henry Ward in Rochester, New York. With a staff of two dozen highly trained taxidermists, modelers, painters, and osteologists, Ward's Establishment became a leading supplier of natural history specimens around the world, with the aim of boosting the quality and educational value of natural history collections. By the end of the century, museums had begun sponsoring their own collecting expeditions (or at least had established the influence and networks needed to acquire wealthy beneficiaries, often avid sportsmen), but Ward's Establishment added a critical push to the transformation of the natural history museum from a purely scientific storehouse into an institution of public education. As Karen Wonders writes, the graduates of Ward's Establishment, and particularly Akeley and Hornaday, "challenged the dominant exhibition philosophy of the time by giving scientific legitimacy to the new 'artistic' techniques of displaying zoological specimens and were thus crucial to the development of the habitat diorama in the USA."[38]

With the ambition of achieving extreme truthfulness in the copying of nature, taxidermists created what became known as the "artistic group." Rather than a single animal starkly posed in isolation, animals of various ages and sexes were grouped together in a reconstructed habitat. Taxidermists left no detail to chance; there was nothing vague or haphazard about the process. Typically, a team of museum taxidermists, naturalists, and artists would set out to collect the desired specimens and their surrounding environmental features. Because dioramas required a broad range of specimens of any particular species—old, young, male, and female were often grouped together within a single scene—more often than not the animals were actively collected to create the particular scene. Photographs and sketches were taken of a particular piece of terrain that most faithfully represented the species' typical environment. Artists and naturalists closely documented the vegetation to be replicated, noting the exact bend of trees, taking molds of the particular texture of bark, recording the colors of leaves and grasses, which flowers were in bloom, and the shape and slate of boulders. All would be replicated, with the added illusion of a painted backdrop that blended imperceptibly with the animals and plants in the foreground.

But taxidermy is never a transparent document of nature. All decisions as to how an animal should be posed are necessarily selective. When a taxidermist is presented with a skin, a whole host of artistic decisions must be made. Should the animal be standing or resting? Small arboreal animals might be posed climbing a branch, or birds arranged with their wings outstretched. Animals might be posed to exhibit "typical" behaviors such as nest building, mating, sleeping, burrowing, or fighting; that is, "typical" is always highly selective. And always, all such choices are never freely made but rather are shaped by available specimens, taxidermic skill, time, money, museums' educational and research agendas, and underlying cultural and political understandings of particular animals and their geographies.

In her magisterial history of habitat dioramas, Karen Wonders outlines the scientific, political, and institutional impulses motivating the genre's creation in the late decades of the nineteenth century. What most concerns us here is the link Wonders draws between dioramas and early environmentalism. The realization that the American wilderness was not an unlimited resource, that rapid urban growth threatened species and their habitats, and that ultimately humans played the decisive hand in preserving or diminishing nature's rich diversity provided natural history museums with an urgent mission. It is fascinating that dioramas initially flourished in only two countries, Sweden and the United States. Wonders presents several reasons for this but argues that, at bottom, the rise of the diorama was fundamentally linked to both nations' concerns about ecological stability and species loss.

> The habitat diorama originated at about the same time that frontier expansion and human exploitation of the wilderness were in an accelerating phase. The national identity of the USA has always been closely associated with the magnificence and vastness of its wilderness regions and with the seemingly unlimited amount of wild game inhabiting these. By contrast, in Europe, with the exception of the Nordic countries, wild nature has disappeared much earlier to be replaced by cultural landscapes dominated by domesticated animals. In other words, in America and parts of the Scandinavian world a more direct and greater awareness of the conquest and degradation of the natural environment by humans may have produced a proportionally greater desire to impart to the museum public an appreciation of the natural-national heritage that was being damaged, diminished or lost altogether.[39]

In America, the nineteenth-century nature movement was spurred on and fleshed out by nature writers, particularly John Muir, Henry David Thoreau, and John Burroughs. Combining nature lessons with raw expressions of intimate experiences of being in nature, they encouraged firsthand contact with nature in order to live life with a more vivid, more intense, more wakeful awareness.[40] When met with soulful appreciation and a sense of wonder, nature was a spiritual cleanser of the ills of modern life. It was this experience of an intimate moment with the natural world and its inhabitants—a sense of nature untouched—that was sought and created by dioramas.

The aim of the habitat diorama was to create an immaculate vision of nature uncontaminated by human presence in order to instill in urban dwellers a deep respect for nature, or what might be described more accurately as a deep longing for a wilderness at the edge of existence. Didactic information was kept to a minimum so that nothing would stand between a viewer and the spectacle of peaceful, pristine, untouched nature. Dioramas tantalized visitors with the possibility of communion with nature, the possibility of experiencing nature's truth. Despite the fact that the animals were all hunted down for the purpose, despite the skinning, the theatrical postures, and the artificial surroundings, dioramas were meant to suggest unhindered access to raw nature.

Dioramas presented nature contained and tamed, in isolation from the world at large, as if in a time capsule, and this was not arbitrary. If the new exhibition philosophy reflected a new ecological sensibility by acknowledging that nothing in nature existed in isolation, it was also driven by the realization that many species were vanishing, and at a rapid rate. As museum professionals often stated, if species were to disappear, at least they could be preserved with taxidermy. The rationale was endlessly advocated by naturalists from the mid-nineteenth century onward. If nature was disappearing, it should therefore be collected en masse and preserved for posterity.[41]

For example, the rapid dwindling of the North American buffalo was the incentive for the Smithsonian's 1886 expedition of buffalo mounted by Hornaday for study and public display. Hornaday's inventory of the Smithsonian's collections revealed a sad series of buffalo specimens: three taxidermied animals (two were no more than "old, badly mounted, and dilapidated skins"), an unmounted skin, and several skeletons.[42] Despite the great scarcity of buffalo, Hornaday hoped to kill and collect between eighty and a hundred specimens of various kinds. In the end, twenty-five buffalo were collected, six of which composed the buffalo group in the Smithsonian. Representing male and female, young and old, the buffalo, posed around a water hole, offered a picturesque vision, complete with sagebrush, sod, and dirt all transported from Montana. "It is as though a little group of buffalo that have come to drink at a pool had been struck motionless by some magic spell," a *Washington Star* reporter wrote in 1888.[43] The magic spell of nature was meant to accelerate awareness, concern, and appreciation. The affectivity of the group depended on a perception of physical closeness, eroding the distance between spectator and the beasts' homeland, and this physical closeness depended on the truth-value of the scene, which was conveyed by real grasses, real dirt, and real buffalo.

Donna Haraway has offered the most decisive attack on such mythmaking in her classic analysis of the American Museum of Natural History's African Hall, opened to the public in 1936. For Haraway, taxidermy was wielded as a fallacious technology of perspicuity and sanctity, tantalizing visitors with the anticipation of communion with nature and offering a curative for the threats and decadence of modern life. "Each diorama," she writes, "presents itself as a side altar, a stage, an unspoiled garden in nature, a hearth for home and family."[44] This truth was constructed, or rather "discovered," by the stance of taxidermic realism, the power of which lies precisely in its magical ability to engineer a truth, a spontaneous revelation. What is so laboriously constructed appears effortless and, moreover, spontaneously found. But far from being spy holes into nature, dioramas of African nature, Haraway argues, reveal the racist, imperialistic, and masculinist motives behind them. To be seduced by the vision is, for Haraway, to be complicit in social relations of domination, of white, robust, wealthy, progressive American manhood over the uncivilized, the dark, the unknown, and the animal.

And yet the strength of Haraway's argument rests precisely on the visual power of the dioramas. The magnetism is, of course, produced by the union of a particular set of social relations and technologies—guns, photographic references, impeccably crafted taxidermy, atmospheric backdrops, exact reproductions of trees, rocks, foliage, etc. However, it is the achievement of a vision of transcendence (whether deceptive or not) that sustains Haraway's analysis of the dioramas' ability to facilitate a fantasy of communion, salvation, and truth. A question that hardly ever gets asked is why stuffed animal skins artificially posed in fabricated backgrounds should be able to concretize and communicate such a cumbersome and intense set of aspirations. But animals, whether dead or alive, are not just any other sort of object, and the emotive power of any piece of taxidermy is driven as much by the sheer, raw animal presence as it is by any cultural incentive.

The thing is recognized as an animal; the nature of the experience may be less recognizable.

—STEVE BAKER, *The Postmodern Animal* (2000), 98

There is a long-standing debate among philosophers, aesthetes, and artists about the relative beauty of human art versus natural wonders and—even more broadly—between the relative merits of human artifacts and natural phenomena.[45] Nature and art have been defined and redefined against each other, generally as two more or less isolated and mutually exclusive terms. In his collection of essays on the aesthetic appreciation of nature, for example, Malcolm Budd argues that any aesthetic experience of nature depends on an "appreciation of nature *as what nature actually is*," that is, nature is appreciated *as nature* in contrast to a human-crafted artifact.[46] And for an appreciation of nature to be "pure," the nature in question must be devoid of any imposed design, particularly any design imposed for artistic or aesthetic effect.

The design and intention in the making of things lies at the heart of most distinctions between art and nature. Natural items are not designed for the purpose of aesthetic or intellectual appreciation. As Budd writes, "given that the natural world is not anyone's artefact, the aesthetic appreciation of nature as nature . . . must be the aesthetic appreciation of nature *not* as an intentionally produced object."[47] This is hardly the case with taxidermy. As Hornaday's taxidermic instructions make clear, every straining muscle, curling lip, and pink tongue is designed and realized by artistic intention. In a sense, the animal has been hijacked, pervaded with artistic intention, made to speak a message. More than other genres of taxidermy we have so far examined, theatrical taxidermy is nature redesigned by desire, a supreme imposition of artistic and cultural intention over the animal form.

One of the crucial differences in the experience of art and of nature is that nature permits or invites an experience, whereas a work of art is intentionally made for an experience.[48] That is, taxidermy can be critiqued as well or badly made, lifelike or wooden, but living animals just *are*. The spontaneous encounter between Dillard and her weasel, discussed in chapter 2, unplanned and unchoreographed, stands in sharp contrast to the patterns of stuffed hummingbirds, hoarded together to accentuate the bijouterie of their tiny bodies, or even the immaculately realized visions of dioramas. Intention and artistry pervade every inch of taxidermy, from choosing which creature to kill to posing and arranging its skin. No one could ever mistake a breathing creature for its taxidermic reconstruction.

Technically speaking, considering the skinning, tanning, sewing, and stuffing involved in both taxidermy and upholstery, a leather chair is not so very different from a piece of taxidermy. But of course they are different. Anyone who has ever stepped into a room containing leather furniture and hunting trophies can attest to that inescapable fact—taxidermy is not mere upholstery. Good taxidermy can capture some sense of the creature's former liveliness and character; exceptional taxidermy may even achieve that uncanny spark of animation that gives viewers the tingling sensation that the hawk might any moment leave its perch or the lion spring through the glass. But even bad taxidermy and old, poorly crafted mounts will evoke a visceral realization that this thing is not just a human-made artifact no different from any sort of product made from animal skins. If aesthetic encounters with preserved animals are distinguished from encounters with living animals, they are also markedly different from encounters with leather chairs. So what sort of objects are taxidermied animals: nature, artifice, or something in between?

Taxidermy is more than a queasy species of trompe l'oeil. Preserved human mummies are not said to be *representations* of humans: they *are* humans. Perhaps this fact is most apparent with the Tsavo lions. Considering that the lions fed on a diet of human flesh for nine months, the skins were at least in part grown on a diet of human flesh. This fact is not irrelevant. It is the reason why visitors linger in front of their display window. Despite the artistic reinterpretation, the visceral impact of two genuine skins of man-eaters remains. The animals have been made to play a role; they have been shot, skinned, and reanimated, surely. But the animal continues to exert the visceral force of its presence. Without the authenticity of the organic material, the diorama loses all its potency. The animals offer the illusion of immediacy, a transparent window onto nature, an unmediated "truth" quite simply because animals are animals. Yet this truth of form rests crucially on artistic intention. That is, through science, chemicals, and art, the taxidermist always strives to create as near an image of living animals as possible. The reasoning is circular but highlights the fact that taxidermy is neither not nature nor not art: it is a bit of both and neither. By straddling the nature-culture opposition, taxidermy obliterates (or at least renders uninteresting) any division between the aesthetics of nature and the aesthetics of art. In doing so, taxidermy requires its own aesthetic vocabulary.

Perhaps the most important feature of taxidermy is an authenticity of organicism. Compare a taxidermied bird with the sort of artificial birds seen frequently in decorative stores, crafted from feathers glued onto Styrofoam balls with glass eyes and wire legs. The feathers have probably come from dead birds, but the encounter is deeply inauthentic.[49] Or consider a lion beautifully mounted but with faux fur. The Tsavo lions make the importance of authenticity viscerally potent: these are the actual skins of two man-eaters. The skins may be old. The taxidermied creatures may be smaller than the lions were in life. But still, these are the actual skins of two man-eaters. A recent study of the types of carbon and nitrogen compounds in the Tsavo lions' teeth and hair reveals that humans made up at least half of the diet of one of the lions in the last months of his life; the study shows that this lion had consumed at least twenty-four people. The other lion had eaten at least eleven people.[50] The skins are not representations of the man-eaters. This is not mere verisimilitude: these *are* the lions, but now blurred with human artistry and intention. An authenticity of organicism does not require that the taxidermy be well executed. Even truly terrible taxidermied animals, with fossilized ears, maladjusted eyes, and shrunken limbs sprouting straw, still convey an authenticity, a realization that these things on display maintain their integrity as animals. Poor craftsmanship does not eradicate an animal's organicism any more than a shrunken head or a mummified body stops being a human. Bad taxidermy might even be said to render the beast's loss of life more abrasively visible.

The visibility of death is the second aesthetic quality of taxidermy. Despite all efforts to capture the liveliness and animation of the animal, taxidermy can never escape being a blatant presentation of death: its realism is deadly. While a leather chair, a steak, and a fur coat offer material evidence of death, they lack that tingling whole organicism that suggests that this thing just might reanimate. Taxidermy offers the unsettling presence of liveliness in the face of death. This organic wholeness despite death endows taxidermy with its eeriness, its uncanniness.

If the necessity of death rubs the electricity of life from stuffed animals, death offers the compensation of time. With taxidermy, time stops. A moment extends for as long as you are willing to look. With taxidermy, you need not worry about what the other is thinking or whether it will act. The weasel will not disappear if you blink, nor will the lion attack or the hummingbird buzz away. Of course, the furtive sulk of a weasel, the potential danger of lion attacks, and the ceaseless flight of hummingbirds—all erased by death—are central to the living encounters with those animals. The thrill of meeting a wild animal is gone, but the animal is not. In fact, the animal might linger for centuries, the fleeting beauty of life hovering immortally behind glass. Time offers a physical intimacy that would be impossible with living animals, whether in the wild, in a game reserve, in a zoo, or even on television. And animal proximity is never irrelevant.

It is this enduring animal magnetism of taxidermied animals—each creature unique and individual—that makes taxidermied animals so serviceable for all manner of propaganda and proclamations of truth. Taxidermy is always a spectacle of human desire for significance and place within the spectrum of life. But always, the perceived truth value of the spectacle rests on the authenticity of animal form.

The next chapter examines a different, more abstract species of animal spectacle: the spectacle of order. With the rise of public natural history museums in the nineteenth and twentieth centuries, nature was increasingly laid bare and ordered for view, without the subjectivity of aesthetic value, personal preference, or political assumptions of nature's significance. In a sense, natural history museums present themselves as spectacles of the human mind working within (or over) nature's diversity. And yet, interestingly, beyond merely preserving skins for examination, taxidermy had a limited role in the making of zoological knowledge from the nineteenth century onward. Rather, the desire to materialize nature's order with real animals—each creature laid out one beside the other—is fundamentally linked to museum pedagogy and public education, not scientific inquiry. And, certainly, the longing to see order in nature is a strange sort of longing. It is a longing to look through what is manifestly visible and to know the truth of a beast, taxonomically speaking. And it requires a specialized sort of looking. But then, the meaning of any particular piece of taxidermy is always a matter of perspective.

ORDER

4

The zebras on display at the Natural History Museum at Tring (thirty miles northwest of London) seem to be resting, posed with their legs tucked under themselves (fig. 17). It is a space-saving tactic used throughout the museum: animals posed as if resting take up less room. Positioned on shelves and stacked up the walls behind glass, zebras relax, elands stretch their necks out, ostriches and emus recline in feathered mounds. But the eight shelved zebras are particularly striking.

With the exception of dioramas, generally speaking, museums display one representative of a species, so why so many zebras? It seems an unnecessary repetition. Perhaps. But if Noah had known his taxonomy as well as he did his divine mandate, he would have welcomed a small army of zebras onto the ark. It is not particularly common knowledge that there is no one single zebra. Three species of zebra have been distinguished—the plains zebra, mountain zebra, and Grevy's zebra—and at least six subspecies are generally agreed upon. Almost all are on display at Tring. On a close look, subtle differences appear: bold black stripes,

"Of every clean beast thou shalt take to thee by sevens, the male and his female: and of the beasts that are not clean by two, the male and his female."

—GENESIS 7:2

The zebras in Gallery 4 at the Natural History Museum in Tring, England. Photo courtesy of Eric Huang.

thin ghostly brown stripes, a tuft of hair on a tail, an unmarked belly. What at first glance seem to be multiples of a single creature blossom into markedly distinct individuals. The plains zebra is distinguished by absent or incomplete leg stripes, while the mountain zebra has a prominent dewlap. The Grevy's zebra has a white belly and more numerous, narrower stripes that create a complex bifurcated pattern on the animal's haunches. And, most preciously, there is the extinct quagga, with its brown rump and striped head and neck. An unexpectedly comprehensive vision of an entire household of relatives unfolds where only one solitary species might have been expected.

Shelves of birds are common enough in natural history museums. Parrots, grouse, hummingbirds, and penguins are often displayed in tight vertical rows in order to showcase their variations in color, size, shape, plumage, or geographic distribution. Small animals—hedgehogs, rabbits, weasels—are also frequently shown on shelves. But large mammals are typically mounted standing one beside the other, not one above the other. Visitors are required to move along the cases in order to see each of the animals in turn, giving each a brief moment before moving on to the next beast. But with so many zebras packed together so tightly—a closeness intensified by the corner configuration—visitors can take in an entire herd while standing still. In fact, the zebras almost force visitors to stop meandering from case to case, to stop and visually absorb animal order. The animals are almost less arresting as individual species than for what they become together—a complete set. There is something compelling in this vision of wholeness, of nature's entirety without the randomness of personal preference or haphazard accumulation.

Certainly the zebras are alluring as individuals, but their arrangement suggests that something more is on display. Most natural history specimens are collected not because of their raw uniqueness or individuality but because they are, in a sense, commonplace: they offer a "typical" vision of their species. The first two chapters of this book examine the exceptionally strange and strikingly beautiful. The third explores lively spectacles of particularly charismatic animals. In contrast, this chapter examines the unexceptional and nontheatrical. These zebras are not displayed because they are particularly noteworthy in any respect but simply because they exist, or rather, because their species exists. The zebras are pieces of a whole—representatives of a slice of organic life. In a sense, all natural history specimens are fundamentally unremarkable, run of the mill. They are not exceptional individuals; they are demonstrations of their kind, nothing more, nothing less, at least in theory.

The quest for order, particularly the urge to find order within the natural world, is a potent human longing. Order gives meaning and clarity. Order defines the contours of objects, illuminating and accentuating their distinctions from similar things. Order can even offer salvation. Consider, for example, that until species that closely resemble one another are distinguished and named, it is hard to know for sure whether a creature has gone extinct. The Grevy's zebra and the mountain zebra are both on the EDGE of Existence program's list of the top one hundred evolutionarily distinct and globally endangered species, while the plains zebra is not in danger. If the various species of zebras had not been distinguished, the plenitude of one would have masked the absence of the others. Order draws animals from nature's tangles, names them, classifies them, and so helps to monitor them as discrete entities.

Collecting is always balanced between salvation and deracination. Salvation can be a judicious selection of items deemed worthy or, like Noah's ark, a comprehensive accumulation. In either case, collecting can be a harboring, a holding together of what would otherwise break apart, or an avaricious hoarding of longed-for items. But at root the collected object is always an object of passion. It has been deemed worthy of safekeeping, and the particular passion always marks its objects. Have the items been collected because of their strangeness or physical beauty? Or perhaps the objects are understood to belong to a set. Or again, the objects are seen to speak to and empower a particular ideology of how the world should fit together. In all cases, the collecting impulse infuses objects with new layers of significance. The items have been particularly chosen and particularly displayed to fit into and fulfill a scheme. They have been uprooted from their natural environments and made to play roles within new settings, and the circumstances of those settings—whether private or institutional, and regardless of the particular ordering principles at work, the aesthetic or conceptual relationships between the displayed objects—fundamentally shape a viewer's appreciation of the things on display.

Over the course of the late eighteenth and nineteenth centuries, public natural history museums emerged as colossal storehouses of nature. The aim was to collect, preserve, and house a representative of every known species of animal, vegetable, and mineral. Even before museums began sponsoring their own collecting trips, collections expanded enormously, voluptuously, aggressively, fed by a constant stream of specimens sent home by adventurous naturalists, colonists, and big-game hunters. By the late nineteenth century about one thousand new species of plants, birds, animals, and insects were identified each year.[1] Until the first decade of the nineteenth century, only one zebra was known to exist. A century later, the number of zebra species and subspecies had swelled to include the plains zebra, Grevy's zebra, Hartmann's mountain zebra, Wahlberg's Burchell's zebra, Selous's zebra, Grant's zebra, Chapman's zebra, Boehm's zebra, and Crawshay's zebra. If ever proof was needed of the close bonds between imperialism and the expansion of zoology, zebra nomenclature would surely offer it.

As historians of science have reminded us, science does not proceed in an idyllic space outside culture. Rather, its practitioners and the objects, philosophies, objectives, and conclusions of investigation are all embedded in the larger social environment. The natural sciences are no exception. As we have already seen, the animal displays in natural history museums are often shaped as much by national, political, and cultural agendas as by the scientific debates of their age.[2] Such histories have been admirably detailed by numerous authors, and it is not my objective here to rewrite their research. Rather, I am interested in the poetics of animal order. How does a natural history specimen—well labeled, well preserved, well arranged within a classificatory scheme—differ from the sorts of beasts mingling in earlier wonder cabinets? How do visions of science contrast with scenes of animal beauty or animal violence? Ordering nature is one thing. Using taxidermy to display animal order is another. As we will see, from the late eighteenth century onward, a fundamental rupture occurs between the acquisition of natural knowledge and its display.

The rise of public natural history museums in the nineteenth century was characterized by two shifts: on the one hand, the specialization and professionalization of natural knowledge, and on the other, a strong mandate for public education. These two impetuses had very different material needs and spatial requirements, particularly with respect to how specimens were preserved, stored, and displayed. In an era before animal documentaries and color photography, museums were a primary venue for the general public to learn about nature, and taxidermy was a primary technology for making creaturely life visible. By the mid-nineteenth century, however, the individuals who were deciphering animal order were beginning to see taxidermy's limitations, and by the early twentieth century animal displays had become exclusively tools for popular aesthetic pleasure and education, not science.

Tracing the subtle interplay between displays of order and visitors' experience of the creatures on display, this chapter ultimately explores the power of animal magnetism. But first, how does taxidermy contribute to the making and display of zoological order? To answer this question, we must first look at the workings of order.

NAMING

It is easy to appreciate why both taxidermy and taxonomy were vital to naturalists from the early eighteenth century onward. If taxidermy came about and improved precisely to preserve material documents of nature's abundance, taxonomy strove to order those documents. In part, a universal system of naming and ordering was required for naturalists to determine whether any particular specimen was a new sighting. Without a standard system of naming, the same species could be given multiple names, perhaps in several languages. Collections across Europe and North America could easily all have the same creature—each named differently in a different language—yet all claim their specimen as a new species. Then again, words and images were often not enough to define a species as new to science. Taxonomy was built with actual specimens. Naturalists had to see the animal, measure its parts, examine its teeth and skeleton, and compare coloration and patterning with other collected specimens, and early taxidermic methods, as we have seen, were frequently less than perfect. Only with reasonably skillful preservation was it possible to see an animal's characteristics clearly enough to compare specimens or confirm whether any particular creature was a new discovery. To use the old metaphor of nature as a book or, better yet, a vast collection of books, early collections were no more workable than a library without a reliable catalogue and plagued by insects and rot.

The system of binomial naming—the use of two Latin words, such as *Homo sapiens,* to mark the genus and species of all living things—was established by the Swedish naturalist Carolus Linnaeus in two remarkable works, *Systema naturae* (System of Nature), first published in 1735, and *Species plantarum* (Species of Plants), first published in 1753, which both went through multiple editions. Linnaeus was an extraordinary scholar. His daunting industry and organizational prowess were matched by an unbounded desire to observe and classify every known species. In the tenth edition of *Systema naturae,* published in 1758, Linnaeus gave binomial names to every known animal, 4,378 species in all. The act was almost biblical: Linnaeus was seen as a second Adam naming the animals again, this time in the international language of science. Everything depended on language.[3]

Language, Linnaeus believed, would harness nature's chaos into a legible and therefore knowable order. And indeed, Linnaeus gave special emphasis to the act of naming. Without a name, a species can hardly be said to exist. As Linnaeus wrote in the introduction to *Systema naturae,* the first step of wisdom is to know the natural bodies, to distinguish them from one another, and to "affix every object its proper name. These are the elements of all sciences; this is the great alphabet of nature: for if the name be lost, the knowledge of the object is lost also; and without these, the student will seek in vain for the means to investigate the hidden treasures of nature."[4] Once named, animals emerged from the unruliness of nature's astonishing diversity.[5]

Linnaeus required a large collection of preserved animals for his research. To create any sort of ordering scheme, naturalists were obliged to look at many specimens of the same species, comparing and contrasting their various parts to determine whether similar but not perfectly identical specimens represented individual variation in one species or belonged to closely related but distinct species. With expanding global exploration and the ever-increasing number of animals known to science, naturalists were often forced to revise their understanding of how the animal world fit together. The anatomical particularities of the platypus caused taxonomic havoc, as did kangaroos, echidnas, and all other creatures that did not conform to established animal order. Monotremes and marsupials in particular provoked considerable taxonomic debate among late nineteenth-century naturalists, who could not quite agree on where to place the creatures. As Harriet Ritvo writes, such anatomical irregularities undermined and even invalidated established systems of classification, and new systems were judged on their ability to accommodate such anomalies: "thus marsupial and monotreme classification emerged as a battleground upon which rival systems and rival systematists could engage."[6] But naturalists had to be able to examine an actual specimen to determine whether any particular creature was new to science or not, and, if new, how it conformed to or disrupted established taxonomic schemes.

Naming is not a vague science. When a species is identified, the newly coined name is attached to a specific specimen. This first identified individual of its kind is known as the "type specimen." There is only one type specimen, one particular preserved creature, for each species.[7] With the new emphasis on giving each species one and only one name (as opposed to the centuries-old chaos of multilingual nomenclature), carefully labeled type specimens became and have remained highly valuable and prestigious reference materials for museums, serving as the models for subsequent specimen identification. Of course, the importance of type specimens means that specimens have to be preserved well enough to withstand repeated examination over decades. If a type specimen disintegrates, a formal piece of documentation is forever lost, and the legitimacy of the description could potentially be cast into doubt. Without the physical proof of the animal itself, words are mere words. In short, taxidermy and taxonomy have remained twin soldiers in the quest for a comprehensive catalogue of nature's diversity. With taxonomy and taxidermy together, the dream of a total ark becomes a possible, or even a thinkable, project.

Since at least the time of Aristotle, zoological classification had used commonly observed differences between creatures, and Linnaeus's *Systema naturae* was no different. The division of nature proceeded by establishing the defining characteristics that all members of a particular group possessed. The organism had wings or fins or four legs. It either had canine teeth or not. By such "logical" physical differences, creaturely life was isolated into smaller and smaller divisions. For example, Linnaeus famously identified and established the thirty-one sexual characteristics of plants as a basis of botanical classification. By analyzing the number and position of stamens, the class of the plant was determined. The number of pistils revealed the plant's order, and its genus was determined by a comparative study of all thirty-one parts together. When confronted with the rather more complex world of animals, Linnaeus was forced to use more than one characteristic (sexual systems hardly offered a nuanced enough view of the animal world), but the same principles applied.

While the notion of genus and species had been established by earlier naturalists, Linnaeus augmented this basic taxonomic structure by adding two levels above (class and order) and one below (variety).[8] Linnaeus began by distinguishing the six classes of the animal kingdom: Quadrupedia (quadrupeds), Aves (birds), Amphibia (reptiles, snakes, amphibians), Pisces (fish), Insecta (insects and arachnids), and Vermes (worms, mollusks, and corals). Between 1735 and 1758, Linnaeus recognized that mammary glands were a far better distinguishing factor than four legs, and Quadrupedia was changed to Mammalia. Mammals were divided into seven orders according to differences in the number and form of teeth and feet. Primates composed the first order and, somewhat scandalously, parceled together man, monkeys, lemurs, and bats, based in part on the observed fact that all have four small front teeth bracketed between two larger canine teeth. Belluae (brute beast) was the sixth order, comprising two genera: *Equus* and *Hippopotamus*. The three species of *Equus* were horse, donkey, and zebra. For Linnaeus, there was only one zebra, *Equus zebra*, now commonly known as the mountain zebra, which Linnaeus defined as a multicolored horse with dusky bands.

Linnaeus's classification produced inevitable disagreement, debate, and out-right antagonism in the zoological world. His main dissenters admitted that the system was neat and tidy but argued that its logic was false or at best perilously arbitrary. It failed to acknowledge the subtleties of nature. It was a tissue of human invention. It grouped together creatures that inhabited different geographies and possessed vastly different anatomical structures. It packaged together human and monkey.

Among the most adamant scientific dissenters were those who sought to understand the relationships among creaturely life. If Linnaeus put animals into an easy, workable system of groups, naturalists increasingly believed that classification should reflect the underlying laws of the natural world. The animal groupings, they argued, should reveal the *true* affinities and differences between animals and not follow some subjective choice of distinguishing parts. Yet without knowing the underlying cause of animal variation, all taxonomies lacked a solid, irrefutable, unbiased foundation. The problem was this: while naturalists generally agreed on the *facts* of nature (the observable biological attributes of creaturely life), these facts could be arranged into an infinite number of organizing systems. Take bats, for example. One naturalist might consider a bat's wings its most defining characteristic. He creates a distinct class for bats between mammals and birds. Another naturalist, noting the physiological similarity of bats and mice (and emboldened by the common French name *chauve souris*), places bats in the same order as mice and small rodents. Another, following Linnaeus, notices that bats and monkeys have similar teeth. She puts bats in the same order as primates and humans. All three agree on the anatomical facts of bats, yet each manipulates the facts into three distinct theorems.[9]

The crucial question remained to be answered: why? Why did certain creatures with similar structures occupy such different habitats? Why did whales have vestigial limbs? Why do humans and monkeys look so much alike? Linnaean taxonomy was certainly useful for containing nature's chaos, but it hardly offered an explanatory theory of variation.

With the research of eighteenth- and nineteenth-century comparative anatomists, particularly John Hunter, Geoffroy Saint-Hilaire, George Cuvier, and Richard Owen, naturalists realized that the function of animals' various parts was vastly important to understanding how species related to or differed from one another, taxonomically speaking. Function described the size, shape, and placement of various parts and determined their uses and benefits to the overall fitness of the animal. By discovering these underlying functional differences—which typically required dissection and structural comparison of skeletons—anatomists believed that they would expose a more coherent, more "natural" taxonomy than any animal order based on visible differences. But what was the cause of this structural variation? The answer finally came with an understanding of evolution as a process of species adaption over millennia. The morphological similarities that naturalists had distinguished as affinities between groups were now appreciated as traits inherited from a common ancestor. With Charles Darwin's *Origin of Species*, the innate truth of animal order was discovered to be genealogical.[10]

For all the inevitable debate, the tenth edition of Linnaeus's *Systema naturae* is internationally accepted as a pioneering work of modern classification and the beginning of modern zoological nomenclature. The system has proved a malleable and workable frame for naturalists to augment and rearrange as new species were revealed, new anatomical similarities were observed, and, most recently, DNA sequencing became possible. From Linnaeus's basic structure of kingdoms, classes, orders, genera, and species, all living things are now ordered in an expanded hierarchy of domain, kingdom, phylum, class, order, family, genus, and species, all of which are frequently further divided into subcategories. Within the animal kingdom, zebras now belong to the phylum Chordata (animals with a supporting rod along the back), the subphylum Vertebrata (animals with bony backbones), and the class Mammalia, distinguished primarily as warm-blooded vertebrates with mammary glands, sweat glands, hair or fur, and three middle ear bones used in hearing. Of the twenty-one orders of mammals, zebras belong to the odd-toed hoofed order called Perissodactyla (from the Greek *perissos*, strange or odd numbers, and *daktulos*, finger or toe). The order splits into three genera: horses and their relatives (*Equus*), rhinoceroses, and tapirs.[11] The *Equus* genus splits into four subgenera, two of which encompass the plethora of zebras. The mountain and plains zebras both belong in the subgenus *Hippotigris*, while the Grevy's zebra is the sole species in the subgenus *Doliochohippus*. And then there are the subspecies. Of the mountain zebra there is the Cape mountain zebra and Hartmann's mountain zebra, while only one species exists of Grevy's zebra. The plains zebra is the most plenteous, with at least five extant subspecies generally agreed on: Burchell's zebra, Selous's zebra, Grant's zebra, Chapman's zebra, and Crawshay's zebra.

Zebras present an interesting case in the history of classification. Their dramatic black-and-white markings easily and obviously marked specimens as belonging to the zebra family: there could be no confusion over what constituted a zebra stripe. But as exploration broadened in the nineteenth century, as discoveries quickened and collections grew exponentially, the comparison of many skins of the same (or supposedly the same) species became possible. It was then that naturalists began to realize that all stripes were not in fact created equal.

The first distinction was made by William John Burchell during his travels in southern Africa between 1811 and 1815. Burchell noticed that some zebras lived only in mountainous regions, while others exclusively inhabited the African plains. Significantly, the two animals had different hooves suited to their different environments, a sufficient anatomical distinction to mark two distinct species. Further, Burchell noted that variations in zebra stripes, which were previously thought to be individual idiosyncrasies, in fact followed particular and distinct patterning. As Burchell wrote of his "new" zebra, "this beautiful animal has been hitherto confounded by naturalists with the Zebra. When these were first described by modern writers, the Quakka was considered to be the female Zebra; while both that and the true Zebra [Burchell's discovery] bore in common, among the colonists, the name Quakka. The *Wilde Paard*, named *Dauw* by the Hottentots, and a much scarcer animal that the other two, was never suspected to be a different species, although it be far more distinct from the Quakka and Zebra, than these are from each other."[12]

To clarify somewhat, Burchell distinguished his new "true" zebra by its leg markings, which continue all the way down to the hoof. In contrast, the mountain zebra (Linnaeus's zebra, or *wilde paard*, from the Dutch for wild horse) has bare legs.[13] Further, Burchell noted that his zebra had paler brown ghost stripes between the dominant black markings, while the mountain zebra had no such ghost stripes. Somewhat strangely, Burchell renamed Linnaeus's *Equus zebra* (the mountain species with a white belly) *Equus montanus* and named his new species *Equus zebra*.[14] To solidify the science behind his discovery, he donated the skins of a quagga and the two zebra species to the British Museum. While field observations were crucial to distinguishing new species, the ultimate truth of animal order rested on the existence of at least one preserved specimen, a physical proof that was available for repeated observation and investigation.

Is the zebra a white animal with black stripes or a black animal with white stripes? I once learned that the zebra's white underbelly had decided the question in favor of black stripes on a blanched torso. But . . . I discovered recently that most African peoples regard zebras as black animals with white stripes.

—STEPHEN JAY GOULD, "How the Zebra Gets Its Stripes," in *Hen's Teeth and Horse's Toes* (1983), 366

The skins were examined by John Edward Gray, the keeper of the zoological collections at the British Museum. Having been struck "with the confusion that exists in the names of the species, part of which was introduced by Mr. Burchell," Gray wrote, he attempted some synthesis, but he only complicated the matter further.[15] Partially owing to the fact that asses and zebras do not have chestnuts (a callosity on the inside of all four legs exhibited by most equine species), Gray concluded that the ass, the quagga, and the two zebra species were more closely related to each other than to horses. He therefore placed them all in the same genus (*Asinus*), and he renamed the three striped animals *Asinus quagga* (quagga), *Asinus burchellii* (Burchell's *Equus zebra*), and *Asinus zebra* (Burchell's *Equus montanus* and Linnaeus's *Equus zebra*). But again, not all naturalists agreed.

Charles Hamilton Smith believed that zebras should form their own genus, *Hippotigris* (from the Greek words for horse, *hippo*, and tiger, *tigris*), thereby again renaming zebras as a new genus. Other naturalists maintained that zebras were too closely related to horses to warrant their own genus and preferred naming the two known species of zebras *Equus zebra* (upholding Linnaeus's name over Burchell's *Equus montanus*) and *Equus burchelli*. Nineteenth-century zoological literature was forced to list all the zebras' names to ensure that readers would know for certain which particular species was under discussion. Since the plains zebra was first identified as a separate species, it has been named *Equus zebra, Asinus burchellii, Equus montanus, Equus zebroides, Equus festivus, Hippotigris campestris, Equus burchelli typicus, Equus burchelli paucistriatus, Equus burchelli*, and finally *Equus quagga*.[16] By the late 1860s, the genus name *Equus* had mostly muscled out its competitors, and just in time, for yet another species was discovered before the end of the century.

In 1882 the Abyssinian emperor Menelek sent a zebra to Jules Grevy, president of the French Third Republic. The animal lived briefly in the menagerie of the Jardin des Plantes (dying quickly of a lung inflammation), but long enough for Alphonse Milne-Edwards, a professor at the Muséum national d'histoire naturelle, to recognize and label it a new species: *Equus grevyi*.[17] The zebra was carefully measured and dissected and its skin mounted for display in the museum. However, some naturalists thought that the new species was nothing but a large variety of the mountain zebra, or even that the animal's long face was evidence of a careless taxidermist. Skins can easily stretch, tear, or shrink, altering the overall size of animals—as with the Tsavo lions discussed in chapter 3.

18 Two zebras at the Field Museum
of Natural History, Chicago.
Photo courtesy of Robert Hest.

But, as always, the beast provided the incontestable proof. Taxonomic debate depends on material evidence. Naturalists realized that the Grevy's zebra had narrower and more numerous stripes than the other two already known species. In addition, far more than individual variation or bad taxidermy, a long muzzle is a distinguishing feature of the Grevy's zebra. The floodgates were opened. Once naturalists realized that zebras came in many stripes and sizes, zebra subspecies proliferated through the late decades of the nineteenth century and remain a turbulent category to this day.

Animal patterning varies between members of a species and often between the two sides of the same individual. Bilateral symmetry is rarely perfect, and no two zebras are entirely alike. Determining zebra subspecies was dependent on figuring out which stripe variations were merely a creature's individuality and which were a sign of subspecies. How to know the difference? In describing South African zebras in 1876, T. E. Buckley noted that "out of five of these animals shot in one herd there were individuals showing variation of colour and markings from the yellow and chocolate stripes to the pure black and white, the stripes in some cases ceasing above the hock, and in others being continued distinctly down to the hoof."[18] In a 1936 analysis of the plains zebra, Angel Cabrera offered illustrations of twenty-one early specimens of the various subspecies in order to compare their patterning. Burchell's first specimen is shown with stripes descending almost to the bottom curve of its belly. A specimen imported live to Paris and described by Frederic Cuvier in 1826 exhibited a much broader white belly and had three streaky stripes on its hocks. A female purchased by the earl of Derby in 1845 had far more complicated patterning across its haunches, while a specimen from the Dresden Zoological Park had body stripes that continued much further down and around the belly. In other words, stripe pattern alone could not confirm a new subspecies.[19]

Although differences in the color and patterning of stripes offer evidence of different species, the ultimate proof of animal order lies under the skin. The distinction between species and subspecies is marked by a variety of features, including overall size, skull and muzzle shape and length, teeth, and geographical distribution. In her study of zebra taxonomy, Debra Bennett used ninety-six skulls and fifty-seven skeletons. Similarly, C. P. Groves and Catherine H. Bell split their zebra analysis between cranial measurements and hide coloration and patterning.[20] Collecting and comparing multiple specimens of entire zebras, including skeletons, teeth, hides, and DNA, helped naturalists clarify the problem of subspecific versus individual variation.

With the research of eighteenth- and nineteenth-century comparative anatomists and subsequent evolutionary investigations, the majority of zoological knowledge was gained from dissection and comparison. Order was a product of expert knowledge. Teeth were counted. Respiratory, circulatory, and reproductive systems were dissected and examined. Skeletons and skulls were measured. Bladders, lungs, hearts, and glands were excised, preserved, and compared. As natural scientists asked increasingly precise anatomical questions, ever more intimate observations were required. In other words, what was going on *under* the skin became fundamental to understanding animal order. So where does that leave taxidermy and the lively representations of animal form?

DISPLAYING ORDER

From the early nineteenth century onward, the new and improved techniques and chemicals for preserving animals at last enabled the creation and stabilization of large research collections. With the discovery of arsenic and other highly effective insecticides, aggressive global exploration, and the rapidly swelling number of species known to science, collections expanded voluptuously over the course of the nineteenth century. However, success brought its own difficulties. How were all these specimens to be stored and displayed? Two separate answers to this question emerged for two distinct communities.

Whereas beauty arrangements of the mid-eighteenth century had been privately owned and shown to exclusive visitors of similar taste and quality, the rise of natural history museums through the late nineteenth and early twentieth centuries coincided with the emergence of education programs. If the majority of early collections had been arranged by individuals for their personal interest, natural history museums were organized for public instruction. Museums became classrooms. Rather than accentuate animal individuality and subjective appreciation, taxidermy displays now presented a scientist's view of nature's underlying structure. The shift from private beauty to public education was a shift from a culture of taste to a system of facts, from aesthetic cultivation to zoological instruction. If earlier cabinets had organized nature to showcase wonder, beauty, and delight (and a fair dose of social pull), displays of systematic order highlighted the workings of the expert mind. The visitor was expected to absorb the lessons that were offered.

Most natural history museums adopted zoological classification as the most informative, most truthful (because there was a right and wrong order, as opposed to good and bad taste), and least aesthetically curious system for organizing collections. The aesthetic pleasure of strange concurrences and beautiful combinations, or the fascination a particularly odd animal might arouse, was well outside the domain of austere arrangement of order. Visually interesting arrangements were replaced by rows and rows of birds, miles of animals laid out one after the other. The emphasis was on representativeness, not rarity, on broad public education, not elite curiosity. And to actuate this new culture of facts, a new curatorial practice was implanted: sameness.

A staunch adherence to order precludes any preferential treatment of any particular species. With an arrangement based on order, all cases ultimately have equal weight, despite their contents. Order confers a democratic sameness to the animals: none is more important or more exceptional than any other. To demarcate these new spaces of orderly knowledge, museum curators endeavored to expunge provocative aesthetic encounters that might deflect attention from the

"Spread eagle" styles of mounting, artificial rocks and flowers, etc., are entirely out of place in a collection of any scientific pretensions. . . . Birds look best on the whole in uniform rows, assorted according to size, as far as natural classification allows. They are best set on the plainest stands. . . . The stands should be painted dead-white, and be no larger than is necessary.

—ELLIOTT COUES, *Keys to North American Birds* (1884)

science on display. Order ruled sensibility. If the austere arrangements were considered dreary and monotonous by some visitors, the educational promise of the new science overcame most objections.

The shift was cultural as much as purely scientific. In fact, systematic classification was viewed as a prime weapon against the elitism and dilettantism of curious collectors. Order was inherently democratic and counteraesthetic.[21] Not surprisingly, this dual value of order (democratic and counteraesthetic) was ardently manipulated at the Muséum national d'histoire naturelle in 1793, after the French Revolution. As Emma Spary writes, the new system involved "a deliberate rejection from the domain of the scientific of all aspects of display which were open to interpretation in a curious manner, no matter how expert. Whilst critiques of curiosity had been around for half a century, moreover, the special conditions at the French Muséum d'Histoire Naturelle were particularly conducive to the institutional victory of the counter-aesthetic movement."[22] Those special conditions included an emphasis on a republican program of public education and an attack on the privilege of aristocratic beauty collections. If the eighteenth-century praise of a well-built private collection had been "how aesthetically pleasing," the greatest nineteenth-century praise of public galleries was "how orderly, how comprehensive."

While the animals as individuals are exemplars of their species, they also combine to make materially manifest the bones of the rules, that is, the relationships *between* animals. The spatial separation in museums of birds and mammals or of zebras and elephants conforms to what distinguishes the classes and orders of the animal world. For example, the close physical arrangement of zebras and asses offers some clues as to what makes this order of animals distinct from others and what holds these animals together. What is on display is as much a system of linking animals as the animals themselves.

With individual specimens of the same family placed one after another, the whole experience of entering collections becomes instructive. With every glance, visitors develop a material understanding of the relationships between animals and their neighbors, that is, their close relatives. Resemblances between animals indicate genus; differences mark species. By following these characteristics—more or less similar, more or less different—through the course of the museum, visitors absorb an understanding of nature's orders almost unawares. The route through the museum itself becomes pedagogical: the orders, classes, and families of nature appear to reveal themselves spontaneously to the diligent museumgoer. The clarity of truth prevails, at least for the casual visitor. Working scientists were increasingly unsure about such taxidermic arrangements.

In his treatise on taxidermy, published in 1840, William Swainson stated that taxidermy was essential for every naturalist: "in order to acquire a more accurate knowledge of their external form, and to investigate their internal structure, it is absolutely necessary to examine them in a dead state. Hence has arisen the art of TAXIDERMY." Without taxidermy, the naturalist could not "pursue his studies or preserve his own materials."[23] Yet Swainson's use of the word *taxidermy* here is rather loose, encompassing both animals artistically preserved as if alive, known as taxidermy or *mounted* animals, and study or *stuffed* skins, which are simply preserved skins stuffed with batting to round out their form.[24]

For Swainson, the typical mid-nineteenth-century displays of birds—rows of individually cased specimens preserved in lively poses—posed serious disadvantages for the scientific naturalist, and Swainson presented technical, economic, and methodological reasons why unmounted study skins were the best for scientific inquiry. First, mounted specimens were more often than not badly done: "it is, in fact, rare to see exotic birds, after they have come from the hands of the bird-stuffer, in a thoroughly perfect state." Second, mounted specimens were expensive to prepare and took up too much room. Last, and most important for the serious scientific inquirer, sealed cases were "unfavourable to a minute examination" of their animal contents and did not allow their defining characteristics, which were essential to scientific description, to be distinctly seen. It is hard to count or examine teeth in a fossilized mouth, and an animal posed climbing a branch is far harder to analyze, compare, measure, and examine than a flat, unmounted skin. In contrast, "when laid upon fine cotton, and arranged in cabinet drawers, [study skins] have a very pleasing appearance; they can be at all times handled, and minutely examined, without the least trouble; moreover, they lay [*sic*] in such a compact space, that, in a cabinet 5 1/4 feet high, 3 feet 3 inches broad, and 1 foot 7 inches deep, containing 36 drawers, we have a collection of near 600 specimens." In short, while the science of preservation—maintaining collections free from decay and insects—was fundamental to the growth and stabilization of collections, the artistic side of taxidermy—setting animals and birds in naturalistic poses—had little if any scientific value.[25]

Charles Darwin had the same thoughts on the matter. When considering the sprawling, cluttered natural history collections housed at the British Museum, Darwin promoted the idea of dividing the collections into two distinct groups. At the time no separation existed, in space or specimens, between scientific collections and public galleries at the museum. Naturalists often worked amid the noise and distraction of visitors streaming through the museums or waited for days when the museum was closed to the public. For the working naturalists, Darwin argued that quiet, private rooms "fitted up with thousands of drawers would cost but little," take up vastly less space than lively mounts, and allow naturalists to work whenever they wanted, undistracted by visitors. For the general public, Darwin advocated a judicious selection of specimens to form a "typical" or popular museum. A well-chosen selection of birds and beasts that exemplified the distinguishing features of animal groups would make nature's orders clearer, more memorable, and therefore more educational. In a letter to Thomas Huxley dated October 23, 1858, Darwin suggested that clearly labeled and well-spaced specimens "would be quite as amusing & far more instructive to the populace (& I think to naturalists) than the present enormous display of Birds & Mammals. I would save expence of stuffing & would keep all skins, except for a few 'typicals,' in drawers. Thus much room would be saved, & a little more space could be given to the real workers, who could work all days."[26] Besides, Darwin wrote to another correspondent, the current galleries of taxidermy were not only a cluttered, inefficient use of space but also exhibited "a sort of vanity in the Curators."[27]

In 1858 Darwin, along with eight other eminent naturalists, including William Harvey and Thomas Huxley, presented a petition to the British government advocating a radical reworking of the display, arrangement, and care of the natural history departments. Basically, they argued for Darwin's concept: to split the collections into a small, well-chosen popular museum for general instruction and a more comprehensive collection for serious study. Without such a division, the writers argued, both the scientific use of the collection and its public appeal were impaired: "the Public are only dazzled and confused by the multiplicity of unexplained objects, densely crowded together on the shelves and cases," while the naturalists were not able to remove specimens from their cases for close examination when the museum was open to the public and so were "deprived of the opportunity of real study." In addition, the specimens themselves suffered from being used for two purposes. The dust and dirt brought into the museum by throngs

19 Flat storage of study skins in the Birds Division at the Smithsonian Museum, Washington, D.C. Photo © Chip Clark / Smithsonian Institution.

of visitors damaged them, yet cases could not be hermetically sealed since those same specimens were required to be easily accessible for close study.[28] Of particular concern were especially precious, rare, or scientifically valuable specimens, particularly the type specimens. Exposed to continuous dirt and light, preserved nature quickly deteriorated, but without any corresponding advantage to the scientific investigator. Without a comprehensive system of descriptive labeling, when crowding forced heterogeneous creatures to be exhibited in the same room (and consequently the specimens most deserving of attention were at risk of being lost among a multitude of bland or defective specimens), the museum could only present a noisy, flawed idea of nature.

On these three points naturalists universally concurred, namely, that (1) the effort to meet two essentially distinct objectives—public education and scientific research—with the same set of specimens was detrimental to both; (2) for the general public, only the best-known, most interesting, most didactic specimens ought to be arranged and labeled in such a way as to convey the greatest scientific knowledge in the most concise manner; and (3) a comprehensive zoological collection for serious scientific study precluded the sort of lively taxidermy mounts so loved by the general visitor. Taxidermied mounts were not deemed inherently unscientific— an animal species was still on display—but they were not ideal tools of science.

Simply put, beyond preserving skins for examination and comparison, taxidermy had a limited function in the making of zoological knowledge from the early nineteenth century onward. The desire to materialize nature's orders with taxidermized animals—each creature laid out one beside the other—is fundamentally linked to public education, not scientific inquiry. Shaping a skin into some semblance of life hardly amounts to the discovery of new knowledge. Taxidermists always rely on previously observed zoological knowledge to sculpt and preserve an accurate vision of the beast. In fact, the artistry of taxidermy can get in the way of scientific work. With stiffened limbs and devoid of viscera, taxidermied animals are inflexible and incomplete and hinder scientific observations. There was no reason that animals could not be stuffed and mounted *after* dissection, but the essential zoological understanding of the animal—its internal structure, the functioning of its parts, what made it a distinct species—is not presented in that state, at least not for the inquiring and knowledgeable zoologist.

Scientific understandings of nature's diverse workings are always liable to change as new information or philosophies are generated, but taxonomic disputes between naturalists are not acted out by sneaking taxidermied beasts into new ordering schemes. Arranging animals is an artistic aftereffect of intellectual work. Biological investigations and taxonomic debate came first, and subsequently the animals were ordered for public education.

This marks a fascinating shift in the history of taxidermy. The animals are not simply on display; they are displayed as representatives of a theory and stand as material proofs of some prior intellectual conception of how the animal kingdom fits together. The order comes first; the beast substantiates the theorem with its bulk. Quite simply, and rather ironically, by the time taxidermy achieved a level of preservation that could be serviceable for natural science, science had surpassed whatever knowledge taxidermy might offer.

The tension between public galleries and working collections persists in museums today. The storage areas of natural history museums house massive collections of creaturely life, all neatly stored in hermetically sealed drawers. But these specimens are not taxidermied, and they are not for public view. The typical museumgoer rarely has the opportunity to see working collections of science. Rather, what is on public view is a pared-down synopsis of what is already known and determined to be of interest. As with the zebras on display in Tring, species are distinguished and classified somewhere else by someone else, and visitors are offered an interesting lesson in zebra diversity.

Of course, there are many exceptions to the rule of sameness in zoological order. Once taxidermy was liberated from the pressures of knowledge making, museums were free to play with ordering principles to teach various lessons and to enliven the potentially monotonous row after row of birds and beasts. Albino, two-headed, or otherwise anomalously shaped or colored animals are frequently presented as informative exceptions and are always accompanied by a disclaimer. Also, select animals are sometimes isolated to make visible various laws of nature.

Between 1887 and 1891 the Natural History Museum in London installed an introductory series of cases on evolutionary theory variously demonstrating species variation under domestication, protective mimicry, albinism and excess pigmentation melanism, and seasonal color variation. Prominently positioned in the main entrance hall, the cases were meant to offer a clear-eyed view of potentially abstract theory with the animals themselves. For example, the case exhibiting seasonal variation was divided into two levels in order to showcase the same animals (an Alpine hare, a ptarmigan, a willow-grouse, a stoat, and a weasel) in their "summer dress" of browns and grays and again in their white winter coats. Both scenes blended the animals with their habitats—white on pure white (faux) snow, mottled browns on lichens, moss, and rocks. Hardly a dry lesson in selective adaptation, as visitors themselves could test the harmony between the coloration of animals and their surroundings by standing back or coming up close. And, as chapter 3 demonstrated, animals can be theatrically arranged in their ecological habitats to exhibit the physical variation in a species and the harmony of plants, animals, and landscapes. The massive African water hole diorama at the Field Museum in Chicago, for example, contains twenty-three animals of six different species gathered around a watering hole. A family of giraffes, herds of zebras and Grant's gazelles, oryx and elands, and black rhinoceroses all face off against a sweeping vista of southern Ethiopia, complete with flat-topped acacia trees, a termite hill, and even a tickbird on the back of a rhinoceros.

Such exceptions to the display of animal order only further accentuate the truth that taxidermic displays are only ever after the fact of science. Theories are built, explored, challenged, and solidified elsewhere. Taxidermy only embodies what is already known—at least in theory.

ANIMAL ATTRACTION

Because species diversity was created prior to humanity, and because we evolved within it, we have never fathomed its limits.

—EDWARD O. WILSON,
Biophilia (1984), 10

For purposes of zoological classification, the visible surface of animals is vital, but not as an end in itself, not for the sheer aesthetic pleasure of a zebra's black-and-white intrigue. The relative beauty of particular animals is ostensibly irrelevant. Instead, physical characteristics become keys or clues. The patterning of stripes and spots, the size of a beak, the shapes of limbs, an absence of claws or horns or glands—all provide crucial pointers that distinguish the similarity and difference of a creature from other species. From the perspective of classification, the physical appearance of animals is only important as a manifestation of zoological order.

As discussed in chapter 1, the wonders cluttering up the sixteenth- and seventeenth-century cabinets of wonder were seen *through* in the sense that each strange exotic was appreciated as a token of its mysterious homeland, somewhere over the horizon. The orderly arrangements of creatures in natural history museums are also meant to be seen through—not through to reveries of distant landscapes but to a theoretical system, from the particularity of this animal on display to a general concept of its species and the species' placement within a classification scheme. Within the pedagogy of display, the creatures are meant to vacillate between visible surface and theory, from material beast to a marker within the evolutionary tree. As if to underscore this fact, museum specimens are typically posed in the most neutral attitudes and positions possible: rows and rows of animals and birds, one after the other, without any suggestion of individuality, personality, or habitat—supposedly just the dispassionate display of nature's diversity.

But no museum could ever possibly display a representative of every species. The diversity of the natural world is simply too astounding. Even the largest museums must always choose which species to display based on the space available. Selection usually begins with broad categories of creatures and moves into smaller groups of genus and species depending on space and available specimens. A small museum might be forced to display only one or two parrots as representatives of the nearly four hundred species of parrots, or just one species of zebra, seagull, or badger.

And which specimen should be chosen as most "typical" of its species? Displaying multiples of each species—male, female, young, old—is usually impossible for reasons of space. If a species varies greatly between male and female, sometimes both sexes will be displayed if space allows. However, usually a male in the prime of life is considered the typical representative. Species with particularly showy males, like peacocks and pheasants, are almost always represented with a male specimen. Such decisions shrink nature down to a more manageable size, which, although hardly comprehensive, is not necessarily detrimental. As Darwin argued, too many animals can be overwhelming, confusing, and chaotic. As with zebras, few visitors expect to see such a plethora of stripes and sizes. The creation and display of any sort of animal order is always a function of the human mind's ability to classify nature, combined with the pragmatics of available species, display space, and skilled preservation. Taxidermy is always a staged spectacle.

Yet the pedagogical power of taxidermy always rests solidly on the visual appeal of the animal themselves. If taxidermy is a silent educator, it is because the animals prove their own truth. Depending on how they are arranged, animals explain laws of nature by their very presence. The success of the lesson depends on the magnetism of the animals. Nothing forces viewers to look except the beauty of material lesson, that is, except the animals themselves. It is animal attraction that engages visitors to look deeply and lingeringly and absorb what knowledge is on display.

Despite the emphasis on order and the precision of arrangement, it is only the excessively conscientious museumgoer who will study each animal in turn, reading each label, noting each feature that distinguishes this species from that. Most visitors are hardly so diligent. Most will wander among the corridors, breezing by some animals, studying others, perhaps stopping to learn facts about classification, or the habits or habitats of certain animals. Perhaps the display will encourage visitors to learn more about a particular creature, but further learning usually proceeds elsewhere—there is rarely room in museums for extended zoological discussion. In the overt sameness of such pedagogical display tactics, what stops visitors in front of any particular creature is an intense animal attraction. What stopped me were the Tring zebras.

With the exception of their being seated, the zebras conform to the neutrality of expression characterizing many natural history specimens: head level, gaze fixed, just a plain, apparently objective series of beasts. And yet the Tring zebras convey something beyond the pragmatics of display and even beyond zoological fact. On the one hand, accentuated by the crisp, modern glass cases, the sight is one of the most stringent order: tight, clean, complete. On the other hand, there is something almost "arkish" in the accommodatingly compact and obligingly restful poses of so many zebras, animals that typically sleep standing. The tranquil vision suggests a lingering, patient waiting. The animals have not been posed as if caught in a photographic flash between one action and the next; this is not captured liveliness as much as a material truth of taxidermy made manifest: death has already happened; material time has stopped, and an alternate timeline extends for as long as the animals will linger. Once ordered, named, and labeled, they remain immortally serene, which for a zebra is something exceptional.

The riotous cousin of the stately horse, zebras are as notoriously unruly as their stripes. An iconic creature from childhood alphabet books, zebras are synonymous with the letter Z. Along with giraffes, elephants, and lions, zebras romanticize the vastness of savannas in a Western cultural imaginary: impossibly lofty, impossibly big, impossibly fierce, and impossibly wild. With the exception of leopard spots, no animal patterning has the visual potency of zebra stripes. A childhood dream beast, a safari icon, a textile blueprint—the zebra is as compelling imaginatively as it is physically, and visitors can never fully disassociate the beast on display from its cultural and poetic aura. Despite the neutrality of posture and the dispassionate aura of classification, despite the overt truth of order, the zebras make obvious a fundamental quality of taxidermy: animals are never just neutral, abstract markers in a classification scheme. The displayed animal always gets in the way of the supposed purity of the animal order. Imagination always blurs into the materiality of animal skins.

The particular and personal appeal of specific animals ruptures all sense of sameness or equality of specimens despite any exhibition's efforts toward taxonomic austerity. The animal and the intensity it provokes are never irrelevant. Some animals are exceptionally beautiful, some birds exceptionally colored. We are entranced by the patterning of zebras, the sheer height of giraffes, the unexpected tininess of a weasel, the hummingbird's astonishing shimmer. Visitors are always stopped by some particular creature. Or again, perhaps it is the way an animal has been prepared, preserved, and presented that causes the fascination. Obviously, dioramas have their megawatt appeal, but individual animals can be equally, strangely appealing. Perhaps the creature is very odd, badly or beautifully mounted. The hindquarters of a giraffe on display at the Harvard Museum of Natural History are sewn together with luridly large stitches and its ancient scrotum is cracked. The case of lemurs and sifakas at the Field Museum in Chicago contains specimens so sensitively preserved that every fingernail, every delicate whisker and eyelash, is beautifully defined, despite the specimens' being more than a century old. Some visitors will notice their beauty; others will not. Some visitors may be more attracted to local species, some to exotic creatures from geographies they will never themselves visit. To stop the typical stroll through a museum means stopping to engage in deep looking, and what visually appeals to any particular visitor is hardly universal.

And then consider that each of the animals is an individual: each has its own narrative both before and after death, the particular trajectory of collector, taxidermist, museum, and display tactics. The collections in Tring, for example, were established by Lionel Walter Rothschild, second Baron Rothschild. Rothschild famously harnessed four zebras to his carriage and drove them into the forecourt of Buckingham Palace to prove that zebras could be tamed. Would it influence visitors to know if one of the zebras on display had been in harness? But the personal histories of animals rarely make it onto the museum's information labels. And although animal celebrities and personalities are often on display in museums, they are usually set apart. For example, the giant panda Chi-Chi is on display at the Natural History Museum in London. Chi-Chi became the star attraction at the London Zoo from her arrival in 1958 until her death in 1972. She is not just a panda but a personality. Interestingly, she is not displayed with her close relatives (taxonomically speaking) but is adjacent to the museum's café.

From the cabinets of wonder hoarders and dilettantes to the public galleries of natural history museums, taxidermy has never really been a tool of zoological investigation but a method of zoological display. Even in the austere confines of a scientific museum, taxidermied animals are always more than flat, neutral, scientific objects. Taxidermy is and always has been firmly rooted in the aesthetic appeal of creatures, in the charm of animals—which is to say, taxidermy is deeply and unavoidably engaged with animal magnetism. Perhaps this is because taxidermy allows visitors to get closer to animals than they ever could in life, or even on television. Perhaps it is because of the immortally immobile liveliness of animals, but whatever the cause, the physical intimacy engenders emotional intimacy: looking at taxidermy is never the same as looking at photographs of animals. The undeniable lingering physical impact of the animal and the emotional encounter it provokes ensure that taxidermy is never just a technology for making nature visible. Comparing your size to the size of a moose or a hummingbird, or seeing the shape of a wombat or a pygmy hippopotamus, is always startling. There is something very personal about encountering an animal face to face, even if dead, even if taxidermied, even if behind glass. The beauty of animals draws us in, but it also increasingly provides a critique of its own existence.

It is true enough that taxidermy is no longer as appreciated as it was during the nineteenth century. In an era before animal documentaries and color photography, museums were a primary venue for the general public to learn about nature, and taxidermy was a primary technology for making creaturely life visible. It also is true enough that museums are no longer uncritically accepted as the cathedrals of nature that they were in the nineteenth century. Contemporary museums do not collect and preserve animals for public display with the same energy as their predecessors. Museums with nineteenth-century roots have been criticized as complicit in the colonial project, their collections branded as imperial archives. Where taxidermy was once considered a vital technology for making nature visible to the general public, it now makes people squeamish; it is seen by many as a gratuitous spoilage, as death on display. In short, all taxidermy, even museum taxidermy, has fallen from grace.[29]

Let me offer a vivid example. Between 1958 and 1960, Gillian Spencer, the curator of the Saffron Walden Museum in Essex, England, successfully convinced the Saffron Walden District Council to remodel and edit the museum's taxidermic displays. In fact, she had been almost ordered to do so. Under the terms of a Carnegie Trust grant that the museum had received for upgrades and improvements, Spencer was required to follow the advice of Dr. N. B. Marshall of the British Museum, who stipulated that only the museum's British specimens and a superior collection of tropical birds should be kept, while the other foreign specimens—mostly collected during the nineteenth-century heyday of natural history collecting—were to be discarded. As Spencer explained in the Saffron Walden Museum Society's 1960 annual report, local museums must exhibit local nature, not the haphazard remains of eccentric Victorian ramblings. The imperial history of the animals was an embarrassment, and besides, the animals were in a "dreadful condition." "Many of them were more than a hundred years old, all very dirty and some very dilapidated," Spencer wrote. "Most of them were so badly stuffed as to be mere caricatures of the creatures they were supposed to represent." Moreover, Spencer argued that "it is felt that television and the zoos now give people, and especially children, opportunities of obtaining a far truer picture of wild life in other parts of the world." And so, after having convinced the council that "nostalgia should be banished in the interests of greater usefulness for the Museum," Spencer sent a letter to every museum in Essex in the hope of unloading what she tepidly described as "foreign mammals which have been pronounced tolerable (though not outstanding) specimens."[30] No museum wanted them. On May 4, 1960, more than two hundred animals, birds, reptiles, and fish were hauled to the city dump and set on fire.[31]

How much nature could possibly remain in a fusty piece of Victorian taxidermy? Grimacing with wizened lips and wooden teeth, the straw-stuffed survivors of the previous century seemed better labeled "cultural relic" than "nature." When Spencer purged the museum, she was sluicing out the imperial heritage of the Saffron Walden Museum, Britain's second-oldest purposely built natural history museum. But if these objects were eradicated because of their ancestry, why not remove other Victorian items from display as well? What makes taxidermy particularly deserving of elimination?

Spencer's purge can be read either as a pragmatic spring cleaning or as a cautionary tale of loss. For the pragmatists, museum taxidermy is an educational tool.

Like all such tools, it is disposable when its didactic value is diminished, undermined, or superseded by improved technologies and display tactics. The Saffron Walden animals failed on all three counts: they were badly stuffed, of questionable imperial heritage, and educationally inferior to television. The opposing cautionary position is more complex, precisely because it is not altogether clear what was burned by Spencer, and without knowing what was destroyed, it is hard to advocate for its preservation. Did the bonfire eradicate animal skins, educational resources, cultural history, or—most nebulous of all—the intimate experience of encountering a long-dead animal face to face?

In recent decades museum taxidermy has been critically reappraised, and not for the better. Among the most forthright examples are the small signs scattered throughout the taxidermy collections at the Natural History Museum in London, which state, "The Museum is concerned about the conservation of animals in the natural world and no longer collects skins for taxidermy displays. The specimens in these displays are from the Museum's historical collections—consequently some are faded or show other signs of their age. We feel it is more appropriate to rely on these collections for display, even though they may not fully reflect the natural appearance of the living animal."

The apologetic signs distance the museum from the acts of killing and mounting. They allow the museum to present a fresher outlook, more in tune with current sensitivities, while nevertheless displaying their collections. The museum's acknowledgment of its own discomfort with the aggressive history of Victorian collecting perhaps makes the displays more palatable to the typical museumgoer, who, living in our current age of environmental awareness, has become acutely sensitive to the human uses and abuses of the natural world and its inhabitants. Yet by undermining the mimetic value of the animals—*they may not fully reflect the natural appearance of the living animal*—and through a barely veiled critique of past collecting practices, the signs suggest that what is on display is not so much nature but another era's vision and manipulation of nature. By drawing attention to the historical depth of these animal-things (and away from their surface appearance), the signs tacitly acknowledge the objects' origins and significance within particular cultural, intellectual, and political practices. In a sense, looking at nature almost becomes secondary to knowing human history: rather than textual description illuminating the intricacies and particularities of the animals on display, the animals now supplement a cultural exegesis.

However, neither a specimen's age nor the skill of its taxidermist reduces the impact of taxidermied animals. Even when hidden in backrooms or stored under plastic, animals retain their alarming magnetism. Despite the acknowledgment that perhaps these animals should not in fact be here to look at, the overall aesthetic of most exhibition galleries—darkly lit interiors with animals beautifully ordered behind glass—entices visitors. In fact, the sheer visual power of the display strangely serves to strengthen a critique of the animals' presence. That is, the

20 Daniëlle van Ark, *Untitled (Zebras 01)*, 2006. Photograph. A zebra lingering in storage at Zoölogisch Museum Amsterdam. Photo courtesy of the artist.

sheer magnetism of the animals compels viewers to look at nature and implicitly encourages them to cultivate an appreciation of the creatures on display and simultaneously to recognize the problematic nature of looking at them within a museum context. Animals are not fixed entities fully explained by the hierarchies of natural order, or by recent cultural or political discourse, but rather are provocative forces, both ruthlessly physical and semantically ambiguous: an overwhelming spectacle of beauty, death, knowledge, and longing.

Taxidermy is always as much a spectacle of creaturely life as it is proof of the fact that, as humans, we need nature and its nonhuman inhabitants to tell us stories about our own place in the world. The innate human need to relate to nature, as Stephen Kellert writes, is not just a need for natural resources, materials, and foods. It is a longing for the emotional, cognitive, aesthetic, and even spiritual sustenance that nature offers. How we use and talk about nature says a great deal about how we understand being in the world. "Even the tendency to avoid, reject, and, at times, destroy elements of the natural world," Kellert writes, "can be viewed as an extension of an innate need to relate deeply and intimately with the vast spectrum of life about us."[32] But, of course, some encounters with nature are more sustaining than others.

And here we return again to the relationship between the ethics of looking at taxidermy, the compelling fascination to look, and the worry about what made that looking possible. The animals did not choose their immortality, and now they can no longer invite or refuse intimacy. The animal is laid bare before any eyes that care to look. There is always an unsettling voyeuristic element to taxidermy, allowing viewers to contemplate creatures that in life would have preferred not to be seen, or at least not seen so closely. After all, part of the elegancy of an animal is its secrecy, and this longing to see what could not, should not, be seen is part of taxidermy's visceral pleasure. The next chapter pushes these features to their limits by considering perhaps the definitive form of taxidermy: the hunting trophy. While taxidermied animals can be manipulated to convey all manner of cultural and intellectual propaganda, they are always strange, unsettling storytellers.

NARRATIVE  5

MY FAVORITE HEAD

On the morning of October 5, 1880, the Anglo-Austrian big-game hunter William Adolph Baillie-Grohman set out alone from his camp in western Wyoming with his 500-bore rifle, the "trailstopper," as he called it, to hunt wapiti, the enormous North American elk. He did not return until late the following evening, having spent one night and almost a second on the trail of an exceptional stag. They were a memorable few days for the hunter and culminated in the acquisition of his most prized hunting trophy. "My favourite head of all," Baillie-Grohman mused in his various hunting memoirs, "is one of over 60 in. with peculiarly long and gracefully shaped tines of good curve. . . . The grizzly old stag that carried it gave me one of the most exciting stalks man ever enjoyed."[1]

It was Baillie-Grohman's third of more than a dozen hunting expeditions to the Rocky Mountains. For fifteen consecutive years he spent the best part of each year in the Pacific Northwest, crisscrossing the Atlantic Ocean some thirty times with the chief ambition to "bag big heads," really big heads. To get a dozen wapiti antlers more than sixty inches in length, or a similar number of equally impressive

I know of few more inspiring sights than a fine stag in his true home, the beautiful Alpine retreats high up on certain of the great ranges of the Rocky Mountains. Scenery, grand as it may be, receives fresh charm when framed in by a noble pair of branching antlers; and I know no trophy of days spent in the far-off wilds that will recall stirring memories in more lifelike and warmer colours, or fill your soul with such longing desire to return speedily to the well-known glade in the forest, where in a fair struggle the bearer of yonder head found in you his master.

—WILLIAM ADOLPH BAILLIE-GROHMAN, *Camps in the Rockies, Being a Narrative of Life on the Frontier, and Sport in the Rocky Mountains* (1882), 121–22 bighorn sheep, Baillie-Grohman explained, "meant the securing of prizes which only a few sportsmen who have visited the Rockies have been able to obtain."[2] Baillie-Grohman was a trophy hunter who sought out what he perceived as a romantic wilderness adventure to test his hardiness, cunning, and animal instincts: meat was not his primary objective. But then hunting is never merely utilitarian. Hunters set themselves the challenge of engaging intimately and passionately with wild animals, particularly with the biggest, boldest, most majestic wild beasts. Driven by the visceral pleasure of stalking and conquest, hunters seek and celebrate a particular sort of animal encounter, the culmination of which is an animal's sacrifice.[3]

Hunting is a broad term that encompasses a vast array of social, cultural, ritualistic, and utilitarian activities. If sportsmen's trophies such as Baillie-Grohman's favorite head are prized personal possessions, they simultaneously participate in a sportsmen's culture: the importance of the hunt is not so much the meat but its symbolic resonance within a particular community. As Roger King explains, hunting is both a personal act, localized in time and space, and a social practice whose meaning is fundamentally shaped by its context. "The aboriginal hunter, the ancient Assyrian king, the medieval poacher, the Victorian trophy hunter, and the modern sports hunter all kill animals. It would be mistaken to suppose, however, that they all perform the same act."[4] How hunts are remembered, if at all, makes these differences in purpose and intention particularly obvious.

While trophies memorialize the performance of a hunt and its successful conclusion, not all hunted animals are commemorated with a trophy. In fact, the number of purposely killed animals that become trophies is exceptionally small. Like any sort of memorial or souvenir, a hunting trophy exhibits the importance of a particular event within an individual's life experience, which is to say, the hunted animal must be highly valued by the hunter or the narrative of its death would hardly need such potent commemoration. Taxidermy is not a quick, easy, or cheap process. Perhaps the animal was the first of its species killed by the hunter. Perhaps it was the most dangerous, the wiliest, or the one that almost got away. Perhaps it was astonishingly large. Or again, perhaps the hunter made a particular trip to kill an individual of a specific species. Among hunters, particular species have distinct auras. From nineteenth-century imperial lion shoots to the romantic American ethos of Daniel Boone, from stags in the Scottish highlands, to kudu hunting in South Africa, to the elusive mountain goats of the Austrian Alps, each species of creaturely life that is regularly hunted is surrounded by customs and rituals, and the trophies of each species have their own significance within the hunting community. For example, "the Big Five" was a term coined by nineteenth-century hunters to designate the most dangerous African creatures to stalk and hunt: lion, leopard, rhinoceros, elephant, and Cape buffalo. Some animals are particularly fearsome, while others are especially elusive or, most tragically, rare to the point of extinction.

Of course, hunting is a charged topic, and my point here is not to debate the merits or deficiencies of animal killing. What interests me here is the material memorialization of the hunter's quest: the hunting trophy. What is this animal-thing? Why does it exist? And, perhaps the strangest question of all, what do trophies become once they are parted from their hunter-creator?

Autumn in the Rockies was prime "whistling time," so called for the peculiar sound that stags emit during rutting time. It was the season when the animals came together in herds of hundreds, old and young, male and female, for "fighting, feeding, love-making, and 'whistling,'" as Baillie-Grohman put it.[5] And, most important, it was the time of year that stags' antlers were at their largest.

Half an hour's walk from camp, Baillie-Grohman sighted a herd of about two or three hundred wapiti grazing peacefully in a beautiful glade below him. He was well accustomed to such idyllic scenes. In the past two months he had seen many thousand wapiti pass in front of his rifle, but he was on the hunt for only the biggest, the most noble of stags. He stalked forward against the wind in the hope of singling out an exceptional animal: "I took a leisurely survey of the deer but I was disappointed; not a single really fine head could I espy." Baillie-Grohman was just about to retreat and try his luck elsewhere when he heard a slight rustling behind him. He turned and there, not ten yards off, just issuing from cover, stood the biggest wapiti he had ever seen. "His neck was nearly black, the rest of the body a grizzly grey-brown, and the antlers of truly gigantic size. We looked at each other for a second; then, still keeping my eyes riveted on his, my hand slowly, very slowly, extended, to where, a foot or two off, my rifle was lying." But the animal was too wary for Baillie-Grohman. He was off into the forest again before the hunter could even lift rifle to shoulder. The whole encounter was over in a second, but even that briefest image of the animal's extraordinary size and the heavy beam of its antlers—outmatching everything Baillie-Grohman had ever seen, let alone killed—kindled a deep lust in the hunter. The animal was to be his. "The reader, if he be a sportsman . . . can fancy that the apparition had awakened in me all the bad passions of the craft, and I determined to bag him, if at all possible" (123–24). In the end, it proved possible, but the hunter was tested. "As the sequel will show, it was destined to be a stern chase." And yet a stern chase is part of the pleasure of a hunt, and certainly a central reason for remembering the animal with a trophy. As always, the best hunting trophies tell the best hunting stories.

The animal led Baillie-Grohman across partially frozen ground, which made tracking nearly impossible. The ground became softer again, but still Baillie-Grohman lost the trail. The wapiti's tracks merged with those of a large herd of six or seven hundred wapiti, which spread out in the valley below him. Some were grazing peacefully. Some were fighting, their huge antlers crashing together in combat. Had his prey joined their number? He was unable to spot his shaggy brown giant. Among the herd he saw several exceptionally large stags. He ignored them. His only interest was the colossal grizzly stag. He waited for several hours, searching the herd with binoculars, hoping, losing hope. He crept closer to the herd, scrambling through a small stand of cottonwood trees surrounded by brush cover. Finally, when the animal seemed lost to him, Baillie-Grohman heard snapping twigs and, clambering down the steep side of the gully, he caught sight of his colossal wapiti again, not more than seventy yards off on the other side.

> He was making down the gully at a double-quick trot, and a sharp corner would hide him the next moment; so, without knowing very clearly what I did, I threw up my rifle and fired. Had I hit him? I knew not, for my shot was a very quick one, and I was standing in a most awkward position on a steep bank, the soil of which was continually giving way under my feet. I imagined I heard the bullet strike, but the distance was too short to make out distinctly that reassuring sound, so well known to the rifleman. The stag had vanished, without a sign or a drop of blood to show that I had hit him. As can be imagined, I was vastly excited, and, I believe, had a grizzly at that moment started up in my path I should probably have shouted to him to get out of my way. (129)

The first thing to determine was whether he had wounded his game. He searched the ground for blood and eventually found evidence that he had punctured a lung with his single shot, a sure sign that the animal would not survive long, though long enough to put several miles between himself and the hunter. It was already late in the afternoon, and Baillie-Grohman tracked the animal's blood trail until night overtook him. Unable to go on, he camped beneath a grove of spreading trees with a small fire and a few drops of whiskey to keep him warm and some bread for dinner, waiting, just waiting for dawn.

At the first show of light, he was on the trail again. Several miles and many hours later, Baillie-Grohman finally found his prey. "It was late in the afternoon when I came up to the monarch of the Great Divide. There he lay, where death had at last ended his gallant flight. He had been dead many hours, for his body was quite rigid, and his eye lustreless and broken" (132). He was the biggest wapiti the hunter had ever seen. His antlers alone would tip the scales at forty-four pounds (fig. 21). But night was again approaching, and rather than spend a second night away from camp, Baillie-Grohman decided to return the following day to claim his prize. He took the animal's tongue and its two enormous canine teeth— sure signs of the animal's impressive stature—and returned to his hunting party at camp.

In the morning, Baillie-Grohman and Port, an American trapper in his early thirties, rode over to the dead stag with a pack horse. Baillie-Grohman had particularly wanted to preserve the unique grizzly-brown hide of the animal, but it was not to be. Bears had discovered and eaten the better part of the fallen stag during the night, and had buried the rest in the frozen ground. All that remained unmauled were the upper portions of the animal. The two men laboriously dug it out with sticks and "and thus rescued not only the best head of my collection, but also the one to which are attached the pleasantest memories" (134). Two years later, as Baillie-Grohman, comfortably settled in his Austrian chateau, wrote his first hunting memoir, it was this favorite head that kept him company:

As I write these lines, which I happen to do in a quiet old Tyrolese "schloss," the arched corridors of which are lined with trophies of the chase in the Old and New World, the shadow of such a great head is thrown across my table, for the low winter's sun is casting its last rays through the quaint old diamond-paned and marble-arched window at my back. It is my largest head. The skill of the taxidermist has not been uselessly expended upon this cherished souvenir of the Rockies, and the grand old fellow looks down with a very lifelike calmness of mien from

My favourite Wapiti Head. Study in Schloss Matzen.

Wm. A. Baillie-Grohman

the broad expanse of the tapestried wall reserved to him, where in stately exclusiveness he has found his last home. (122)

Certainly, hunters frequently preserve the entire bodies of animals. Also, various parts of hunted animals are fashioned into household items—skin rugs, elephant foot tables, antler chairs, and deer-foot lamps. But here I am interested specifically in the quintessential hunting trophy, the sort of souvenir that Baillie-Grohman's favorite head typifies: a severed head of an animal mounted on a wooden plaque and displayed in a domestic space, perhaps above the fireplace or in a study.

Whole taxidermied animals require large rooms—especially as hunters seek out the largest animals and decidedly not small beasts such as rabbits and hedgehogs. Heads, however, particularly antlered heads, offer a shorthand proof of the age and overall splendor of the animal. With just heads, a larger number of animals can be packed together. And, to be crassly pragmatic, heads offer an important spatial advantage for domestic displays. From a decorator's perspective, mounting heads on walls frees up floor space for furnishings. Just heads comfortably fit into a decoration scheme surrounded by paintings, portraits, chairs, mirrors, books, and side tables.

But trophy heads, obviously, speak to deeper issues than merely spatial constraints. Displaying the entire bodies of five deer would require a separate room. The herd would potentially impart some sense of a diorama's stillness and quietude, and perhaps turn visitors' thoughts to the animals' beauty, fragility, and form. In contrast, just the heads of these same five deer underscore the essence of their message: a hunter desired, stalked, and killed these beasts. As memorials of hunters' triumphs, trophies should make those triumphs blatantly visible.

With the exception of big cats, which are often depicted snarling, mouths open, fangs exposed, most sporting trophies are crafted with calm expressions. (Perhaps the ferocious depiction of felines is because cats are more expressive facially than ungulates. Certainly, their teeth are more impressive.) Buffalo, deer, elk, wild boars, mountain goats, and moose are almost always endowed with "a very lifelike calmness of mien," as Baillie-Grohman put it, and almost never with fear or anger. A severed head with a serene aspect bespeaks a peculiar mythology. Carefully crafted docile features are meant to convey acceptance, as if the animal was at peace with its own termination, as if the animal acknowledged that a competition between two heroic rivals had occurred, and, even more peculiarly, as if the animal

21 William Adolph Baillie-Grohman pictured with his favorite wapiti head in his study in Schloss Matzen. Frontispiece to Baillie-Grohman's *Fifteen Years' Sport and Life in the Hunting Grounds of Western America and British Columbia* (London: Horace Cox, 1900).

acknowledged that by losing, it proved itself valiant, dignified, and worthy of the hunter's quest.

A preserved severed head can never be a neutral object. After all, a head is the essence of an animal's magnificence and individuality. Its presence is raw and primal. This rawness is accentuated by the fact that trophies are never placed behind glass in the home. They are always touchable, always available for intimate encounters. With no barrier between death and domesticity, you can look into the animal's glass eyes. What has this animal become, hanging on its hunter's wall?

With antlers spanning five feet, the wapiti is a wonder of nature, an extraordinary, superlative beast that could easily be included with the exotica filling early modern cabinets of wonder. But majestic size is not the exclusive reason why the wapiti is hanging on Baillie-Grohman's wall, although if the creature had been smaller, it might have escaped its fate.

The animal was also an incontestably beautiful creature—a perfect specimen of a regal species. But compare the wapiti trophy to the conglomerations of beautiful birds so avidly collected in the nineteenth century. Collectors displayed whole creatures, not parts. The lively poses of the birds expressed a longing to capture the beauty of animal form wholly and completely, *as if the birds were still alive*. Only a head remains to tell the story of the wapiti's majestic size and dignity, and a bodiless head is not a nondescript object. The fact that trophies exist without bodies distinctly mark them as something different from all other genres of taxidermy.

Notwithstanding its physically partial nature, the wapiti head shares most in common with the theatrical lions exhibited at the nineteenth-century world exhibitions. The lions also embodied bloodlust and the thrill of the chase. Yet the violent spectacles expressed something of the beast, or at least a fantasy of the beast. And while some scenes may have been accompanied by a hunter's narrative, the spectacles ultimately sidestepped the specifics of a particular animal's death and participated in a larger imaginary of imperial pleasures and self-appointed license over colonial landscapes. A trophy head is similarly a spectacle of prowess and similarly ties into cultural assumptions of license over nature. But there is a sharp difference. The death of the wapiti was a very personal affair, for both hunter and prey. On an otherwise pleasant autumn day, this wapiti ran for its life across frozen ground with a punctured lung, but ultimately failed to escape. Baillie-Grohman stalked, fatally wounded, and tracked this particular animal. He ignored all other wapiti on his quest to kill this noteworthy individual. He hung the head of this particular creature on the wall of his study. This wapiti was an individual, and its individuality enabled it to be transformed into a "cherished souvenir" of one man's very personal, very visceral encounter with a very specific animal.

All taxidermied animals are particularly desired for their unique qualities and characteristics. Through preservation and display the animals are burdened with a cumbersome significance: they became objects of longing. But they are not necessarily souvenirs. As a token of authenticity from a lived experience, souvenirs are infused with narratives of personal significance. In the case of hunting trophies, it is a human story about a quest to kill an animal. These narratives set hunting trophies apart from other genres of taxidermy. Although each animal has its own particular narrative of how it came to be taxidermied, the intimate details and circumstances of its death are not crucial to the meaning of its display. In contrast, trophies speak volubly about their deaths.

ANIMAL SOUVENIRS

All taxidermy embodies a longing to perpetuate an animal's aesthetic presence, and this desire is infused through the animal by the process of preservation. Simply put, taxidermy merges animal form and human desire together immortally, inseparably. Desire and beast become one. As such, taxidermy is always necessarily marked by and indelibly inscribed with the human longing to perpetuate a particular animal's beauty, form, and presence. There can be no taxidermy without desire.

But if desire motivates all taxidermy, taxidermic longings are stirred by a variety of wants or interests. As we have seen, William Bullock's hummingbird cabinet made his passion for hummingbird beauty tangible and, in a sense, memorialized Bullock's longing to contain, to own, and to possess. But hunting trophies push possessive desire in a different direction: they bespeak not just a desire to perpetuate looking but a desire to immortalize a powerful narrative of personal significance. For Bullock, the hummingbirds were their own reason for existence. It hardly mattered how they died or by whose hand. For Baillie-Grohman, the wapiti head is treasured *because he killed it.* But more, *because of the stories it is able to tell the hunter about himself.* While most hunting narratives have the same plot, they are all deeply and distinctly shaped by the particular details that make them personal, intimate, and memorable. The head told the story of Baillie-Grohman's

The souvenir must remain impoverished and partial so that it can be supplemented by a narrative discourse, a narrative discourse which articulates the play of desire.

—SUSAN STEWART, *On Longing: Narratives of the Miniature, the Gigantic, the Souvenir, the Collection* (1993), 136 uncertain chase over frozen ground, of losing the beast and finding it again, of his night under a grove of trees in the cold autumn air, of his stalking, his tracking, and finally his conquest. The wapiti was taxidermied *because* it put up a battle, a worthy chase, but ultimately fell to Baillie-Grohman's weaponry, skill, and violent desire. At the moment of seeing a beast, the hunter initiates a possessive, desiring relationship with the animal: "I determined to bag him, if at all possible." Of the genres of taxidermy, hunting trophies are the souvenirs and the storytellers, which is to say, of the genres of taxidermy, hunting trophies are among the most deeply personal and so perhaps necessarily the rawest.

Souvenirs are only fragments of ever more distant experiences. The object—a ribbon from a wedding dress, a plastic Eiffel Tower from a Paris honeymoon—can evoke powerful memories of experiences that can never be relived or fully recouped. In fact, if souvenirs *could* somehow recoup events, strangely enough, their power would weaken. The partial nature of souvenirs is the very source of their magic. Their incompleteness means that they *must* be fleshed out with narratives that explain why these particular objects are particularly valued. Without a story, the wedding ribbon is just a random piece of ribbon, no different from any other, and a ribbon is not an inherently valuable thing. With the story, the ribbon becomes infinitely valuable because it is irreplaceable.[6] Because we only take souvenirs of personally significant events that we wish to remember, the stories attached to souvenirs are always narratives of desire and longing, of authenticity and possession. These are my stories, my souvenirs; they are my history in material form, my longings, my deeds. Souvenirs are always deeply personal possessions enfolded in our sense of identity, desires, and authenticity.

This is as true of hunting trophies as of wedding ribbons. Any object can become a souvenir. But some objects are purposely crafted as souvenirs. Photographs, locks of hair, bronzed baby shoes, trophy cups, tombstones, and hunting trophies all belong to a particular class of objects that have been created specifically to focus and retain memory. Even if the individuals in nineteenth-century photographs are unidentifiable, or centuries of rain have eroded the names on tombstones, the knowledge that something important was being memorialized lingers on. For such objects, meaning and materiality are forever merged.

Obviously, hunting trophies stand apart from most other sorts of mementos, with the exception, perhaps, of tombstones: the material existence of both signifies loss of life. However, even here a sharp distinction exists. If tombstones are commissioned from grief, trophies are commissioned from triumph. Animals have been vanquished and broken, and their fragmented forms accentuate the raw fact that trophies are souvenirs of termination. And it is this celebratory display of deliberate death that inclines most nonhunters to see trophies as nature destroyed, not nature displayed.

When most people think of taxidermy, they think of hunting trophies. In a sense, trophies epitomize everything that is disliked about taxidermy in general. All taxidermy makes death overt, but just heads are decidedly deader. The eerie sensation of immortally motionless liveliness becomes even more eerie with trophies. Any fantasy of reanimation can only be a nightmare of a disembodied head.

Abhorrence is understandable in vegetarians, animal rights activists, and any community that believes that there is no excuse for killing an animal. But for meat eaters and anyone who owns leather shoes, bags, or furniture, the sharp negative reaction to taxidermy is less straightforward. What is the difference between a steak, a belt, and a trophy? In all cases an animal has been killed, dissected, and reshaped, and yet a distinction exists in contemporary opinion. What makes hunting trophies so particularly objectionable?

It could be argued that trophies are more appreciative of animal form than leather belts, since trophy heads preserve some semblance of the beast. Belts, which are nothing but strips of cured, tanned, dyed skin, offer nothing of the cow's form, no sense of its size or physical characteristics. The animal has been reduced to a bit of functional material, easily discarded and completely disassociated from the animal it once was. In other words, a belt could seem more disrespectful to the animal than a trophy mount, which preserves at least part of an animal's form. Adverse reactions to trophies potentially highlight a hypocrisy for anyone who routinely uses products made from purposely killed animals. From shoes, to baseball mitts, to cooking shows on television, it is impossible to live a day without encountering animal parts. And perhaps this is partly why hunting trophies have the potential to make even leather-wearing carnivores highly uncomfortable. Most meat eaters do not kill animals themselves and rarely seek out the grisly truths of the meat industry. As discussed in chapter 3, belts and steaks hardly offer the tingling sensation that the animal might just be reanimated and scarcely make death as visible as a preserved head does. Trophies give bold and individual faces to the pervasive desire for animal death that underpins so much of culture.

But this is not the way debates usually go about the moral merits of belts versus trophies. It is the particular way the animal died that offends, not necessarily the product that is made afterward.[7] Leather belts are typically made from the hide of cows that have been raised specifically for their utilitarian benefits to humans, which is to say, leather belts are the products of cold, anonymous killing. The death is planned from birth and conducted in a sterile space. Garry Marvin writes that slaughterhouse workers maintain an emotional distance between themselves and the animals they kill: "this is a detached and impersonal, non-individualized relationship."[8] Trophies, on the other hand, are the products of passionate, hot-blooded, very personal killing. The hunter has specifically sought out the opportunity of killing an animal. He or she has stalked this particular animal, and the trophy head is a memento of that desiring encounter. Belts are not mementos of anything: not of the cow, not of the person (or machine) that killed the cow. Belts erase everything about the cow, its life, and its death. Hunting trophies bring it all into focus.

A degree of respect is always due to the dead. Parading or desecrating dead bodies is as morally reprehensible as violating the living. That is, just because we may eat an animal, this does not mean that we want to see its death memorialized. And this gets us closer to the heart of nonhunters' dislike for trophies. Trophies are not anonymous deaths: they are souvenirs of a passionate, deadly personal desiring. The animal's life and body have been ruptured by a hunter's longing to make nature tell the story of its own vanquishing, its own termination. In contrast to the anonymity of slaughterhouse animals, the hunted animal is an individual, although its individuality rests crucially on its death. If it had not been killed, it would remain *a* wapiti, not *the* wapiti, and certainly not Baillie-Grohman's favorite head. Trophies arouse negative reactions not simply because they are evidence that a human killed an animal. More deeply, they are evidence of a human's *desire* to kill an animal. If most taxidermy manifests an unfulfillable longing (such as Bullock's desire to capture the shimmering beauty of the ever-moving hummingbird), hunting trophies offer satisfaction. To see a hunting trophy is to see a longing and its fulfillment both glorified and immortalized.

Trophies are extremely eloquent objects. A full-bodied taxidermied animal might have been preserved because it was the last living specimen of a now extinct species, or the type specimen of a newly identified species. It might have been shot because it was terrorizing a village, or maybe it was a beloved companion.

A posture or surrounding diorama might give viewers some clue as to why a particular animal was preserved, but nothing speaks its message as clearly as a severed head. Materiality and meaning are one, and because the trophy's ruptured form literally embodies hot-blooded human desire for animal death, trophies will continue to speak their message, no matter how they are subsequently altered, used, or displayed.

These issues are central to the work of British artist and animal activist Angela Singer. Much of Singer's work involves a process that she calls "de-taxidermy." By deconstructing, concealing, or embellishing old, discarded, or donated taxidermy mounts, Singer creates pieces meant to challenge society's blindness and indifference to animal death and suffering. Her work is provocative precisely because she accentuates the power of looking and of being seen. Partially hidden under blankets, spilling out blood-red buttons from open wounds, or adorned with porcelain flowers and jewels, Singer's animals have a powerful effect simply by being highly and disturbingly visible.

Singer's most direct and perhaps most successful works involve reclaimed hunting trophies. Part of their success arises from the hunting trophies themselves: a severed head of a hunted animal endowed with a calm expression bespeaks a very particular mythology, and this is precisely their potency for Singer. *Sore* (2002–3) is among the most violent and difficult pieces, although, oddly enough, no animal parts remain. By peeling the skin off a deer trophy, removing the antlers, and drenching the underlying taxidermy form with red wax, Singer re-creates the frighteningly bloody original death of the animal. (The hunter who donated the trophy explained that while he was sawing off the antlers, a gush of blood had drenched both hunter and stag.) By subverting the trope of a hunting trophy's expression of placid acceptance, Singer animates the nightmare of a living severed head. Broken down, peeled apart, covered in "blood," disassociated from all parts of the animal that once was, the animal nevertheless continues to gaze steadily at any viewer willing to look.

Such intense visibility of trauma can arouse repulsion or empathy, depending on how it is handled. In contrast to the extreme horror of *Sore*, Singer's *Thorn* (fig. 22) offers something approaching a funereal memorial for Bambi. With oversized eyes and surrounded with porcelain flowers, the little fawn has an almost cartoonish beauty. Yet it is only a severed head, and its skin is cracked, torn, and covered with dead flies and cockroaches. Again, what animates the piece is the

Angela Singer, *Thorn*, 2004.
Recycled vintage taxidermy fawn
and mixed media. Photo courtesy
of the artist.

simple original truth of the hunting trophy: it is a memorial of an animal's death. No amount of sweetness and flowers can erase the violence that caused the trophy mount to exist. The damage is already done. Decorating death only makes it even more abrasively visible.

But Singer's work is not about sweetness. Her process of "de-taxidermy" brings its own brutality, which is meant to accentuate the original violence. Like many of her pieces, the fawn in *Thorn* was donated to Singer by its hunter (now an ex-hunter), who was able to narrate its story. As a boy in the 1930s, the hunter often accompanied his father and uncle on hunting trips. While the men hunted stags and does, he would shoot the fawns. The fawn was only a month or two old, and it had been preserved as a full body mount. In other words, the fawn was not originally a trophy head. Over the passing decades, a dog chewed off an ear, and its body was too badly damaged for Singer to work with it as a complete mount. Singer sawed off the head and peeled the skin back around the eyes, making them more prominent.[9] Doe-eyed yet defiant, dead yet abrasively enduring, the fawn simultaneously signifies and critiques its existence as a souvenir of deadly desiring.

No matter how much damage has been done to a trophy, no matter how its original message is challenged, a hunter's longing to tell stories about himself or herself through animal death can never be emptied from an animal souvenir. Simply put, taxidermy permanently embeds human longing for animal form within animal form. The narrative of desire remains as long as the animal exists.

From a focus on hunter versus prey, let us now examine the broader cultures of hunting. Hunting trophies are never simply evidence of hunter versus beast. For hunters, trophies are cultural symbols that position their owners in particular ways within particular communities. Certainly, hunting is always an expression of individual prowess, conquest, and dominion, but it is also always an expression of belonging within a particular culture. Hunting is a social practice as much as it is an individualistic exploit. Broadly speaking, there are two main hunting cultures that have influenced what trophies have meant at various times to various communities: the European aristocratic tradition and the freedom of the North American wilderness. Nineteenth-century hunters like Baillie-Grohman straddled both cultures. If European aristocratic hunting was in his blood, he extended his prowess to the New World, particularly to the Rockies, an area of near-unrestricted license: "there he found his paradise."[10]

The importance of hunting lies in its symbolism, not its economics.

—MATT CARTMILL, *A View to a Death in the Morning: Hunting and Nature Through History* (1993), 28

In his history of hunting, Matt Cartmill outlines the requirements for an act of animal killing to be classified as hunting. "Hunting is not just a matter of going out and killing any old animal; in fact very little animal-killing qualifies as hunting. A successful hunt ends in the killing of an animal, but it must be a special sort of animal that is killed in a specific way for a particular reason." First, the animal must be wild, as opposed to domesticated and docile, and able to run away: killing a dairy cow or a lion in a zoo is not hunting. Second, hunting is a directly inflicted act of intentional and preplanned violence: putting out poison or running over an animal with a car is not hunting.[11] Nor is killing an animal in self-defense properly labeled hunting unless the engagement was initiated by the hunter, who was then cornered or wounded during the chase.

Further, the spaces of hunting are set apart from everyday living. The hunter enters wild terrain in order to find, stalk, and kill a wild animal: killing an animal that has wandered into your backyard is not properly classified as hunting. Moreover, as Baillie-Grohman's narrative made clear, the hunter's success must be not guaranteed. In fact, the more difficult the chase, the more uncertain the prize, the more challenging the animal and the terrain prove to be, the more enjoyable the memories of the hunt. A hunt is retold with the narrative devices of a good story: it is plot driven and filled with conflict, suspense, drama, and tragedy. And this marks a fundamental difference between hunting for food and hunting for sport. If all a hunter requires is sustenance, the easiest meat is the best. Sport hunters elaborate the contest. "Rules, regulations, and restrictions are imposed and willingly followed," Garry Marvin writes, to create the necessary challenges for hunting to be considered a sporting activity and not mere slaughter.[12] Hunting must be a personal challenge and a test of skill. For the hunter, the trophy stands as a symbol of his or her vigor, hardiness, sportsmanship, and backwoods know-how. An easy or unfair kill would hardly require memorialization. These are the basic codes of the sportsman. Machine gunning herds of deer might qualify as hunting, but no self-respecting sportsman would condone the behavior.

Hunting is also defined by the particular animal species pursued and killed. Shooting gophers, squirrels, rats, or creatures labeled pests or vermin is not considered hunting. Only species that have been designated as "game" can properly be said to have been "hunted." "Game" is a fascinating word. It means amusement, delight, and sport; the object of pursuit; wild animals; the flesh of animals used for food; and the defining spirit, fight, and courage of game animals. That is, the word means the enjoyable sport of pursuing a wild, tough, and gallant animal to the death. Game animals have variously been hunted for their dangerous nature (lions, wild boars, elephants), nobility (stags), momentous size (moose, wapiti), or elusiveness (mountain goats). To hunt an animal is always to designate the animal as being worthy of attention.

To hunt is also to engage in a relationship with the animal's landscape. Animals exist within their particular ecological climates—some inhabit densely wooded terrain, others, wide open savannas. Some are local to the hunter's district; others are on the other side of the world, and all such distinctions are not irrelevant. The hunter's cultural and political relationship to the animal's geography underlies the meaning of the hunt as much as any ensuing trophy does. As we have seen, the nineteenth-century imperial lion and tiger hunters were not just hunting lions and tigers but were marking their sovereignty over Indian and African landscapes. Likewise, wapiti hunting in the Rockies, chamois hunting in the Alps, or stag hunting in the Scottish highlands all underscore particular relationships between hunter, animal, and landscape. Hunting is always an exercise of dominion, and traditionally trophies spelled out a hunter's rights over particular geographic terrains as much as human mastery over beast.

In Europe, from the Middle Ages onward, stag hunting emerged as the sport of kings. The dark and savage forests populated by man-eating beasts were already shrinking. In particular, dangerous animals such as wolves and bears, which once roamed freely across Great Britain and western Europe, were forcibly driven toward extinction. What forest areas and beasts remained were slowly being transformed into exclusive aristocratic playgrounds. Prized hunting grounds and royal preserves were forcefully restricted. Game was carefully tended and protected by gamekeepers who were endowed with the liberty to punish any poacher, whether human or animal.

Born into an estate, the landlord—literally lord of the land—maintained exclusive rights to its woods and copses and all its creature inhabitants. In a sense, the ability to shoot a stag (outside of illegal poaching) was a birthright and an exercise in social status, and European hunting evolved from a chase for meat into a symbolic performance formalized with strict custom and ritual. In turn, the stag was surrounded by a chivalrous romance, embodying purity of heart and daunt-less courage. In fact, something of a cult developed around the majesty, nobility, courage, and—of course—tragedy of the stag.[13] Alongside a violent desire for the beast is always a violent love for the beast.

The exclusivity of European hunting preserves continued well into the twen-tieth century, and in some places into the twenty-first. In Baillie-Grohman's day, shooting rights in the Bavarian highlands remained almost entirely in the hands of the Austrian nobility and royalty, and as far as Baillie-Grohman was concerned, such exclusivity had saved the animals from extinction. In his opinion, the Aus-trian Alps, with their large estates and sport-loving landed aristocracy, offered much more inviting hunting fields than Switzerland, "where the republican spirit and peasant proprietorship make the preservation of game by individuals almost impossible." In North Tyrol, he wrote, "some of the best preserves in the world are situated, five royal shoots almost abutting on each other."[14]

If the mere ability to hunt connoted land ownership, the remembrance of those hunts similarly signified political affiliation and social status. Not surpris-ingly, hunting halls came to occupy a special place in the castles of Europe from the fifteenth century onward. Early trophy collections did not contain taxidermied heads. Rather, trophies typically consisted simply of bone: either just the antlers or the antlers still attached to bleached skulls. As we have seen, the early history of taxidermy and preservation hardly encouraged the mounting of full heads until the nineteenth century. This type of trophy—antlers and the top of a bleached skull mounted on a wooden, shield-shaped plaque—is still referred to as a European mount. Usually the details of the hunt would be recorded on the shield below the antlers. The date would be noted as well as the hunter's name, particularly if he or she were a noble guest, perhaps a visiting duke or prince. The extraordinary hunting hall of the archbishop of Olomouc's castle in Kromeriz in the Czech Re-public, for example, displays forty-one trophies from the hunt organized for the momentous occasion of the Russian tsar's visit in 1885. The hunt, of course, was in the archbishop's own forest. The trophies make known the expansive lands of the bishopric and royal favoritism, a sure sign of power, wealth, and social position.

Generations of hunting trophies decorating hunting halls were read as evi-dence of generational status: rows and rows of antlers demonstrated that the cur-rent owner was nobly born. In a sense, collections of antlers functioned symboli-cally like portraits of ancestors. Both portraits and trophies endowed descendants

23 The hunting hall in the Agricultural Museum in Vajdahunyad Castle, Budapest. Photo courtesy of Michelle Enemark.

with the weight and prestige of an ancestral lineage. Both fulfilled the demands of witness, nostalgia, and memory. Authority and authenticity lingered in both objects. In a sense, both were storytellers for future generations, who could say, Here is evidence of my status, and my father's status, and my grandfather's before him.

A cosmopolitan Anglo-Austrian, Baillie-Grohman had grown up hunting the famous deer and chamois in the royal preserves about his grandfather's chateau on the banks of Wolfgangsee Lake in Upper Austria: Baillie-Grohman was a well-connected, wealthy man. His grandfather, a distinguished Viennese banker, had acquired the chateau, formerly an abbey, in the early nineteenth century. Although it had not been in the family long, the chateau had a noble heritage, a weighty symbolism that was conferred on the family. The holy Roman emperor Maximilian had been a frequent visitor to the chateau, and it had once served as a refuge for Emperor Leopold. One of Baillie-Grohman's earliest memories was of sitting on the knees of Elizabeth of Bavaria, empress of Austria and queen of Hungary, during a royal visit to his grandfather's estate. In fact, it was on his grandfather's estate that Elizabeth had become affianced to Francis Joseph, emperor of Austria.[15]

The chateau of Baillie-Grohman's grandfather was sold owing to a reversal in family fortunes during the politically turbulent 1860s. However, in 1873 Baillie-

Grohman's mother acquired one of the gems among historical Tyrolean castles, Schloss Matzen. It had been home to some of the most distinguished members of Austrian society, including the Fugger family, the famous banking dynasty. Once again, although the chateau had not been in the family long, Baillie-Grohman transformed it into a traditional theater of status, origins, and authority, but with a twist. Only *his* trophies were displayed. As Charles Landis writes in the introduction to Baillie-Grohman's *The Land in the Mountains, Being an Account of the Past and Present of Tyrol, Its People and Its Castles*, "That the corridors, halls and rooms in the beautiful old castle, where many hundreds of Baillie-Grohman's trophies are kept, make a most suitable setting for these choice records of a hunter's life, need hardly be pointed out. Amongst these spoils of the chase there are heads that hold the world's record, and there probably exist few better dual collections of the mountain game of Europe and America, in the pursuit of which it is safe to say no man has shown more persistence."[16] If traditional hunting halls spoke of family lineage, the heads spoke exclusively of Baillie-Grohman's own exploits, which were made more refined by their backdrop.

Over the course of the nineteenth century, a romantic culture of imperialistic hunting developed. In the search for raw wilderness, European adventurers such as Baillie-Grohman sought out bigger, bolder beasts in North America, Africa, the Arctic, and India. The rapidly expanding knowledge of the world's fauna, populating vast uncharted landscapes, beckoned the wealthy nineteenth-century hunter, and particularly aggressive hunters who sought out the wildest terrains emerged as nothing short of heroes. With preservation techniques rapidly improving, for the first time the full-head trophy mount took deep roots among hunters.

Hunters who could afford overseas hunting expeditions made every effort to prepare their kills properly for shipment home. In fact, many taxidermists issued instructions on how to best preserve a skin for shipment, outlining the best techniques for skinning animals and the powders and astringents that could preserve skins for potentially a month of travel in order to avert decay, staining, and hungry insects.[17] Hunters festooned their billiard rooms, studies, hallways, and libraries with their exploits, which were read as evidence of their social status, hardiness, and conspicuous expenditure on foreign travel. As the nineteenth century progressed, hunting trophies littering the walls of country homes coalesced with imperial power and self-appointed license.[18] It is tempting to say that the improvement in taxidermic techniques encouraged the nineteenth-century mania for exotic hunting. Previously, the fleshy heads of big cats, wapiti, elephants, and buffalo had been difficult if not impossible to transport back home. With the new techniques, overseas triumphs could be proved, and they came to define a hunter-explorer's sense of verve, vigor, and reputation.

Hunting was a different experience for North Americans. In contrast to European land enclosures and generational privilege, hunting was the unrestricted pleasure of all citizens in North America for much of the nineteenth century. The vast areas of rugged American wilderness stretched out in a seemingly endless expanse, populated by seemingly endless herds of buffalo, deer, moose, and wapiti: a sportsman's Eden, overflowing with superlative game. If only an elite sector had traditionally been privileged to hunt in Europe, in North America hunting became a declaration of democratic values, and the American wilderness emerged as a paradise for the hardy, adventuresome, industrious, and independent spirit.

Although hunting had a contested history for early colonists, by the early nineteenth century it had become entrenched as a cornerstone of the American identity. In claiming the landscapes, a new nation claimed dominion over all its inhabitants (animal or otherwise), and thereby made them American. Cities might have been marred by social conflict, Daniel Herman writes in *Hunting and the American Imagination*, "but the ideal world of the wilderness seemed true to the republican vision."[19] American hunting was infused with the romance of the buckskin-clad frontier adventurer epitomized by hunting heroes such as Daniel Boone and Davy Crockett. Hunting spoke of freedom from ancestral rights and privilege. It made manifest the natural fertility of a blessed land, a land of plenty, liberty, openness, and independence. As Jennifer Price writes, "To hunt meant so much more than mere utilitarian gain. To go hunting was to tap into the continent's bounty, to supplement the table, to exercise your skill with a shotgun, perhaps to band together with neighbors after plowing. You also expressed your rights or ideals in a fledgling polity. Hunting was at once an ecological, economic and political thing to do, a social event and a sport. It was like telling a story to yourself *about* yourself."[20]

And the taxidermied heads of American species—wapiti, bald eagles, bighorn sheep—that populated private homes, banks, saloons, and country stores all told this story of rugged American individualism (fig. 24). They spoke of the self-reliance of men and women who found and made their identity within the American landscape. Hunting trophies are always a show of prowess and dominion over the

24 View of front desk area in the Meeker Hotel, Meeker, Colorado, in 1903. Photo courtesy of the Denver Public Library, Western History Collection.

natural world. But if the traditional European display of rows of antlers signified social privilege, land ownership, and wealth, the American trophies told a story of belonging to and ownership of a new nation.

Of course, despite such rugged backwoods values, American hunting cultures nevertheless gained importance from the European tradition. Codes of hunting remained tied to connotations of gentlemanly exploits, and hunting's popularity in the nineteenth century was strengthened in part by its elite and privileged associations. If trophies spoke of democratic rights, they also spoke of culture and taste. "With the growing fondness for Taxidermy," Joseph Batty wrote in the preface to his *Practical Taxidermy, and Home Decoration* (1885), "many ladies are endeavoring to master the art, and in the variety of work necessary to perfect it, feminine taste and skill can be brought effectively into play. The collector can learn to mount his own specimens, the schoolboy his game, and in the general household, a buck's head in the dining-room, or a bright oriole in the parlor, presents a pleasing contrast to the other ornaments."[21] In contrast to such polished associations, on the facing page is an image of "Our Author in Costume," dressed in buckskins and canvas legging, leaning on his rifle in front of a vast, empty wilderness: the epitome of a frontier hero. The flyleaf depicts a beautiful, gentle-eyed wapiti with two rifles crossing its antlers and surrounded by wisps of ferns, butterflies, and a leg-hole trap. As if to explain the image of elegance and violence, the publishers themselves added a few words. "The appreciation and love of 'Home Decoration' increase with the growing taste and culture of the American people. Our author's chapters upon this subject are very timely, and will be keenly appreciated, especially by ladies."[22]

Of course, the cultures of hunting are far more nuanced and complex than I have conveyed here. Particular customs surround almost every species of animal considered worthy of hunting. Almost every culture that hunts has its own traditions, and a detailed history of these is well beyond the scope of this project. My objective is not to write a history of hunting but rather to paint broadly certain themes or narratives within Western hunting traditions. The European aristocratic mount, with its associations of privilege, wealth, and cosmopolitanism, and the backwoods American trophy, redolent of rugged individualism and of belonging to the landscape, have remained two dominant themes for interpreting the cultural meaning of hunting trophies. Oddly or not, such poetics continue well beyond hunting culture and into the most unlikely places.

RECLAIMED TAXIDERMY

All taxidermy has a life of its own. Any particular piece is hardly rooted to the particular circumstances of its creation. These animal-things persist. After all, they have been transfigured into quasi-immortals, easily outliving their original owners by decades, by tens of decades. Consider the trophies in Baillie-Grohman's Schloss Matzen. The schloss has been transformed into a bed-and-breakfast by American owners. Many of Baillie-Grohman's trophies still grace the walls, creating the heavily romantic aura of a traditional European chateau for guests. The heads are no longer animal souvenirs of one man's conquests. They no longer have Baillie-Grohman to infuse them with his desiring remembrances of stern chases

All Camp objects, and persons, contain a large element of artifice. Nothing in nature can be campy. . . . Rural Camp is still man-made, and most campy objects are urban.

—SUSAN SONTAG, "Notes on 'Camp,'" in *Against Interpretation and Other Essays* (1961), 279 and conquests. Baillie-Grohman is long dead, and his descendants have long since left the chateau. With the passing decades, the stories of the individual heads have been lost, or at least partially lost, which is to say that these heads shift out of the realm of souvenirs and personal storytellers and take on new identities. They become period pieces, blurring into the overall decorative scheme of the chateau to create an atmosphere of history and times past.

Since they are still displayed in his home, Baillie-Grohman's trophies retain their connection to their hunter. But even when all details of the hunt are lost, hunting trophies retain their aura as memorials. Like old tintype photographs and nameless tombstones, secondhand hunting trophies remain souvenirs, but they are *somebody else's* souvenirs. Mute, closed off, half-forgotten yet still redolent of significance, they mark the passage of time while standing outside time in the way that dusty, once-cherished objects in forgotten attics are suspended in a temporal limbo, neither fully explainable in this world but no longer part of their own past era.

If nineteenth-century black-and-white photographs encapsulate the vague melancholic nostalgia of faded elegance (hardly what the photograph meant to its original owner), somewhat improbably, hunting trophies have become equally prone to stylization. In fact, a solid and nuanced culture surrounds secondhand taxidermy. From Austrian bed-and-breakfasts, to bowling alleys, to stylish Brooklyn homes, vintage taxidermy has taken on new life and new meaning in the twenty-first century. Rummaged from thrift emporiums, eBay, or antique stores, songbirds under bell jars, Victorian stuffed dogs, and hunting trophies have become the new chic.[23] Open any home decoration magazine and you are likely to find at least one vintage trophy incorporated into a decoration scheme. At the very least, you will probably see a modern reworking of a trophy head fabricated from cardboard or plastic or carved from wood. The crucial point of these reappropriated trophies, however, is that they were not killed by the current owner. Collectors sidestep the rawness of hunter versus beast in order to focus on the aesthetics of the display.

Broadly speaking, secondhand trophies fall into two distinct styles: either a flaunting of all things crass and backwater or a Victoriana aesthetic. In both cases, the trophy slides away from an individuated animal souvenir and toward a camp sensibility: a ribald enjoyment that simultaneously glorifies and mocks the outmoded and the flamboyantly outlandish.

A 2006 television commercial for cheese by the Dairy Farmers of Canada depicts an elderly couple feverishly overhauling their adult son's bedroom. Their inspiration seems to be 1970s motel décor: jaundiced floral wallpaper, a brown-and-yellow bedspread, a Hawaiian lamp, various tacky paintings, pillows, knickknacks, and an enormous moose head mounted above the bed. The parents hope to get their son to leave home by redecorating his room, but their plans fail. The punch line of the commercial: "Want your kids to leave home? Stop cooking with cheese." In other words, the son would rather—literally and aesthetically—eat cheese.

While the mammoth moose head dominates the room, it seems to blend seamlessly into the décor. Reactions to the commercial's moose head are not "disgusting: you've killed a moose" but "disgusting: what bad décor." Wall coverings and lamps go in and out of style, but when does nature become tacky?

In the North American imagination, secondhand hunting trophies have long been synonymous with all things hick, kitsch, or tongue in cheek. Dusty heads and antlers mounted in restaurants, gas stations, and bowling alleys are as much a part of the backwater American landscape as plastic pink flamingos and velvet paintings of Elvis. The heads offer that peculiar aura of failure and ruin—what Celeste Olalquiaga describes as the "stoic refusal of things to depart once their usefulness is exhausted"—that characterizes all things kitschy and campy.[24]

This kitschy aura of secondhand trophies arose as a shadow fell across hunting in the twentieth century. If Joseph Batty could claim in 1885 that a buck's head presented a "pleasing contrast" to other household ornaments, this was hardly the case a century later. As Daniel Justin Herman writes, the negative stereotype of American hunters developed not because Americans as a whole become more urban, affluent, and divorced from the necessities of hunting for food, but because hunters have come to be seen as less urban and affluent. Hunting "loses popularity today—at least among middle-class men—because of its association with working-class and rural folk. Hunting, to be blunt, seems backwards."[25] And these rustic backwoods and backward associations linger in secondhand trophies. For some, this aura is reason enough to loathe trophies: they represent everything there is to hate about rural America. For those with a darker sense of irony, trophies like the cheese commercial's moose are transfigured into crassly beloved relics of frontier America. They are collected in part for this gauche anachronistic flair, despite the fact that hunters are still hunting and trophies are still being made. Crucially, these trophies are of indigenous American species. Otherwise, they would not be able to exude that particularly American flavor of cheese: the Daniel Boone aesthetic. Part tall tale, part Old West, part diner décor, the Boone aesthetic belongs to log cabins and hunting lodges, red plaid shirts, lamps made from deer hooves, and, of course, tacky taxidermy.

Perhaps the king of the Boone aesthetic is the jackalope. A mock totem of the Old West known as the "warrior rabbit," the jackalope is a jackrabbit endowed with horns. "Indigenous" to Douglas, Wyoming, the jackalope was born in the 1930s when two teenage brothers, Douglas and Ralph Herrick, returned home from a hunt and tossed a dead rabbit next to a pair of antlers. The accidental pairing sparked Douglas's creative imagination. The brothers had studied taxidermy by mail order, and Douglas set to work to create his legend: a cross between a pronghorn antelope and a jackrabbit.

Frontier stories of the jackalope's particularities abound, and they are always frontier stories. The jackalope has an uncanny knack for mimicking the human voice and in the old days was known to join in singing sad cowboy songs around the campfire. It is highly aggressive but can always be mollified with whiskey. You can also purchase a jackalope hunting license from the Douglas Chamber of Commerce, although regulations stipulate that hunting can only occur on June 31 between midnight and 2:00 A.M. and that the hunter must have an IQ lower than 72. If you fail to conform to the mock regulations, you can always buy a jackalope trophy from the Douglas Area Chamber of Commerce Jackalope Store for $79.95. Also for sale are jackalope postcards, jackalope earrings, and a carton of jackalope eggs for $2.00.

Although a jackalope is fabricated from a real rabbit, the surrounding kitsch culture deflects viewers' attention from the raw realities of a severed rabbit head. Death is softened by the mail-order delivery (no hunting necessary), the hoax legend, and add-on antlers. The mythology of the hunting trophy is turned upside down, since the jackalope is not a lived reality but a stylized extravagance, foolishly amusing and altogether disengaged from the ethics of animal death. We interpret the jackalope not as a piece of nature but as a tacky piece of décor.

A victory of style over content and aesthetics over ethics, camp deposes the serious with playfulness. Its hallmarks are flamboyance and artifice. Camp is always too much, too outlandish, over the top, and passé. But, as Susan Sontag observes, camp is not a love of old things as such but an appreciation of the detachment old things offer. Things become campy "when we become less involved in them, and can enjoy, instead of being frustrated by, the failure."[26] We can indulge in irresponsible fantasies when they are not of our own era, which is partly why the jackalope's accompanying narrative is so successful. Even jackalope trophies that are made in the twenty-first century nevertheless date to the bygone era of cowboys.

Most important, nature is not campy. Like the merging of a jackrabbit and an antelope, nature must be transformed, exaggerated, and stylized to become camp. As with the jackalope, the tragedy of an animal's death is muted or at least blended into the overarching spirit of ribald extravagance. Ethics and camp do not sit well together.

In contrast to tacky taxidermy, consider the heads displayed in the loft of sisters Hollister and Porter Hovey in Williamsburg, Brooklyn. The Hoveys' apartment was featured in a 2009 *New York Times* article titled "The New Antiquarians: Cultivating a Late Nineteenth-Century Style at Home." The windowless, black-walled apartment is decadently overstuffed with all things outmoded yet belonging to a highly stylized Victorian aesthetic: fencing masks, nineteenth-century natural history prints, pith helmets, oak desks, vintage bicycles, silver ice buckets, leather-bound books, and old taxidermy, all objects that exude a palpable nostalgia for another era. It is not by chance that the Hoveys' antiquarian aesthetic references a period when taxidermy was a common household object. If the collector plays with narratives to structure his or her collection, the Hoveys find their metaphors among the Victorian salon.

Again, the animals offer an anachronistic flair. However, in contrast to the Daniel Boone frontier aesthetic, the trophy heads and vintage taxidermy help create an Old World aura of contemplation, politesse, and leisure. Together with the other antique objects, redolent of upper-class world-traveling Victorians, the trophies complete a vision of the dilettantish aesthete. Flamboyantly outdated and overcultured, saturated in a baroque arrangement of infinite detail, these trophies are still playfully ironic, but they exist at the other end of the spectrum, conveying not a kitsch aesthetic of a backwater bowling alley but a new style of dandyism.

The Hovey sisters are hardly unique. For the past decade, vintage taxidermy has been appearing in high-end boutiques, chic restaurants, and private homes of the style-conscious. Why the new interest in taxidermy? In part it speaks to disenchantment with sameness and reproduction. In a sense, taxidermy is the ultimate antimodern object. Objects that have been serially produced and industrially

25 An inside view of the Contemporary Zoological Conservatory in Toronto. Photo by Christopher Bennell. Courtesy of the Contemporary Zoological Conservatory, Toronto.

manufactured have clean lines and smooth surfaces. Taxidermy is beautifully, sensuously, intensely textural. If modern objects are defined by their function, taxidermy is defined by memory and longing. If manufactured goods are endowed with a replaceable sameness, each piece of taxidermy—just like each and every animal, human or otherwise—is inherently, potently, uniquely itself and utterly irreplaceable. If modern objects self-consciously sidestep the moral weight of history and tradition, vintage taxidermy—like all antiques—resonates with a deeper symbolic order. All antiques fulfill the yearning for nostalgia, memory, and authenticity. It hardly matters if the histories of the objects are unknown. They still impart, to use Jean Baudrillard's lovely phrase, the "moral theatricality of old furniture."[27] And more, if modern objects are plainly knowable (in the sense of being newly manufactured goods without the history of previous owners), taxidermy always holds a secret back. Taxidermy is always ambiguous and haunting, yet honest in a way that a manufactured product never could be.

While there is something darkly provocative in this postmodern reappropriation of hunting trophies as fashionable items of home décor, there is also often a softer salvage sensibility at work. Since the animals are already dead, for some collectors it seems more disrespectful to let them molder into oblivion than to display them as cherished animal-things. This salvage mentality is the driving principle of the Contemporary Zoological Conservatory in Toronto, run by Morgan Mavis (fig. 25). Mavis has collected more than eighty vintage taxidermied animals, including deer head trophies, two standing bears, a fox, a beaver, and various birds salvaged from antique stores, purchased at auctions, or donated by others, which she displays in her apartment-turned-museum. For Mavis, the animals are storytellers, although their narratives are usually long forgotten, an absence that gives the animals a certain melancholy. "I am interested in the preservation of discarded memories. Taxidermy is the embodiment of a story. Most of the pieces are hunting trophies. But it's a memory for someone, and they either preserve it themselves by stuffing it, or commission a taxidermist, a son inherits it, doesn't want it, it gets discarded. So rather than focusing on the act of killing years ago, I look at it as rescuing the animals from a junk shop or someone's basement and giving them an afterlife."[28]

On the one hand, the Contemporary Zoological Conservatory might seem to gloss over the ethics of animal killing by glorifying its animal products. On the other hand, Mavis has arranged the collection to focus attention on the animals, and not on her own sense of style. The walls are bare and white, and the space is sparsely decorated with a few pieces of furniture, which allows the animals to be seen with a clear-eyed gaze. In a manner fundamentally different from Angela Singer's, Mavis is also engaged in a process that subverts traditional trophy rooms. Mavis's salvage/salvation process reindividuates the trophies. They are not abstracted as symbols of human abuses of nature or as icons of a particular period or style. Rather, these trophies are displayed as noteworthy and individual animals that have lived full lives in the afterlife.

Whether hunting trophies are loved or loathed, they maintain some dignity of the animal. A hunter is not mocking the creature by preserving its head for personal display. These are animal souvenirs of personal significance, and the narratives attached to the prized trophy are of pride, not sarcasm. In contrast, the following chapter explores the second lives of waste animals: kittens, squirrels, gophers, and guinea pigs. As we will see, such tiny unwanted creatures have been fashioned into darker, stranger, more troubling allegories of dominion.

ALLEGORY

BEAST FABLES AND ANIMAL DESIRES

The beast fable belongs to the ancient tradition of telling stories about humans with animals. Not just any sort of stories, but stories about needs, weaknesses, and desires purified and pared down by the perfect simplicity of animal form. Fables offer a true-for-all-times-and-places sort of knowledge and point to a moral truth that is believed to hold throughout the natural world, irrespective of time, place, or culture.[1] They offer something resonant, something deep, something that could not be expressed quite so clearly without other animal species. The art of fabling beasts captures the potent and seemingly irrepressible human act of articulating experience through the medium of animal life.

At the heart of the beast fable is a narrative built around a dialogue between animals, all variously expressing their needs, urges, and fears while endeavoring to avoid or capitalize on those of other animals. As such, fables require an interaction between different species in order to highlight diverse character foibles and follies. More important, encounters between species make glaringly obvious the dangerous

We are not just rather like animals; we *are* animals. Our difference from other species may be striking, but comparisons with them have always been, and must be, crucial to our view of ourselves.

—MARY MIDGLEY, *Beast and Man: The Roots of Human Nature* (1979), xiii paths such follies cut: the silly goose who lets herself be flattered might just get eaten by the wily fox. From Aesop's fables, to Beatrix Potter's stories, to George Orwell's *Animal Farm*, and, more recently, movies such as *Babe* and *Bambi*, animals have talked, and in talking they have told us about human proclivities and transgressions. The fable's humor is the knowing, dark humor of recognizing one's own shortcomings.

Before a dialogue can occur, characters must exist, and the animal characters that populate beast fables are not assigned behaviors randomly. In the forest, foxes and rabbits are different species, with distinct moods, inclinations, capacities, and dietary habits, and so too in fables. This leads us to ask what sort of animals populate fables. Why these animals and not others? Although exotic creatures do find their way into fables from time to time, generally speaking, fables are told with familiar animals, farm animals, and wild animals that raid the barnyard: rabbits, foxes, dogs, chickens, geese, and weasels. Beast fables draw from intimate lived experience with animals and depend on reasonably fixed communal expectations about animal behaviors. In a word: proximity. The way we live—or do not live—with other animals shapes the sorts of stories that can be told and understood.

Nicholas Howe suggests that fables originated in the juxtaposition of house, barnyard, and wilderness. The fable's symbolic setting involves interplay between two clearly demarcated spaces—the safety of the home and the precarious unknown of the wilderness—and, crucially, makes use of the intermediate zone between the two: the barnyard. "This sense of place does not govern each and every fable ever told," Howe writes, "but it does underlie the fable's sense that the human and animal exist together as something other than a rigid binary opposition." Put another way, caught between the domestic and the wild, the setting explains "how it is that humans and animals can do what is so palpably obvious they do: speak to each other." This experiential knowledge is always based on cultural conventions, but it remains rooted in observed behavior. As Howe puts it, when "we lived and worked in barnyards and knew animals as something other than pets or exotica, we understood that the beast fable could have a moral function. This knowledge came with belonging to a group defined at least in part by its knowledge of animals, knowledge not strictly speaking scientific but rather traditional or experiential."[2]

In his classic essay "Why Look at Animals?" John Berger uses Homer's celebrated animal metaphors to explain the use—even need—of speaking through animals. Book 17 of *The Iliad* begins with Menelaus standing over Patroclus's body to prevent the Trojans from stripping the corpse. Homer writes, "Menelaus bestrode his body like a fretful mother cow standing over the first calf she has brought into the world." Menelaus then kills a Trojan who threatens him, and nobody else dares approach: "He was like a mountain lion who believes in his own strength and pounces on the finest heifer in a grazing herd. He breaks her neck with his powerful jaws, and then he tears her to pieces and devours her blood and entrails, while all around him the herdsmen and their dogs create a din but keep their distance—they are heartily scared of him and nothing would induce them to close in." Here, Berger suggests, Homer uses animals as metaphoric references to convey "the excessive or superlative qualities of different moments. *Without the example of animals* such moments would have remained indescribable."[3] Animals animate our language and imaginings by giving shape to our experiences in the world.

Quiet as a mouse, a bull in a china shop, a lion's courage, the boxer who floats like a butterfly and stings like a bee, crying wolf, owlish, a peacock, a rat, as cunning as a fox. Why are sports teams named after big cats and other man-eaters (lions, tigers, sharks) and not zebras, hummingbirds, and weasels? Why does the expression "too sly for his own good" bring to mind a fox? Certainly, not all animal metaphors carry the same intensity. The imaginative strength of speaking through animals is nurtured by a multiplicity of causes—historical, cultural, habitual, proximate—that affect the immediacy of what can be said and the depth of truth expressed. Yet, in their varying degrees, animal metaphors endeavor to capture qualities shared by humans and animals and extrude those qualities through the elegant simplicity of animal purpose. Such *animalizing* is grounded in the biological while not being fully reducible to the biological. It emerges from experiential encounters with animals but has been transposed onto an alternate plane of experience, from literal animal to animal archetype.[4] In some ways, we need animals to express the inexpressible, to give shape to subtle emotions, to steady the more tenuous and vague corners of our experience of being in the world. Of course, on a literary level beast fables only ever play with sameness between humans and other animals. Ultimately, they make no arguments for or against our resemblance to the rest of the animal world. Fables have never been lessons in animal rights. Rather, it is the moral lessons at the heart of beast fables that are to be taken sincerely. After all, allegory's power resides in the space *between* the literal and the figurative, between concrete imagery and abstract concepts. Whether that potency remains when fables are portrayed with real dead creatures is another question entirely.

26 Hermann Ploucquet, *The Ermines' Tea Party*. Photo © V&A Images / Victoria and Albert Museum, London.

This chapter examines several forms of taxidermied fables—from nineteenth-century narratives acted out with dead animals to unsettling animal hybrids crafted by twenty-first-century artists. Despite their obvious historical, material, and conceptual differences, the works all demand the viewer's participation to make sense of the scenes. What is on view is not primarily an animal species but a darkly mischievous reflection of human desires, longings, and anxieties. After all, allegory is always cultural before it is natural; its imaginative potency resides in its more than material meaning, beyond any knowledge that might be elucidated by simply describing physical forms and properties. And, as we will see, transmuting human desire through the materiality of animal bodies reveals a great deal about ourselves and often little about the animals themselves.

We begin with the strange and supposedly humorous world of anthropomorphic taxidermy: setting up little animals in mundane human scenarios such as a kitten tea party, squirrels playing cards, or toads on mechanical swings. Known as grotesques, the genre first emerged in the mid-nineteenth century and continued to delight audiences throughout the century.[5] For Victorians, it was love at first sight. Instructions and ideas for setting up the little scenes appeared in most taxidermy manuals from the mid-nineteenth century onward. One of the better-known creators was Edward Hart, whose *Prize Fight* was also shown at the Great Exhibition of the Works of Industry of All Nations in 1851. Consisting of five individual cases, *Prize Fight* depicts two squirrels in various stages of a boxing match, until one of the squirrels is knocked out.[6] Other well-known anthropomorphic taxidermists include George Swaysland, William Chalkley, and of course the now infamous Walter Potter. But it was a taxidermist from Stuttgart who brought the genre to life for English audiences. Although Hermann Ploucquet may not be the genre's inventor, he was most certainly its popularizer and the first to create an extensive collection of theatrical dramas: a full-blown storybook in fur and feathers.

ANIMAL EXPRESSIONS

A declaration of love between two weasels, a dormouse duel, hedgehogs ice-skating, wrapped in gray coats for warmth, and six kittens serenading a piglet beneath her window were just a few of the miniature dramas that charmed Victorian audiences at the Great Exhibition of 1851 in London. The scenes were created by Hermann Ploucquet, taxidermist at the Royal Museum of Natural History in Stuttgart, and exhibited down the length of a long wall in the Württemberg Court in the Crystal Palace.

The list of scenes continues. Six cats mourning the death of a relative. A lady cat in crinoline with her howling monkey husband and baboon footman. Six thieving hares caught by a fox policeman. An evening by the Stuttgart fountains with four dogs in uniform flirting with four young geese, while another eight geese, spurned and jealous, cackle scandal around the fountain. The easily flattered geese, the jealousy of their kin, the silly vanity and impending doom are all the stuff of traditional beast fables, except that here the beasts belong to the material world. Allegory is made corporeal.

The fable as a form explores those regions where human and animal overlap, where it becomes not only hard but also counterintuitive to separate them.

—NICHOLAS HOWE, "Fabling Beasts: Traces in Memory," in *Humans and Other Animals* (1995), 236

To a generation familiar with the technological wizardry of *Babe* and its talking pig, it seems ridiculous to say that the appeal of Ploucquet's works rested squarely in their innovative technology. In the mid-nineteenth century, well-crafted, lively taxidermy was still something impressive. The lively postures and animate gestures heightened Ploucquet's already admirable technique, transforming the works into dazzling and delightful visual amusements. Ploucquet's comical creatures were among the highlights of the Great Exhibition. Newspapers regularly ran delighted descriptions of the miniature scenes. "We have on more than one occasion—and we have not by any means been singular in that respect," wrote a correspondent for the August 12, 1851, edition of the *Morning Chronicle*, "directed the attention of visitors to the Exhibition to the consummately clever collection of stuffed animals, or miniature representations of animals, engaged in performing human occupations, and seemingly influenced by human motives, hopes, and fears." The stall at which Ploucquet's creations were exhibited was "one of the most crowded points of the Exhibition." Truly, Ploucquet had delighted English audiences with his novel creations: "nothing can be more genuine than the admiration, or more hearty than the laughter, with which the civilized animals are greeted."[7]

Among Ploucquet's most popular works were a series of eighteen tableaux illustrating the German fable of Reineke the Fox, based on Wilhelm von Kaulbach's etchings of Goethe's version of the medieval trickster tale. Reineke's exploits are cruel and vengeful, and yet when rendered in fur, the scenes were pure delight, and Victorian audiences could not get enough of them.[8] They were "admirable," "ludicrous," "exquisitely funny," and "irresistibly droll." Reminiscing several years later, James Anthony Froude noted that the appeal of Ploucquet's vision of Reineke incited a craze for the neglected fable: "Everybody began to talk of Reineke."[9] A run of Reineke fables occurred, with at least three translations being printed within a decade of the exhibition.

Ploucquet's technical facility at crafting animal expressions and his imaginative flair achieved such celebrity in Britain that a book of engravings was published even before the exhibition had ended, so that "one of the cleverest and most popular displays in the Great Exhibition . . . may be long perpetuated." The preface claimed that "everyone from Her Majesty the Queen down to the charity boys, hasten to see the Stuffed Animals." At a price of three shillings and sixpence (or six shillings with color plates), the book of engravings, with text by David Brogue, was as greatly admired as the original animal creations. "To whom, old or young, will it not be welcome?" the *Examiner* exclaimed over the etchings. "Who has not, young or old, seen, laughed at, revisited, and brought away pleasant recollections of the Stuffed Animals?"[10] The *Morning Chronicle* even suggested that the book was likely to become a treasured piece of memorabilia: "we have little doubt that many an urchin still in petticoats will in future years associate his most vivid recollection of the Great Exhibition of 1851 with Mr. Brogue's perpetuation of the 'Comical Creatures from Wurtemburg.'"[11]

The theatricality of Ploucquet's works, their phenomenal popularity, and the hearty amusement they inspired might suggest that Ploucquet was appreciated more as a showman than as a serious naturalist, and that his creatures might best be categorized as whimsical entertainment. Yet, as delightful as the scenes were, they were not mere fancy to Victorian audiences. In particular, anthropomorphic poses were not seen as masking the creatures' innate characteristics. In fact, it was quite precisely Ploucquet's achievement of this double identity—human behaviors and animal expressions—that earned him such praise. "The animals borrow exaggerated expression, without losing their brute looks," a reviewer for the *Morning Chronicle* wrote, "and the *rationale* of the irresistible risibility which they excite, is the wondrous union of brute face with human expression." The sly fox was still a fox; the placid rabbit, with his "honest hairy face . . . is also a rabbit still."[12] After all, Ploucquet was a highly skilled museum taxidermist: along the wall facing Ploucquet's anthropomorphic scenes were his superlative series of taxidermic tableaux of animals engaged in the drama of survival. Ploucquet's anthropomorphic works consisted of "comicalities, not caricatures," the distinction resting in the "truth and spirit of expression and attitude" that Ploucquet had captured. "Our [English] artists would do well to note what constitutes the inimitable expression of these small animals."[13]

Indeed, 1851 became the defining moment in English taxidermy, the moment when, as Montagu Browne claimed almost half a century later, the "slumbering" English taxidermists had their eyes opened by the teachings of foreign exhibits, particularly Ploucquet's anthropomorphic scenes, or what Browne called the German grotesque school.

> Though taxidermy flourished . . . for some years previous to the Great
> Exhibition of 1851, yet that decidedly gave a considerable impetus to the
> more correct and artistic delineation of animals, especially in what may
> be called the grotesque school instituted by the Germans, which, though

it may be decried on the score of misrepresenting nature in the most natural way possible, yet teaches a special lesson by the increased care necessary to more perfectly render the fine points required in giving animals that serio-comic and half-human expression which was so intensely ridiculous and yet admirable in the studies of the groups illustrating the fable of "Reinecke the Fox."[14]

It was this skill in modeling the varied expressions of hope, fear, love, and rage in squirrels, hedgehogs, weasels, and foxes that was such an immense step in the advance of the "old wooden school" of taxidermy, which Browne described as gaunt birds "staring, round-eyed, at nothing" with stiff legs and overstretched necks. And for Browne, if thoughtfully handled, a little indulgence in anthropomorphic taxidermy had significant merit for taxidermists. The art form encouraged taxidermists to stretch their imagination and use some artistic flair rather than mechanically repeat the same standard, humdrum construction of solitary birds stuck on pedestals. Likewise, comic scenes such as a mouse wielding a sword or a pouting frog demanded a much better understanding of anatomy (and its limitations and possibilities) and a greater attention to the minuscule details that guaranteed a work's success. In short, anthropomorphic taxidermy was instructive, enlightening, and imaginative. But, Browne warned his readers, "these caricatures are not artistic taxidermy, and they are only allowable now and then as a relaxation."[15]

Browne's artistic taxidermy, as we have already seen, is taxidermy that re-creates and conveys a poetic appreciation of an animal's essence—what makes a dove a dove and a lion a lion. In a sense, artistic taxidermy seeks to capture and convey a perceived "truth" of an animal as expressed through its engagement in "typical" behaviors. Although rooted in animal behavior, this truth is ultimately a representation, and *representations* of animals, as Nigel Rothfels argues, are rooted in human *expectations* of particular animals.[16]

Expectation is an aptly chosen word. It makes no claim to truth or verisimilitude. Rather, it connotes a waiting, an anticipated arrival, a supposition nurtured by personal experience, imagination, cultural assumptions, or, most probably, an amalgam of sources.[17] The term also allows for a clash or disjointedness when divergent sets of expectations collide. After all, representations of animals are rarely one-dimensional. More often they are paradoxical, ambiguous, and inconsistent.

Anthropomorphic taxidermy offers particularly convoluted representations of animals. At first glance, Ploucquet's theatrical scenes would seem to be an overt denial of any expectation of animal behavior. Kittens do not fall in love with piglets. Hedgehogs do not ice-skate. However, dogs and foxes do take advantage of geese and rabbits. To understand Ploucquet's animal representations and those of subsequent anthropomorphic taxidermists, it is useful to distinguish between the various scenarios being portrayed. Ploucquet's tableaux can be divided into two broadly defined categories or styles. The first depends on the actual behavior of animals to clarify the message of the tableau—foxes eat rabbits, not the other way around. The second substitutes arbitrary animals in various human activities—there is nothing particular about hedgehogs informing a tableau of hedgehogs ice-skating. Kittens or squirrels could easily be substituted. The first style belongs to the harsh world of animal fables and usually involves a sinister narrative of death and disappointment. The second depicts a frozen moment of miniature sweetness. Both styles endeavor to capture animals' attitudes, and Ploucquet probably would not have made a distinction between the two. But a distinction can and should be made, since, as delightful as Ploucquet's Reineke was to Victorian audiences, the genre made a distinct turn away from animal fables in the later decades of the nineteenth century and has never returned.

As with all animal fables, Ploucquet's animals "speak" to one another. Although they do not say a word, viewers know exactly what the uniformed dogs are saying to the geese to woo them away from the safety of the fountain. And—again true to fable form—in "speaking," Ploucquet's animals nevertheless exhibit a degree of anatomical fidelity. Although humanized in their theatrics and upright postures, the creatures were anatomically correct. As Browne wrote, anthropomorphic taxidermy was not a denial of anatomical knowledge; it merely pushed that knowledge in a particular direction. The animal form has not been perverted. Modeling the faces of serenading kittens required the same delicacy of touch needed in fashioning snarling lions, simply on a smaller scale. Ploucquet's fidelity to animal form was particularly important, considering the species being portrayed. Most of his audience would have seen a living goose going about its business and would have recognized the physical attitudes of foxes and rabbits. The scenes were not just fables materialized but fables materialized with the anatomical knowledge of a highly skilled taxidermist.

The near-human expressiveness of the animals was not necessarily at odds with nineteenth-century naturalistic descriptions, and particularly not those offered by popular natural history literature. Published at the end of the eighteenth century, Thomas Bewick's *General History of Quadrupeds*, the granddaddy of Victorian popular natural histories, sought to enlighten readers about "the various instinctive powers of animals—that hidden principle, which actuates and impels every living creature to procure its subsistence, provide for its safety, and propagate its kind."[18] Throughout the text, attention is drawn to the proximity of animals and humans. While human superiority is never in question, the text acknowledges that the basic needs and desires of humans and other animals are not so very different. The description of each creature reads as a sensitive character study. Animals are industrious, courageous, gluttonous, indolent, clumsy, devious, and cunning. They all have their own particular reasons, their own inclinations, and pursue their lives with an intuitive and energetic precision. These were not anthropomorphisms—there is no reason why humans should have the corner on industry or gluttony.[19] Rather, such animal studies expressed a shared animal experience of being in the world and engaging with surrounding species—some are dangerous to you or your kin, some provide your dinner, and with some you live in harmony. Like the beast fable, popular natural histories of local species drew from an intimate lived knowledge of the animals themselves.

Interestingly, the same view was held of John Tenniel's illustrations for Lewis Carroll's *Alice's Adventures in Wonderland*, first published in 1864. As a cartoonist for *Punch*, the highly popular satirical newspaper, Tenniel was very experienced in the subtle expressive blurring between humans and beasts: animal caricatures of public figures were *Punch* favorites. The humor of the Wonderland animals, like that of Ploucquet or *Punch*, lies quite precisely in the realism of representation. Tenniel often copied postures for his illustrations directly from natural history texts. The Wonderland creatures were merely earthly beasts that spoke. Perhaps they wore waistcoats and walked on their hind legs, but they nevertheless remained earthly beasts. Tenniel even conformed to the natural history technique of using natural background elements—flowers and mushrooms—to remind readers of the physical scale of Alice and the other animals. A review of children's books published in the *Times* in 1865 praised the illustrations in language reminiscent of the reviews of Ploucquet's animal scenes: the illustrations were "clever and funny," and despite their fantastical flourishes nevertheless expressed a remarkable " truthfulness . . . in the delineation of animal forms." The illustrations were successful because Tenniel drew his creatures straight, or nearly straight.[20] And therein lay the humor and pleasures of fables and fairy tales come to life.

And it is here, in the animal knowledge offered by fables and natural history, in the imaginative world of talking beasts and the physical world of living beasts, between animal expectations that are partly fabulous, partly experiential, partly satirical, and partly earnest, that Ploucquet's animal fables exist. A crucial question remains: what is the difference between fables told with narrative and fables told with animal skins?

The humor of fables is a dark humor centered on the raw realities of survival. Many of Ploucquet's scenes involve an eat-or-be-eaten mentality: the foxes and dogs are always circling, always waiting for their opportunity. Fables narrate a world in which opportunism is king; sly cunning and wily tricks, not decency or fairness, win the prize. But then, the barnyard is not fair. Foxes raid the henhouse. Wolves steal the foxes' dinner. Even in the less deadly fables, some creature is always losing his cheese or grapes; another beast wins the battle of wills. It is these habitual, unfair, unavoidable realities of life that power the beast fable.

Taxidermy might seem particularly suited to portraying this eat-or-be-eaten world. After all, the typical fable themes are pathos and Pothos: suffering and longing. Yet with the materialization of allegory, its potency is lost. Or rather, the meaning of the fable is transmuted into something altogether different. When reworked with dead animals, the playful truism of the fable is stripped away. Humans have killed and mastered animal form, and in the process the animals have become playthings to be looked at by a disconnected, detached observer. The conclusion of the traditional narrative beast fable lies in the reader's moment of recognition of him- or herself in the story. In contrast, allegories made material with dead animals necessarily fall flat. Death is too bluntly visible. It is hard to imagine yourself into a dead, stuffed, stiff fox, which is to say that humans can no longer be implicated in the drama. With dead animals, a spatial and species divide is established and solidified. The hazy blur of imaginative sameness is gone, and with it the suggestive depth of meaning that gives allegory its potency, that flicker of moral truth that connects us, even if only for a moment, to the rest of the animal world. The taxidermy scenes do not point toward a moral or significant truth but rather to the material fact of dead animals. In this sense, Ploucquet's work represents a dark terminus to the fable tradition: the animals have lost the fight.

Perhaps there is a fundamental incompatibility between the play and potency of the beast fable and its reworking with dead animals. Some subjects are best dealt with symbolically or imaginatively. Perhaps the truth of allegory dissolves if we approach it too directly or, in this case, too viscerally. And, interestingly, all subsequent anthropomorphic taxidermists turned away from depicting fables. Gone are efforts toward narrative and interaction between animals. In their place are scenes of summer idleness, sports, and pleasure: guinea pigs playing cricket and squirrels fencing. We have moved from cautionary tales to cutie-pie pleasures. But why use dead animals to act out scenes of human idleness and mirth? For the answer to this question we must turn to Walter Potter, the veritable king of anthropomorphic taxidermy.

KITTENS IN DRESSES

The diminutive is a term of manipulation and control as much as it is a term of endearment.

—SUSAN STEWART, *On Longing: The Miniature, the Gigantic, the Souvenir, the Collection* (1993), 124

Walter Potter was born on July 2, 1835, in the village of Bramber in Sussex, England. After a brief schooling, he worked in his father's inn, the White Lion, and pursued taxidermy as a hobby in a workshop above the stables. Potter's first subject was his pet canary. Typically enough for a first attempt, the result was poorly executed: a yellow feathered lump. But Potter was not disheartened. The fastidious process of skinning and stuffing suited him, and by the time of his death at the age of eighty-three, Potter's museum contained approximately six thousand of his taxidermied birds and animals. Most of Potter's taxidermy conforms to the quintessential Victorian aesthetic of bottling birds under glass domes with a few sprigs of foliage for ambience. However, the fame and origins of the museum center on his anthropomorphic works.

Potter's inspiration came from his sister, Jane, who showed him an illustrated book of nursery rhymes with the well-known poem "The Death and Burial of Cock Robin." Seven years later, in 1861, Potter finished his own rendition and exhibited *The Burial of Cock Robin* in the summerhouse of the White Lion's garden. The taxidermic tableau included ninety-eight British bird specimens and a miniature bull constructed from fur stretched over a wood form. True to the poem, a rook with a white collar and a prayer book acts as the parson, a dove is the chief mourner, and the bull tolls the bell of the Bramber church, painted in the background, making the churchyard the same as that in which Potter himself was

buried. The trees overhead are filled with sorrowful birds, some with glass bead tears in their eyes. Acting the part of the gravedigger, a barn owl stands beside the open grave with a few disinterred bird remnants spread on the ground. A long, melancholy procession of birds in black neckties winds through the graveyard, past a few little graves, up a sloping path, and out of sight.

The delighted reception of the tableau encouraged Potter, and in 1880 a museum was built across from the inn to display his expanding body of work. One tableau contained seventeen taxidermied kittens sitting around a laid table pouring tea and offering each other cake on tiny china plates; in another, twenty kittens enjoy themselves, some playing croquet, some watching the game under parasols, one riding a bicycle. In another tableau, eighteen red squirrels play cards, sip port, or enjoy cigars in their exclusive clubhouse. This "upper-crust" scene is contrasted

27 Walter Potter, *The Rabbits' Village School*. Photo © Marc Hill / Alamy.

with *The Rats Den*, crowded with fifteen large brown debauched gambling rats. One rat has fallen asleep with too much drink. Others have turned over their chairs in a fight, and policemen are just entering the hall. In *The Rabbits' Village School* (fig. 27), forty-eight white-and-brown rabbits learn their lessons. Another tableau stages a guinea pig cricket match alongside a guinea pig brass band. Potter also created a myriad of smaller scenes: toads on mechanical swings and seesaws, squirrels fencing, and rats stealing wine.

All of Potter's scenes are distinguished by his painstaking, near-obsessive attention to detail. The rabbits have rabbit-sized slates for their sums. The squirrels deal carefully painted miniature cards. The rats play with tiny dominos with perfect white dots. The croquet mallets, bicycles, and cricket bats were all made by Potter, as were the instruments for the brass band. Unable to find ready-made tiny trumpets and French horns, Potter labored for six months to make the delicate accessories. Perhaps most famously, Potter made a wedding dress. Completed in 1898, *The Kittens' Wedding* was Potter's last large work (although he was working on a squirrel court scene before his stroke in 1914, from which he never fully recovered) and the only one in which the animals are fully dressed. The lady kittens have cream brocade gowns, gaudy beads, and earrings. They even wear frilly knickers under their dresses. The scene includes eighteen kittens, a parson, an altar, and a rail. The bride has a brass ring on her finger, and the groomsmen sport wild, woolly heads and morning suits. All have oversized kitten eyes made of glass.

With kittens wearing dresses, we have a complete deviation from the beast fable. There is no moral portrayed, no sense that kittens are somehow like us—or we like them. There is no nuance between various character wiles and follies. The animals tell us nothing about themselves, and no viewer could pretend otherwise. What, then, are these scenes? And how should we read these animal-things on display?

In contrast to Ploucquet's scenes and Potter's earlier nursery rhymes, Potter's later tableaux include only one species. Different creatures never interact. Squirrels and rats do not belong to the same club. Only guinea pigs play in the brass band. This species specificity is a clear step away from the *interaction* between species that was a cornerstone of the fable tradition. Here animals merely replace humans, without commenting either on humans or on other animals. In the schoolroom, for example, rabbits are both studious and cheating; one has smudged his work, while another mocks him. There is nothing particular being said about rabbits. The scene could as easily be portrayed with kittens, squirrels, or hedgehogs—though perhaps not with rats. (Potter did make one distinction between species. The rats in their drinking hall and the refined squirrels in their gentlemen's club are clearly designed to exhibit different rungs on a "class" ladder. They could not occupy each other's establishment. But then, rats hold the unique position of being the object of near-universal human loathing.) There are no narratives being enacted, no implied storylines of what is about to occur. Rather, these are arrested moments, tableaux frozen in time. By eliminating the narrative thrust of species interaction, the scenes become more literal, concrete, and static. These are not figurative allegories but pretty postcards of human pleasures. They belong to the contained, motionless realm of miniatures and not to the rollicking story world of barnyard fables.

If there is nothing particular being said about the behaviors of these particular animals, nevertheless there is nothing irrelevant about which species are present. Most obviously, the animals are all small and stout. In great part the choice is logistical. If similar scenes were created with larger animals—sheep or caribou, for example—the tableaux would have required significantly more labor, expense, effort, and space for display. In addition, unlike sheep or caribou, Potter's squirrels, guinea pigs, rats, rabbits, and toads have "hands" and a facility to stand on their hind legs in order to swing a croquet mallet or play a tuba in a way that caribou never could. Also, with the death of fables as a motivating narrative, birds and barnyard fowl disappear from anthropomorphic taxidermy, presumably because of their limited facial expressiveness and lack of hands—no croquet mallets for a goose.

More important, besides being small and chubby, the animals all belong to a particular category of creature based on neither biology nor scientific classification but rather on the animals' proximity and expendability to humans. It is hardly imaginable that a taxidermist might pose a lion pouring cups of tea, and not only because of spatial constraints or anatomical limitations. Some animals are too "noble," exotic, or esteemed to be manipulated in such mock scenarios. In distinction to all other genres of taxidermy previously discussed, anthropomorphic taxidermy uses animals that have been deemed disposable: small, expendable, local, plenteous creatures, abundantly available and physically familiar yet without any sentimental attachment. Unlike the swollen triumph of the colonial lion hunt or a stern chase for a superlative wapiti, there is no glory perceived in these animal deaths. Foxes, dogs, geese, hedgehogs, rabbits, kittens, vermin, livestock, lunch, barnyard predators, waste: these were not trophy kills. These animals were not killed to exhibit their beauty or wonder. They were not useful to science. Their deaths were just part of the routine functioning of country life. If Ploucquet, Potter, and all subsequent anthropomorphic taxidermists had not used their skins, their bodies (with the exception of the geese) would probably have been discarded as unwanted refuse. Potter's kittens, for example, came from a local farm. His rabbits came from Mr. Feast, a rabbit breeder in a nearby village. The squirrels came from a local park where (according to a guidebook to Potter's museum) "the Red Squirrel was plentiful, and just as troublesome, in those days, as the more ferocious grey variety is to-day."[21] The origins of the guinea pigs are unknown, but the rats were killed by a dog during corn-threshing season.[22]

Expendability does not mean that these little animals were not considered endearing or cute when dead and stuffed. Cuteness is typically designated by a series of roly-poly physical attributes strongly associated with baby mammals: short, plump limbs, large, forward-facing eyes, a proportionally larger head in relation to the body, and the teetering walk of babies. Cuteness suggests harmlessness and vulnerability and stimulates a tender, pitying love. But cute is as much a term of control as it is of endearment. Cute things are never big or powerful or dangerous or impressive. They are small and vulnerable and pretty and sweet. But when does a dead kitten become cute?

The late nineteenth-century attitude toward cats was particularly nuanced and included both barnyard mousers and feminized pets. Cats were not commonly kept as pets until the eighteenth century. Once they became household companions, their fond owners frequently oversentimentalized them into declawed, defanged prettiness devoid of all predatory instinct. The impulse to rehabilitate cats from past criticism—traditionally cats were sly, lecherous, selfish, hypocritical, ruthless—often led to mawkish exaggeration of their prettier qualities. Highly popular artists and writers like Louis Wain and Beatrix Potter (no relation to Walter) depicted anthropomorphized cats as innocuous little people engaged in all manner of darling human activities. They went to school; they got married; they played golf.[23] In short, cats became cute. And yet, while cats evolved into the cutest of creatures, becoming the very image of domestic bliss, few farmers thought twice about drowning excess litters. Cats were working members of a farm, but only a few were needed. For example, the guidebook to Potter's museum makes the following comments:

Most of the kittens came from Ward's Farm at Henfield, where a number
of cats were allowed to run wild in the barns. Under such conditions,

each female cat might raise a family of at least ten kittens every year, and it would therefore be impossible to retain them all, otherwise they would soon prove to be a greater menace than the mice they were intended to destroy. One kitten of each family was usually retained, and the others put to sleep. Walter Potter was then allowed to choose any that were suitable for preservation, and the remainder were buried.[24]

Despite the raw fact that the kittens populating *The Kittens' Wedding* and *The Kittens' Tea and Croquet Party* were euphemistically "put to sleep," no dark truths of animal desires are meant to be read here. Rather, the scenes are supposedly laced with enough droll whimsy to veil the death on display. With their dead cute kitten bodies, the creatures offer snapshots of an idealized, delightful world in which all inhabitants have the leisure time to enjoy tea parties, play croquet, and listen to a band on the village green. In Potter's fantasyland, even potentially dangerous moments—the police raiding the rats' drinking hall—become quaint and defanged. The scenes embody a longing for a moment of plenitude, a yearning for the peace and simplicity of summertime idleness, and—crucially—a desire to see such pleasing human experiences gently reflected. The impeccable details of the little scenes steady, comfort, and confirm familiarity. All is right in the world, at least on the surface.

The *idea* of a kitten wedding belongs to the enchanting childhood world of storybooks, but its actualization in material form is hardly so delightful. It is quite precisely the ostensible sweetness of the imagery and the perfection of its miniature details that make it provocative for twenty-first-century viewers. Dollhouses, toy soldiers, fairies, kitten stories, and all such diminutive sweetness are set apart from the world of lived realities by a reduction in scale. They offer a miniature model of a just-so world, while always suggesting hidden realities: "the daydream of life inside life, of significance multiplied infinitely *within* significance," as Susan Stewart puts it. "Once the toy becomes animated, it initiates another world, the world of the daydream. The beginning of narrative time here is not an extension of the time of everyday life; it is the beginning of an entirely new temporal world, a fantasy world parallel to (and hence never intersecting) the world of everyday reality."[25] The secret life of anthropomorphic taxidermy, however, is all wrong. Potter's scenes become disquieting through their meticulous precision in miniature form. It is hard not to think of Potter skinning the kittens, easing their fur around body moulds, inserting glass eyes, shaping little mouths, and affixing tiny earrings and cravats.

All taxidermy is unsettling, but anthropomorphic taxidermy achieves a higher degree of eeriness *because* its subjects are so domesticated and demure. Potter's scenes would not be quite so unsettling if he had chosen subjects other than kittens and rabbits and composed them in scenarios other than nursery rhymes, domesticated spaces, and spaces of leisure. But he chose to craft visions of "Babes in the Wood," "The House That Jack Built," and homely scenes of everyday life. Taxidermy and nursery rhymes should never meet. In the hands of Potter, the two not only met but morphed and engendered a hallucination of unsettling cuteness.

What, then, is the difference between such scenarios as depicted in literature and as realized in material form? Like all taxidermy, anthropomorphic taxidermy blurs imagination and materiality by fusing human desires with raw animal form. As we have seen, raw animal form is reworked and manipulated to condense and concretize the longings always working within human encounters with the rest of the natural world. But kittens in brocade dresses embody an altogether different sort of fantasy from the theatrically savage lions discussed in chapter 3. With anthropomorphic taxidermy, the mastery of animal form is presented as a mockery, not a triumphant accomplishment. These discarded animals are meant to endear us to them by embodying the happiness of golden moments. And yet their death seems more conspicuous because their postures could never be performed by living creatures.

There are several possible avenues for exploring the vast popularity of late Victorian anthropomorphic scenes. We might see them as exemplars of a moment of transition in attitudes toward nature. As has often been noted, a profound cultural shift in Victorians' relationship with the natural world occurred during the nineteenth century. By midcentury, the cult of Victorian pet keeping was solidly established, as was a sentimental genre of animal art, perhaps epitomized by Sir Edwin Landseer's *The Old Shepherd's Chief Mourner* (1837), portraying a doleful sheepdog resting his head on his master's coffin. Animal welfare groups, particularly the Society for the Prevention of Cruelty to Animals, were created. Animal cruelty acts were debated in Parliament, and antivivisection rallies were common in the 1870s and '80s. While such changes tended toward endowing animals with human sensitivities, emotions, and experiences, Charles Darwin's work pushed the debate in the opposite direction. Darwin was not suggesting that animals are like us but rather that we are like them. In *The Expression of the Emotions in Man and Animals* (1872), Darwin went so far as to compare the emotional lives and expressions of humans with those of other animals. He described the sounds uttered by impatient dogs, how snakes inflate themselves when irritated, and the facial expressions of monkeys when jealous, dejected, angry, sulky, disappointed, enraged, or astonished, in order to prove that the instinctual behaviors and expressions of animals and humans share a common origin. (And yet, the popularized form of Darwin's thesis was frequently expressed anthropomorphically, e.g., apes wearing pants.)

However, anthropomorphic taxidermy should not be understood to express any anxiety about humans' status or position within the animal kingdom. As already noted, the scenes express nothing particular about their animal inhabitants except that these inhabitants were otherwise superfluous to humans' needs. While nineteenth-century popular natural histories, pet keeping, and animal rights activism all expressed degrees of behavioral fellowship between humans and other animals, anthropomorphic taxidermy perverts that fellowship. When waste animals—killed simply because they were a nuisance—are mockingly transmuted into humanoid dolls, the divide between species is not narrowed but rather deepened: humans remain supremely and undeniably king. Anthropomorphic taxidermy offers a queasy material fable of human supremacy wrapped up in witty cuteness. The humor is not a knowing humor of dark truths revealed with deceptive simplicity but rather the unsettling drollery of dead bunnies doing sums.

Potter has emerged as the most famous anthropomorphic taxidermist owing in no small part to the longevity of his museum. After Potter's death, the museum was left to his daughter, Minnie, and then to his grandson, also named Walter. Walter's widow sold the collection, which passed through numerous owners until it finally was bought in 1986 by John and Wendy Watts, who moved the collection to the Jamaica Inn (made famous by novelist Daphne du Maurier) on Bodmin Moor in Cornwall. With the advice and help of Pat Morris, a leading taxidermy authority, and Mike Grace, resident taxidermist, the Wattses restored, maintained, and augmented the collection, which received about thirty thousand visitors a year. However, with the death of Grace and the retirement of Mr. and Mrs. Watts and the curator, and after unsuccessful attempts to sell the museum in one piece, the collection was finally split up and sold at Bonhams Auction House. On September 23–24, 2003, the contents of Walter Potter's Museum of Curiosities was auctioned off, item by item, at the Jamaica Inn. Ordered into 691 lots, the parade of Potter's taxidermied ark lasted two days and in total sold for an astounding £529,900—more than twice the predicted sum. The highest-selling items were *The Burial of Cock Robin* and *The Kittens' Wedding*, each of which sold for more than $30,000.

The celebrity of Potter's pieces today perhaps stems from the current popularity of Victorian kitsch and its exaggerated aesthetic of nostalgia. The scenes of golden pleasures that Potter portrayed, of brass bands on the village green, tea parties, and croquet matches, have themselves eased into history. They are no longer typical pastimes (if they ever were), and even without the kittens they hold a certain nostalgia for simpler, sunnier days. As much as the kittens themselves, the activities portrayed encapsulate something very Victorian. In fact, *The Kittens' Wedding* was exhibited at the Victoria and Albert Museum in London as part of a 2001 exhibition on the Victorians called Inventing New Britain—The Victorian Vision. And when those simple pleasures are fused into the dead bodies of kittens, they develop the aura of cultural fossils—at once glorified and mocked. The kittens seem doubly dead: once because their lives were cut short, and twice because they have been reduced to the kitschy posturing of crusty Victorian dolls.

Potter's scenes are also iconic of a peculiar Victorian obsession with denaturalized nature. No longer truly part of nature but nevertheless exuding the authenticity of genuine animal skins, the scenes are strange allegories of the late nineteenth-century consumptive love of the natural world. Living in aquariums or herbariums, bottled up in jars, and fossilized behind glass, coral, seaweed, birds, butterflies, beetles, ferns, and orchids were everywhere collected and transformed into little vistas. Lost yet glorified, nature became an icon of itself and was transformed into the perfect commodity. Such containable, subordinated, imperishable miniature worlds were always open for contemplation and were always a source of both aesthetic pleasure and endless longing.[26]

THE SECRET LIFE OF THE DISCARDED

From the late nineteenth century to present-day creations, the genre of anthropomorphic taxidermy displays a surprisingly consistent set of scenarios: scenes of pleasure, idleness, and silliness. Although its appreciative audience has narrowed over the past century, the genre has not disappeared. In fact, several museums center on such droll animal theatricalities. The two best-known collections can be found at the Torrington Gopher Hole Museum in Alberta, Canada, and in the basement of the Cress Funeral Home in Madison, Wisconsin. Interestingly, both are exclusively limited to one family of animals: squirrels and their close relatives, chipmunks and gophers. Small and sturdy, with nimble hands, inhabiting both urban and rural landscapes, plentiful yet short-lived, cute and fuzzy but also a potential pest, the squirrel is the perfect creature for anthropomorphic taxidermy.

In the basement of the Cress Funeral Home, along with a collection of giant stuffed fish and dozens of mammals, Sam Sanfilippo set up a perky world of dead animal fun. Some of his dioramas, such as the squirrels who rock back and forth in chairs, are mechanized, but most just seem to be having a good time on bucking broncos or watching half-naked chipmunks at the Topless Girlie Show.

Similarly, the Torrington Gopher Hole Museum, just north of Calgary, exhibits seventy-one gophers wearing tiny outfits and doing various things no gopher has ever done before. There are a police officer and a bank robber, three Olympic winners (fastest grain eater, fastest car dodger, and fastest hole digger—all wave gaily from their podiums), a butterfly catcher, and a fireman. There are forty-five little dioramas in all, and some have the added theatricality of cardboard bubble phrases attached to their heads. "I'll see your 5 and raise your 6," one gambler says to another; "This beats your mother's burrow," the groom says to his new bride. The museum is housed in a small, squarish white building with green trim and a pitched roof, resembling a prairie one-room schoolhouse. The dioramas themselves are likewise simply built: two-foot square beige boxes stacked randomly, each with an oval front revealing a glowing, strange, yet highly familiar little world. Interestingly, such anthropomorphic scenes never depict foreign or fantastical situations. There is never a gopher superman or a gopher from another culture. The scenes and the characters are always the most familiar and the best known. This is not an exploration of difference but a confirmation of self and the commonplace.

All taxidermy engages animal expectations. Anthropomorphic taxidermy plays with those expectations, reverses them, transposes them, and sometimes even mocks them, but always while stamping animal nature with human desires. Using the dead bodies of discarded animals to depict scenes of pleasure suggests flaccid allegories of human supremacy. There is no sense of a hovering truth, no deeper understanding to decipher. There is no room for allegory to work because there is no space for the imagination to play. At first glance, anthropomorphic

The animal is a reminder of the limits of human understanding and influence, but also of the value of working *at those limits.*

—STEVE BAKER, *The Postmodern Animal* (2000), 16

taxidermy might suggest a longing for reflection or resemblance between humans and other animals. But at root it is what it seems to be: a queasy expression of mastery dressed up as whimsy.

If the power and purpose of allegory is to make us read beyond, to question, or to engage more deeply with a cultural value, such kitschy scenes of everyday life hardly move beyond the obvious. However, there is a genre of contemporary taxidermy that offers what might be called postmodern beast fables. The narrative structure is broken down. All is ambiguous and troubling, yet tales are being told of humanity and animality and the confusion between the two. And, like all good beast fables, these strange fictions could not be expressed—or at least not expressed as powerfully—without the abstraction of animal form. If fables explore the regions where human and animal overlap and where it becomes almost counterintuitive to separate them, these next-generation beast fables force viewers to confront the deeper significance of human-animal encounters.

On the white floor of a gallery, a lioness is sleeping, her head resting on her crossed paws, her ears softly turned downward. She is relaxed, at peace, without worry. But there is only half of her, the front half, which disappears into globules of gold arching away from her middle section. The work is a collaborative creation of two Dutch artists known as Idiots (Afke Golsteijn and Floris Bakker) and is evocatively titled *Ophelia*, after the tragic heroine of William Shakespeare's *Hamlet* (fig. 29).

The presence of a real animal in a gallery space, especially half an animal, is disconcerting, to say the least. If the lioness were not so flawlessly taxidermied and so gently posed, *Ophelia* would seem better described as road kill than as art. But the visual magnetism of the work—the animal's raw beauty—lulls viewers, and the lioness's almost human pose almost allows us to imagine ourselves into her position. Hiding the seams hides the violence inherent in taxidermy.

But *Ophelia*'s meaning hardly seems confined to its materials. Lion: dun-colored predatory mammal native to African savannas and Indian forests. Gold: atomic number 79, soft, shiny, yellow, malleable, dissolved by mercury. Rather, *Ophelia* seems to exist somewhere between its concrete presence and its allegorical significance: the lioness and the gold, the queen of beasts, the king of metals and money. The work offers a vision of a world where fantasy and reality merge into infinite possibilities and unanswered questions. Is the lioness liquefying or coalescing? Has she fallen under some enchantment, or is she dreaming herself into existence? Is this an alchemical vision of matter being transformed into the highest and purest of elements, or a most sinister allegory of the human transformation of nature's vitality into raw capital? Is this aesthetic hedonism or a material tragedy?

In writing about their work, the artists draw attention to the frailty of the line dividing observed reality from poetic imagination. Combining their skills with glass, metal, embroidery, and taxidermy, the artists decorate and adorn real animals, transfiguring them from regular creatures—rabbits, hedgehogs, swans, mice, birds—into the tragic figures of contemporary fairy tales. Taxidermy always undergoes a transformation, and it is difficult not to think about death when looking at half a lion. But for Golsteijn and Bakker, the morbid is transformed into something beautiful and beautifully provocative. "The striking beauty and the vividness of the animals that figure in the works, conjure powerful emotions of awe and inspiration before giving way to our morbid curiosity surrounding death, which leads us ultimately to think of our own mortality. This contrast between beauty, luxury and greed coupled with the mystery of death, timelessly preserved, transports one into a transient state of mind, in which anything is possible."[27] The works oscillate between brutality and beauty, between flesh and allegory. The piece seems informed by desire, but desire for what? And what is the cost of such longing?

As Steve Baker has argued, much contemporary animal art draws a potency from the animal's thereness, its embodied thingness, its literalism: the way the animal-thing stands in the same space as the viewer as a confrontation and perhaps even a goad.[28] After all, taxidermy is as much an encounter as an animal-thing. Yet at the same time, the animal of *Ophelia* is obviously manipulated to engage a more than material meaning and to provoke unsettling questions about the nature of human-animal interactions. At work is an unexpected tension between viewers' visceral and imaginative reactions. Ultimately, viewers are left to make meaning of the pieces from their own reservoir of images. The meaning is there. You can sense an understanding, but you cannot always draw that understanding into concrete language.

And this is the power of allegories. Their imaginative potency always resides in their more than material meaning, in what lies beyond any knowledge that might be elucidated by simply describing physical forms and properties. To read allegory is to dream, to read within and beyond the text, to read oneself, to rely

on one's own profundity to illuminate the interwoven meanings of the narrative. After all, the ultimate conclusion of an allegory is not in the text but in the understanding—perhaps even the conversion—achieved by its readers. It is the reader who draws out a personally resonant truism from the text's play and possibilities and discovers greater truth than words alone could express. Allegorical truth cannot be spelled out. It is a realization, a sort of quickening experienced by each individual.[29]

The animal art of Iris Schieferstein perhaps offers even more enigmatic allegories of organicism and desire. Fusing together the parts of road kill and other dead and discarded creatures, Schieferstein creates disquieting hybrids that offer haunting commentaries on beauty, necessity, longing, and death. In *Life Can*

29 Idiots, *Ophelia*, 2005. Taxidermy lion, ceramics, and glass. Photo by Karin Nussbaumer. Courtesy of the artists and the National Museum of Oslo.

Be So Nice, Schieferstein combines the parts of little pigs, birds, snakes, cats, and other small creatures to create new series of species, each of which hovers upright in clear liquid against a white background, without context, without history (fig. 30). Their poses are almost ritualistic, restless yet immortally motionless, and not unlike the creatures seen in the illuminated letters and images of medieval bestiaries. But looking more closely, viewers will see that each animal forms a letter with its hybrid body. A little pig with a feather ruff uses his kitten paws and chicken feet to form the upper and lower curves of the letter C. What appears to be a rabbit kicks out a wing, a leg, and a cat's tail to spell the letter E. Together, such idiosyncratic characters spell the letters and words of a refrain from the Prince song "Life Can Be So Nice." Prince's lyrics are unambiguously blissful: "It's a wonderful world, sweet paradise / Kiss me once, kiss me twice / Life can be so nice, so nice." Transmuted in animal flesh, the refrain becomes something different, not darker or sadder, exactly, but filled with a searing sort of reality, a haunting, enigmatic truth.

And perhaps allegory always becomes more powerful when it is broken down into oblique, vague, fragmented, inchoate forms. Schieferstein's dream beasts are most likely to resonate because they are both within and external to the material world of creaturely life. They haunt us precisely because they both are and are not animals, both are and are not imagined. They exist between. Schieferstein engenders an entirely new fantasy world, forever beyond the everyday world of lived reality yet constantly referring to the known and knowable.

With Schieferstein's work, there is always the sense that something more lurks in or between the material bodies of the little beasts. Some truth is opaquely present, but it is not an easy truth or one that is easily deciphered. *Life Can Be So Nice* would not be the same if she had spelled the letters with "real" animals. Something extra and not quite communicable is conveyed by the fact that these dream beasts literally spell out a yearning for a simple paradise on earth.

The little beasts become hieroglyphs, and as with *Ophelia*, the meaning of the work ultimately lies within each particular viewer's reaction. This polysemic quiver and only ever half-revealed meaning of contemporary animal art offer endless possibilities and interpretations. On the one hand, the fragmentation and recombination of the creatures could be understood to disrespect further already discarded and abused animals. On the other hand, the already broken little beasts have been elevated to an alternate plane of existence, perhaps even transformed into devotional icons. Schieferstein's works provoke viewers to flesh out the work's

30 *Life* and *Nice*, from Iris Schieferstein's *Life
Can Be So Nice*, 2001. Animal parts, glass,
formalin, distilled water. Photo by Stephan
Rabold. Courtesy of the artist.

profundity for themselves. There is no one meaning. From disgust, to melancholia, to a more philosophical analysis of the horrors and beauty of life, each viewer will find his or her meaning, if he or she is willing to look long enough. After all, the creatures have been recombined precisely to engage an empathetic response in viewers. Perhaps mythic in significance, perhaps ethically reprehensible, such animal art can leave no viewer unchallenged. They purposely make us uncomfortable. They exude a sense of uneasiness, a queasiness, a sense of wrongness, of rightness. They become brutal allegories of the endless human quest to achieve resonance and place within the natural world and the destruction humans will cause to find meaning.

All taxidermy renders animals immortal, and through that immortality they exist apart from lived reality while still physically lurking in this world. This is taxidermy's psychological potency: dead yet still animate, these animal-things offer something more than words alone can describe. Taxidermy is always experiential. At its most basic, taxidermy is an encounter between a viewer and a reconstructed animal. This encounter might be cast as educational or culturally significant. It may be private, emotional, disturbing, repulsive, or awe-inspiring, but at root taxidermy enables encounters with an animal presence. And when that animal presence is fragmented, rearranged, and recombined, an additional layer of significance is added. The play and multiplicity of meaning carries beyond the actual animals themselves. Viewers must move from materiality to emotionality, from what is present to the eyes to what cannot be presented in material form.

The final chapter of this study explores one of the more intimate and perhaps necessarily the most perverse strain of human longing to find meaning within nature: the perpetual pet. Of all the taxidermy we have considered, no genre has sought to capture much beyond the physical form of the species. Stuffed pets, however, exist because their owners miss the spirit or character of their dead pets, which means that with stuffed pets, the temptation of enchantment is always lurking. But you must believe if the enchantment is to work, and belief is dependent on two factors: an excessive sentimental attachment and an indulgent disregard for loss.

REMEMBRANCE

7

There are many species of sadness, each with its own particular weight and shadow—the gloom of homesickness, the maudlin tears of self-pity, the distress of grief or empathy with another's loss—each shifting the weight of sadness toward a place or person that once was but is no longer, or, more abstractly, toward what might have been. But while sadness for a failed dream is bitter, sadness is most acutely linked with the real physical loss of a person or thing that has passed forever from view. With this loss comes remembrance, and with remembrance a longing for the departed and, in its absence, a sentimental yearning for a token, an object, something that can be felt and touched: a material souvenir of what is no longer but lingers everlastingly in memory. "After an emotional catastrophe," Susan Pearce notes, "it is always the sight of a scarf which the absent lover used to wear which enables us to enter more profoundly into our sense of loss, showing ourselves to ourselves in ways which nothing else can do."[1] Objects of remembrance are private things filled with a personal and at times incommunicable significance.

Loulou was established on a part of the chimney-piece which jutted into the room. Every morning, on waking, she saw him in the light of dawn, and recalled the days that were gone and insignificant events down to their smallest details, without grief, full of tranquillity.

—GUSTAVE FLAUBERT, "Un coeur simple" (1877)

Strangely, objects of remembrance give us the freedom to forget. They allow us to move on in life, to do other things, to put certain memories out of mind for a while. Hidden in boxes, squirreled away in drawers, these memory-laden objects are always ready to be retrieved, fondled, and re-remembered, and then to be put out of sight again. Such objects are an individual's possessions, not in the way that books, toasters, and shoes are possessions but rather like prosthetic limbs: they are ours, an extension of our individual self; they fit into a hole that has been left by loss while embodying the very evidence of that loss. In this way, souvenirs of loss bring the past into the present. They make time personal and intimate.

A souvenir that belonged to a departed loved one is powerful, but a souvenir that once *was* a beloved is potentially intoxicating. How intoxicating? That explanation is best left to Gustave Flaubert and his short, sad tale "Un coeur simple," published in 1877.

Flaubert's tale recounts the series of deaths and departures that compose the life of a simple housemaid named Félicité. Her father dies, then her mother, and the sisters are dispersed. She is beaten by a farmer who let her keep cows in his fields. Her fiancé is harsh and deceitful and leaves her heartbroken. She begins life again as a servant for Madame Aubain and her two children, Virginia and Paul, whom she serves for half a century with the unswerving devotion of a nun. But one by one they all leave her—her long-lost nephew, the children, an old man with cancer living in a pigsty. They all forget her or die, even Loulou, her beloved parrot. But Loulou Félicité has stuffed. Jauntily posed with one foot in the air and a gilded nut in his beak, Loulou becomes more than just the stuffed shell of Félicité's beloved bird.

Over the years Félicité transforms her little attic room at the top of Madame Aubain's house into a shrine cluttered with religious icons and relics of all her departed loves: rosaries, holy virgins, a holy water basin made out of a coconut, a picture of the Holy Ghost with flaming red wings, Virginia's little plush hat, artificial flowers, a box of shells from her nephew. Loulou, her only real treasure, is the central figure. The difference between religious objects and objects of remembrance blurs, and together these mementos provoke a sad yet rapturous passion in the housemaid. She begins to suspect that the Holy Ghost—the "Giver of Tongues"—was really a parrot, not the dove that is conventionally represented. Logic is certainly on her side: parrots and the Holy Ghost talk; doves only coo.[2] And when Madame Aubain dies and Félicité is completely alone in a crumbling house, deaf, almost blind, and nearly mute, she begins mumbling her daily prayers kneeling in front of the parrot. After all, another name for the Holy Ghost is Paraclete, from the Greek for one who consoles, or comforter. The comforter, the giver of tongues: only the lonely could understand the solace. When the glint of the sun falls through the window on Loulou's glass eye, it seems to ignite a spark in the bird that sends the simple woman into ecstatic reveries. At this point, Loulou is really no more than a mass of feathers with a broken wing and batting sprouting from holes eaten by worms. But none of that matters to Félicité. As she finally passes from this world to the next, holding Loulou tightly to her bosom, Félicité thinks she sees a gigantic parrot hovering in the opening heavens above her, welcoming her home.

Is Flaubert mocking Félicité, as she dies clutching a rotting parrot? Is this the final, pathetic act of a simple-minded, emotionally overwrought individual? Perhaps. Perhaps not. Underlying the absurdity of Flaubert's tale is a keen image of the everyman, of the universality of loneliness and the objects we shore up against loss. Of course, not all of these objects are equal. Some are more poignant, more precious than others. Some are sentimental, others tinged with irony. But how we choose to remember the dead and departed is not arbitrary.

Flaubert himself was not immune to the emotive powers of objects. His novels are infused with a tender regard for even the most mundane things: combs, cigar cases, little plush hats. Such simple objects are transfigured into seducers and comforters, fragrant with memories and human longing. Consider that Flaubert's beloved younger sister, Caroline, died tragically just nine weeks after their father's death in 1846. On the morning of the funeral, Flaubert, devastated beyond words, cut a few locks of her hair and had a plaster cast taken of her face and hands. "I saw the great paws of those boors touching her and covering her with plaster," he wrote to his friend Maxime du Camp. At least, he added, "I shall have her hand and her face." From the death mask, Flaubert commissioned a white marble bust, which sat with him through the passing years in his writing room. A month before her death, Caroline had given birth to a baby girl named Caroline. Flaubert nicknamed his little beloved niece Loulou.

Death souvenirs have fallen out of vogue since the nineteenth century. Death is now put away, cleanly and promptly. Any mixing up between dead and living things is a contagion, miscegenation. In contrast, Flaubert's era was not so squeamish. After all, individuals were born and died at home. Death was intimate and

9 Septembre 1919

Perroquet "Amazone

ayant servi à Flaubert
pour écrire le Conte
"Un Cœur Simple"

« Mardi, j'ai eu à déjeuner Pouchet
« et Pennetier. Il y a huit jours,
« j'avais été au Muséum lui
« demander des renseignements
« sur les perroquets, et actuelle-
« ment j'écris devant un "Ama-
« zone" qui se tient sur ma
« table, le bec un peu de coté
et me regardant avec ses
yeux de verre .

Correspondance de Flaubert
Lettre à sa Nièce Juillet 1876
Edit Conard. T. V. p 410

ce perroquet figure dans les Collections du Muséum
(Photo par LeRoy)

frequent. But neither were locks of hair or marble busts thought to be gruesome tokens. Unlike the macabre memento mori of earlier times, nineteenth-century death souvenirs focused attention quite precisely away from the grim realities of death and toward the mourners' own emotional experience and eventually toward comfort and consolation.[3] Take the nineteenth-century vogue of "sleeping beauty" postmortem photography. The dead were posed peacefully, as if merely sleeping. Children were surrounded by flowers or memorialized holding their favorite toy. The suffering of death was eased by sweetness. The same held true of preserved animal companions. The physical remains of the animal were posed and carefully tended to allow mourners to remember the joys of life and the golden companionship.

But postmortem photographs, death masks, locks of hair, and stuffed parrots are not all the same sort of objects. The first two are copies of the departed, captured either by traces of light or reliefs of facial contours; the other two *are* the departed.

Organic materials have the potential to be far more haunting souvenirs than manufactured objects. And haunting is the right word. By staving off the finality of material dissolution, preservation endows bodily souvenirs with an impoverished yet resolute immortality. They literally are the flagrant emotional drama in which all earthly creatures unavoidably share: of life, its inexplicable terminus, and the materiality that remains.

Nothing determines that bodily relics will be desired or, once taken, cherished. They should not exist. They should have been burned, buried, or floated out to sea, but instead they remain. As such, death relics exhibit a strange kind of material longing: a desire to remember in a physical, tangible way, a longing, if you will, to *possess* remembrance itself. It is a longing that easily becomes incontinent. Or perhaps it is inherently incontinent, saturated by languishing, overwrought emotions that can only be soothed by eternal proximity. And certainly few of us would find emotional solace in a stuffed parrot eaten by worms. But then, Félicité's fanatical hold on the dead, glossing over all material collapse, is as fictional as it is oddly touching. Part devotional object, part wistful souvenir of better days, Loulou, for Félicité, becomes hope and love materialized. Such is the potency of all objects of remembrance: they become whatever we need them to be.

Memories may make the souvenir, but the object's physical form is never irrelevant. While both Flaubert's lock and Félicité's parrot are bodily relics, locks of hair and stuffed parrots are not the same sort of thing. To state the obvious, one is a whole bird; the other is a piece of a human. Part versus whole. Human versus

31 The stuffed parrot that allegedly perched on Gustave Flaubert's desk as he wrote "Un coeur simple," 1876. © Roger-Viollet / The Image Works.

animal. Why the difference? Is whole more affective than part, or is part more eloquent than whole?

All souvenirs arise from the insatiable demands of nostalgia: the longing to look back and inward into our past, to recount the same stories again and again, to speak wistfully. But nostalgia cannot exist without loss, and souvenirs are always only fragments of increasingly distant lives and experiences. Yet fragments sometimes speak more clearly than wholes. "Their very fragmentariness helps evoke the past," David Lowenthal writes in a meditation on architectural preservation; "engaging the viewer's imagination, fragments activate myriad connections between what is and what was."[4] Ruins evoke the unstoppable passage of time. Ruins have lived. They have struggled with life, and the struggle is everywhere materially apparent. Fragmented, partial, incomplete, all souvenirs are in a sense ruins, never fully recouping but always evoking the past, encouraging nostalgic dreams of significance. The souvenir is a potent fragment that erases the distinction between what actually was and what we dream or desire it to have been.[5]

What, then, does the whole souvenir evoke? "The whole souvenir": the phrase is almost a contradiction. Does it still conjure up the same tales of nostalgic longing? Is it possible to remember someone who is still fully physically present, albeit rather stiffly? It is one of those arcane philosophical questions, at once profound and profoundly trite, but it is a question worth keeping in mind. As there are many species of sadness, there are many shades of remembrance, some more focused on loss, others leaning toward tribute or regret. The remembrance at work with stuffed pets is peculiar quite precisely because, with the powers of preservation, the departed is not wholly departed. In fact, as Loulou exemplifies, the departed is still present enough to offer comfort to those left behind.

In a sense, this strange duality of presence and absence characterizes all taxidermy. The animal is dead but not gone, refashioned but fundamentally still available. As this book has argued, the various genres of taxidermy were all created to satisfy a variety of longings for continued connection. The desire to capture beautiful forms, to tell stories about their importance, or to offer lessons in natural history all fundamentally shape how the resulting animal-things will be perceived and understood. But of all the longings so far considered, none has been motivated by personal loss and teary-eyed partings. Most of the animals have been anonymous creatures that were either shot in the wild or died in zoos. Perhaps a few were named and appreciated as individuals, but none were loved as friends.

Stuffed pets make up a particularly strange genre of taxidermy. With all other genres, the act of preservation is focused on capturing the animal's physicality, not its personality. Even habitat dioramas exhibiting a species' typical behaviors do not accentuate the individuality of the particular animals on view, except in rare instances such as the Tsavo lions. In contrast, animal companions, mascots, and animal stars and heroes are preserved because of *who* the animal was, not *what* it was, that is, not because of its species or beautiful plumage, not because it was in any way rare, strange, or notable, but because it was loved as a companion. And, as with all beloved companions, the physical appearance (whether in terms of beauty, species, or race) is largely irrelevant to whether or not it was loved in life, which begs the question: what precisely is being remembered with the stuffed pet?

The question is not easily answered. The sort of emotionality at work turns away from a pure remembrance of the departed (after all, the beast is still present) and veers dangerously toward an enchantment characterized by excessive sentimental attachment that refuses to be broken by death. And for this reason, perhaps, it is not too surprising that the vogue of preserving deceased pets reached its height during the Victorian period, an era cluttered by lockets filled with hair and other such sentimental pieces of mourning jewelry, which were valued as comforting surrogates of lost loves.

ENCHANTED WHOLES

Loulou is a fanciful exception to the rule: stuffed pets are rarely transfigured into the Holy Ghost. But Flaubert's depiction of Félicité's tender regard for Loulou despite his gradual physical dissolution is hardly a fictional conceit. The softer, more sentimental emotions cultivated during the nineteenth century also nurtured a new passion for pets and pet keeping. As luck would have it, the soaring popularity of pets coincided with the nineteenth century's obsession with the preservative powers of taxidermy.

Pet keeping had always delighted the privileged upper classes and those who could afford animal care and food for no other reason than companionship and affection. Royalty and courtiers were captivated by exotic pets, frequently posing for portraits with a monkey or parrot imported from distant lands. In the sixteenth and seventeenth centuries pet keeping began to establish itself among the middle

"She was there! But she was a corpse."

—ALFRED HITCHCOCK, *Psycho* (1960)

classes. In urban areas, pet dogs, monkeys, parrots, tortoises, canaries, otters, rabbits, and squirrels multiplied, and in the eighteenth century, as sympathies widened, there were pet hares, mice, thrushes, cuckoos, and even pet hedgehogs, bats, and toads.[6] But it was not until the nineteenth century that the cult of pet keeping reached full swing.

Pet keeping rapidly developed into a mainstream passion in the nineteenth century. Inviting dogs, cats, and birds into the home and even the bedroom was a solace against the tensions and tedium of daily life. But pet keeping was—and has remained—a means for owners to communicate who they were, socially, culturally, and stylistically speaking: our animal companions have always allowed us to talk about ourselves without saying a word.[7] By the mid-nineteenth century, dogs in particular had become the cliché accessories to modern life, and dog breeds continued to mushroom throughout that century and into the next. In 1788 the French naturalist George-Louis Leclerc de Buffon described fourteen breeds. By the end of the nineteenth century, more than two hundred breeds could be distinguished: sheepdogs, Great Danes, bulldogs, collies, proliferating subbreeds of poodles and lapdogs, all reflecting their owners' class, style, and sensibilities. Dog-care manuals, canine coiffure, combs, embroidered collars, and pet cemeteries filled with sentimental epitaphs likewise emerged to complete the transformation of the dog from a working companion into an essential domestic figure. And into this denatured world of fantasy and control, add the popularity of having a deceased pet's head mounted on a plaque, trophy style.

Although stuffed pets were immensely popular in the nineteenth century, the practice was not universally appreciated. Alfred Bonnardot, inventor of the pet-care book in France, was certainly not a fan. "This mode of remembrance repulses me," he wrote in 1856. "It is a sad thing to see one's little companion whose look was once so lively and bright forever immobile and staring. Moreover, if one kept all his successors this way, one would end by having a somewhat cluttered and encumbered museum." The mode of remembrance Bonnardot recommended was a photograph or painting taken of the pet "at the time of his brilliant youth," although just its coat, Bonnardot added, "as long as it had not lost its silkiness," was also a nice piece of memorabilia.[8]

In England the mania for pets and for preserving their carcasses was a source of constant spoof and lampooning by satirical newspapers like *Punch* and *Fun*. A weekly series titled "About Taxidermy," published by *Fun* in 1882, gives a good jab

ABOUT TAXIDERMY.—5. THE LIFELIKE PET.

How beautiful and touching a trait of human character is the untiring affection for, and belief in the lifelikeness of, the effigy of a departed pet!

Fun knows a lady who had her pet spaniel stuffed. Honouring the above-named touching trait, whenever Fun enters that lady's room, he starts in violent bodily fear, and exclaims, "W-w-will he b-b-bite?" on which the lady regularly and reassuringly says, "Oh, no! he isn't alive. You would never suppose he was stuffed, now, would you?"

"Look!" she says; "I'll put him in the garden, and you notice how he terrifies all the cats!"

And when Fun and that lady are hoary and decrepit, and that pet will not hold together much longer, Fun in his gallantry will still exclaim, "W-w-will he b-b-bite?" and the lady will still believe in its lifelikeness and put it out to terrify the cats!

at the rising fashion of stuffed pets and the poor quality of Victorian preservation. In "Episode 5: The Lifelike Pet," the character Fun exclaims, "How beautiful and touching a trait of human character is the untiring affection for, and belief in the lifelikeness of, the effigy of a departed pet!" Fun himself, in his jester's suit, encounters a stuffed pet spaniel seated on a stool in a lady's parlor. Oblivious to his unnaturally bulging glass eyes and patches, his owner proudly exclaims, "You would never suppose he was stuffed, now, would you?" Even many years later, when both the lady and Fun are decrepit and the dog's eyes have fallen out and his paws are sprouting straw, the lady still believes in his lifelikeness. The joke is not only her delusional faith that the dog is physically unchanged. Far more nonsensical is her insistence that her pet still exudes a lively persona: "you notice how he terrifies all the cats."[9]

What exactly is being remembered? The pet itself, or the good times the owner enjoyed while her spaniel was alive? We remember departed companions because of their spirit, their charisma and personality. Once dead, this liveliness departs, and all that remains is a husk. Preserving that husk and claiming that it is still the creature is a disturbing confusion of corporeality for presence, or worse: it suggests that what has departed is not particularly missed. As *Fun* makes clear, a stuffed husk can be just as amusing as the living spaniel it once was.[10]

Jokes aside, there is no reason to suppose that the loss of an animal companion is less difficult for any particular individual than the loss of a human friend. Our pets share our emotional lives; we allow them the sentiments, intelligence, and dignity usually reserved for our fellow humans. Some might argue that the desire to stuff a pet—to refuse to be bodily parted by death—reveals a heartfelt, heartbroken attachment that surpasses the typical human-pet relationship: this animal was truly, deeply loved. Yet this sort of thinking presents a frightening categorical confusion. If the pet *were* human, taxidermy would be unthinkable. Indeed, taxidermy, like eating meat, marks an unbridgeable chasm between humans and other animals. In the regular course of things, we do not stuff or eat our own species.

However, in the regular course of things neither do we eat our domestic animal companions. In fact, a cannibalism taboo surrounds which animals can and cannot be eaten based on their intimacy in domestic life.[11] In the Western world, we can eat a cow or a pig but not a cat or a dog, and the idea that dogs are dinner in other parts of the world is horrific. It is not that cats and dogs taste bad but that cats and dogs are species that have been designated "almost human" and part of family life.[12] And, perversely or not, it is *because* they are part of family life that we sometimes have them stuffed.

CANINE LOVE

The popularity of preserved pets waned in the twentieth century. In fact, many taxidermists today are wary of taking on pets precisely because of the intimacy and depth of emotion surrounding the animal. Sometimes a bereft owner reconsiders preservation with a calmer mind after a few months and refuses to claim or pay for the preserved pet. Or sometimes the owner is horrified that the animal no longer resembles its former self. As with our human companions, it is the little quirks and expressions that make a pet a uniquely loveable character, and a taxidermist unacquainted with the animal in life must struggle to capture the animal's idiosyncratic charisma in death.

However, a new technology of deep-freezing and dehydration has in great part replaced traditional taxidermy for pets. The process involves freezing the animal in a vacuum chamber. Frozen moisture is slowly extracted from the animal in a gaseous state, leaving the tissue, bones, and all internal organs intact and unaltered. Once all moisture (the source of all organic decay) is removed, the animal is returned to room temperature, perfectly and eternally preserved. The process is not quick. Small animals require anywhere from six to ten weeks, while large dogs may take as long as six months. But advocates claim that the procedure produces results vastly superior to the traditional method of rebuilding the creature almost from scratch. In addition, freeze-drying allows the owner to choose the exact pose in which the pet will be immortalized, and—perhaps best of all—many owners are comforted by the thought that their pets have not been skinned. With the artistic interpretation and craftsmanship of taxidermy eliminated, freeze-drying gives the impression that here is the whole pet as it once was, complete with bones and guts. As with traditional taxidermy, eyeballs are replaced with glass replicas.

Pet Preservations, a Colorado company that freeze-dries pets, and Perpetual Pet, another freeze-drying company whose slogan is "the perfect plan for the perfect pet," have posted letters of appreciation from their customers on their websites. The letters narrate tales of love and friendship during life, total devastation after a pet's death, and joy at having the pet home again. Being "together" always

The pet can be—and usually is—loved as an individual creature, distinct from notions of species or any other category. A pet is a pet first, an animal second.

—ERICA FUDGE, *Animal* (2002), 32

and forever is a constant refrain of owners. One writer describes unbearable emotional pain and an inability to put her beloved Lacie, a fluffy white Maltese, into "the cold dark worm infested hole in the ground" her husband had dug for Lacie's burial: "My heart told me we couldn't part this way." Several months later, after summoning the courage to open the box from Pet Preservations with beloved Lacie inside, the owner was overjoyed. "I can't describe the realm of emotions that overwhelmed me, from spooky to a sense of peace and love. . . . I couldn't take my eyes off of her. After a couple of hours I began to brush her and talk to her like I used to. To most of you this story sounds very strange. But to me, I believe Lacie never wanted to leave my side in spirit or body."[13]

Other letters describe comfort in the process itself, in knowing that a preserved pet is not simply a skin shell: "We were so distraught when our darling Jenny passed away. We did not want to bury her and lose her forever, and we did not want to have her 'outsides' put on over a form as they do in taxidermy. We wanted our whole kitty to be with us forever. It was a blessing to have found your website and the services that you offer. We love having our dearest little one with us in our home. Seeing her each and every day, sleeping so sweetly has eased our anguish over a life that was much too short."[14] A whole kitty forever: the enchantment is complete.

The letters express a strange relationship with these animal-things: the actual creature is preserved precisely to alleviate the owner's sense of loss of the creature. This is the whole souvenir at its emotionally perverse extreme. At the first stab of sadness, the pet is always there to comfort, to be stroked and cuddled until the sadness of loss eases. As the owner of Choko, a Bichon Frise, wrote to Pet Preservations, "I am able to see my beautiful precious dog every day, & I am able to hold her & pet her. . . . I can see that she's safe; her presence comforts me."[15] What sort of longing is this—the material remains of a pet becoming a consoler to a grief-stricken owner? In a sense, Choko encapsulates the same enchantment as Loulou. By glossing over the inconvenience of death while nevertheless always highlighting the trauma of loss, both parrot and Bichon Frise erase their owner's pain and, in a sense, remove the need for memory. The transfiguration of pet into heavenly comfort has a particular charm in fiction. In reality, it is an unsettling exhibition of excessive sentimental attachment.

The real proof of a whole souvenir's enchantment comes with a continued desire to touch. Taxidermy might endow creatures with a peculiar second life but never with pristine immortality, and aging skins cannot possibly improve the remembrance of a beloved animal companion. Old taxidermy gets dirty. Skin becomes brittle and cracks, especially the delicate skin around the eyes, lips, and muzzle. The vibrancy of fur and feathers fades in sunlight. Perhaps a few teeth fall out. Lumbering along for decades in a semi-immortal state, gathering dust in the corner, surely the creature is not thrown away when it gets musty. But what happens to the perpetual pet when the owner herself dies? Several clients of Pet Preservations have thought about this. When her beloved raccoon Suggie died, Dana C. had him preserved with "the technology that will allow you to be with me always," she writes in a letter to Suggie. "I didn't want to get you taxidermied because I want you to be you.... Not your fur on a Styrofoam frame. When I look at your picture and ache so to touch your fur, I am able to. When it is time for me to go, you will be buried with me. We will be together forever."[16] Lacie the Maltese will also be buried with her owner when the time comes.

While all taxidermy transforms animal vitality into a material thing, perpetual pets take the process one step further: the material thing is imbued with deeply personal living memories of the animal and its vivacity and charisma. Pets are not preserved in order to ease their journey into the afterlife or to capture some spiritual essence. They are stuffed so that their owners might find solace. One creature's individuality is transfigured into another creature's indulgent desire for a tangible remembrance. Refusing to be bodily parted by death, this longing is the ultimate proof of ownership.

An impressive number of deceased animal mascots, famous friends, stars, and heroes have been preserved. Just the briefest list includes Trigger (Roy Rogers's sidekick Palomino), Jumbo (the elephant star of P. T. Barnum's circus), Dolly the cloned sheep, Top (Dante Gabriel Rossetti's pet wombat), Grip (one of Charles Dickens's ravens and the avian muse for Edgar Allan Poe), and Phar Lap (the Australian thoroughbred legend). Perhaps the animals that have been most frequently preserved are dogs. Some were heroes in life, while others were champion athletes or even celebrities; that is, they were stuffed because they exhibited admirable characteristics that are valued in all animals, humans or otherwise. If Choko and Lacie were stuffed to satisfy a surfeit of emotion, canine heroes, movie stars, and athletes are preserved for public remembrance. In a sense, to see a stuffed dog is always to know that a significant biography lurks behind the creature. Whether

33 The dogs of Gallery 6 in the Natural History Museum, London. Photo © Natural History Museum, London.

posed for posterity in a museum or in a private home, the dog was respected as an individual and not just a species. Or, to put it another way, to see a stuffed dog is to see the underbelly of doggy love.

Some dogs are displayed in museums because they exhibited exceptional heroism, whether voluntarily or not. At Moscow's Memorial Museum of Astronautics, visitors can see the dogs Belka and Strelka, the first animals to survive orbital flight. (Laika, onboard Sputnik 2 in 1957, was the first animal to go into orbit, although she did not survive the journey.) In 1960, Sputnik 5 was launched, with Strelka and Belka inside, along with a gray rabbit, forty mice, two rats, flies, and a number of plants and fungi. After a day in orbit, the landing capsule returned to earth with all passengers alive and well. Belka and Strelka are in separate glass cases, both rather wistfully posed gazing upward toward space. At the Cleveland Museum of Natural History, the Siberian husky Balto is on display. Balto was the lead dog on the final leg of a desperate journey in the winter of 1925 to carry the diphtheria antitoxin into the icebound town of Nome, Alaska. The extraordinary thousand-kilometer run—through blizzards, across a frozen inlet, and in temperatures that dipped below minus sixty degrees—made Balto a national hero, and he has also been commemorated in several movies, books, and a bronze statue in New York's Central Park.[17]

Dogs are also sometimes preserved because they exuded charismatic star power. For example, alongside Trigger, Bullet the Wonder Dog also starred in the Roy Rogers Western television series. Both Trigger and Bullet were on display at the Roy Rogers and Dale Evans Museum, along with a wide variety of memorabilia from Rogers's life and times.[18] Owney the stray mutt turned postal mascot can be seen at the National Postal Museum in Washington, D.C. As a puppy, Owney wandered into the Albany post office in 1888 and began traveling across the country with the mail. Since no train ever derailed while he was a passenger, he was adopted as a mail mascot. In 1895 Owney even made a round-the-world trip, traveling with mailbags to Asia and Europe. But Owney grew irritable with age. He bit a reporter and was shot on June 11, 1897. He is posed wearing his custommade jacket, adorned with all the dog tags he was given on his travels.

And then there are the exceptional athletes and champions. At the Natural History Museum in Tring, several champion English greyhound racers can be seen. Mick the Miller was idolized by British greyhound race goers and won nineteen consecutive races in the 1930s, while Fullerton won all but two of his thirty-three races in the 1890s. The dogs are part of a rather unusual exhibit known as the Dog Collection, which includes eighty-eight dogs of various breeds. Almost all of the dogs were champions of their breed and kennel club winners. For example, Brownie the Pomeranian was the winner of eight championships and eighty first prizes in her breed. Marquis of Lorne, a Scottish deerhound, won continuous prizes in the 1890s. Most of the dogs date to the beginning of the twentieth century and were collected by zoologist Richard Lydekker in order to create historical documentation of the rapidly expanding number of breeds and to offer the public a visual education in selective breeding. The dogs are posed in the classic posture of a natural history specimen—standing and attentive but with a neutral gaze—although several dogs are lying down or sitting and a few, including a black and tan spaniel named Nina Advocate, are displayed trophy style, with just their heads on a plaque.[19]

The Dog Collection is displayed in a long glass gallery case with a pebbly floor. The length of the case and the expansive sheet of glass allow most of the dogs to be seen in a single look. To see so many dogs together, all immortally immobile, all staring out at visitors, is disconcerting. Despite the enormous number of other species on display at Tring, the dogs stand apart, and not merely because they were champions and athletes. Part of the reason that dogs are not regularly on display in natural history museums is that no one breed could offer a typical representation of the species. From feral dogs and dachshunds to teacup poodles and Cuban mastiffs, dogs are too astonishingly variable to fit into the regular exhibition constraints of most museums. No one dog could represent all dogs in the way that a Grevy's zebra could stand in for all zebras.

In fact, dogs, cats, cows, horses, pigs, sheep, and other domesticated species are only rarely on display in natural history museums, in part because such creatures are not naturally occurring species, untouched by human culture. Their various shapes, sizes, aptitudes, and abilities have been fashioned and refined by selective breeding. And when they do appear, we know one thing for certain: they were not hunted. They either died naturally or were euthanized in old age. In either case, the animals lived, died, and were valued within a human world. And we know they were valued. Otherwise they would not have been preserved.

However, from a less pragmatic perspective, a preserved dog will always stand out as something different. Of all our domestic companions, dogs are among the most universally loved, and perhaps for this reason there is no more troubling animal-thing than a stuffed dog. Taxidermy is driven by a longing to hold on to what could or should not otherwise persist, and all taxidermy exudes a disquieting liveliness within death. But that uncanniness is necessarily heightened with dogs and other close domestic companions.

Most pet owners would never consider having their pet preserved. The emotional intimacy we share with our domestic companions ensures that they are never "just" animals. They are friends, and the transition of friend into animal-thing is unsettling and perhaps even unseemly. While the emotionality surrounding perpetual pets makes them particularly disturbing, even the dogs in the Dog Collection at Tring are disquieting. Dogs are our companion species, our ancient partners in work and life, and probably humans' first nonhuman friends. Perhaps the human-dog bond is too intimate for such postmortem bodily invasion. Or perhaps the uncanniness of stuffed dogs arises because most viewers know the manners and movements of dogs far more intimately than the behavior of almost any other creature. We know exactly how they would shake themselves awake from immortal death.

The queasiness that preserved dogs and other stuffed domestic familiars arouse in most pet owners raises emotional and ethical uncertainties about taxidermy in general. Why do we perceive a stuffed dog as something different from a stuffed weasel, hummingbird, or lion? What does this disquietude reveal about our attitudes toward taxidermy in general?

As animal rights activists, academics, and, more recently, animal artists remind us, our relationships with animals are full of contradictions and inconsistencies. Pet keeping is a particularly powerful expression of cross-species intimacy and potentially highlights our mistreatment of other, less familiar, less loved creatures. Pets are friends first and animals second. We invite them into our homes and we are horrified when they are treated with nonchalance.

Several contemporary animal artists use dogs, cats, bunnies, and other cute domesticated species in their works as inflammatory provocations to examine precisely such use and misuse of animals. Perhaps the most notorious pet artist is Katinka Simonse, known by her artist name, Tinkebell. A Dutch performance artist and provocateur, Tinkebell became infamous for making her own cat into a handbag, and for creating *Popple*, a reversible cat-dog purse (fig. 34). Her work is unnerving, jarring, and unswervingly focused on drawing attention to the hypocrisies in our relationships with different species. Why is a cat purse more distasteful than a cow purse? Why are we outraged when the skin of a little dog is made into a utilitarian object?

And viewers have certainly been outraged. After she produced the handbag, an artwork she titled *My Dearest Cat Pinkeltje*, in 2004, Tinkebell was overwhelmed with thousands of vehement, explicative-laden, hate-filled e-mails, mostly in response to the artist's transparent admission that she personally euthanized her dying cat (rather than leaving the task to a veterinarian), skinned it, and reworked her pet into a practical and handy thing. Admittedly, the work is designed to incite controversy, but the e-mails Tinkebell received are violent in the extreme, variously threatening to maim, torture, skin, rape, and kill her, rip off her head, disembowel her, and cause unimaginable suffering and pain.

Fascinated by the outrage, Tinkebell, in collaboration with Dutch artist Coralie Vogelaar, researched the identity of the senders, hunting out intimate details that the senders themselves posted online. Most of the writers were American teenagers, although the e-mails were tracked back to men and women of all ages from across the world. The result was *Dearest Tinkebell*, published in 2009. The massive volume is an uncomfortable combination of shocking hatred and the commonplace. Each e-mail is presented in violent hot pink and accompanied by any information Tinkebell and Vogelaar could find: name, age, e-mail address, telephone number, likes and hobbies, and photographs of the writers posted on Facebook and MySpace.

By turning her own cat into a handbag and transforming a cute kitten and lap dog into a reversible purse, Tinkebell certainly succeeds in highlighting the vast discrepancy in the ways we love or use different species. There is no reason why a cow cannot be deeply loved, but Tinkebell's work is successful because she uses the iconic creatures of domestic companionship. A cow bag is an everyday occurrence. A cat bag warrants thousands of death threats. But while Tinkebell's work highlights the hypocrisy in valuing the life of a cat over the life of a cow, it also emphasizes the importance of deciphering the longing behind any particular piece of taxidermy. *My Dearest Cat Pinkeltje* was horrifying to many viewers not simply because it was a cat but because it was the artist's own cat and presumably a once-loved companion. The idea that a pet owner could viscerally manipulate her own pet into a conceptual project was simply too much: it is not just the species that causes discomfort but also the sentimental attachment.

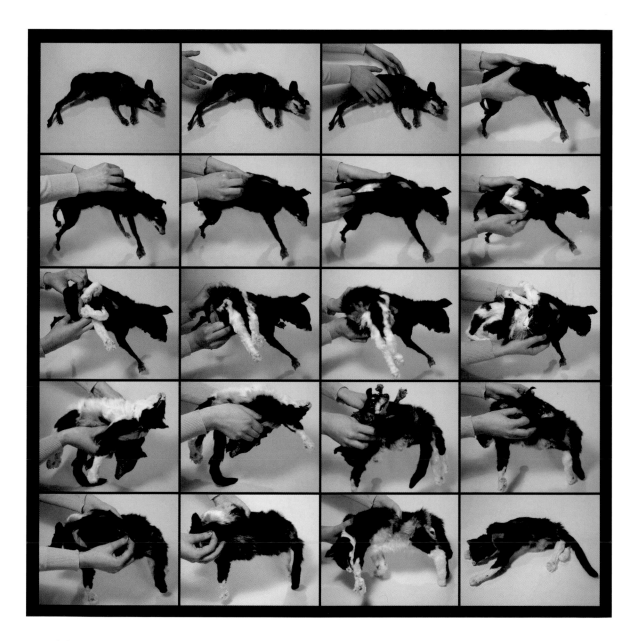

34 Tinkebell, *Popple*, 2008. Taxidermied cat
    and dog, felt, fake eyes, zipper. The name of
    Tinkebell's *Popple* is derived from a series of
    plush animals manufactured in the 1980s.
    The toys are transformed into balls by
    inverting the animals into pouches on their
    backs. Photo courtesy of Torch Gallery,
    Amsterdam.

While exceptionally strange and disturbing, Tinkebell's work nevertheless draws us back to the fundamentals of taxidermy. The meaning and materiality of any piece of taxidermy are always dependent on the species preserved and the motivating desire.

All taxidermy is caught in a web of interactions between culture, desire, and nature. It is always an unsettling fusion of animal form and human longing. Stuffed pets accentuate the uncanniness of all taxidermy, but they also highlight the importance of understanding the longing that inspires the making of any piece of taxidermy. Was the creature preserved so as to document its strangeness or in order to showcase its spectacular beauty? Is it being used for a political statement or to present a philosophy of how the natural world fits together? Or do the longings take a darker shade by transmuting animal flesh into souvenirs of human deeds and desires? Perhaps more important, stuffed pets reveal that the particular longing always leaves its trace in the resulting animal-thing. Longing is always deeply inscribed.

THE TEXTURE OF MEMORY

Much has been written on the hollowness of souvenirs, their intrinsic sadness and the ultimate futility of collecting things in an effort to remember places and events. Perhaps none is more poignant than that which is plucked from "nature," that thing that once was living and now is dead or redundant—a shadow of what it once was in life.

—BRYNDÍS SNÆBJÖRNSDÓTTIR, MARK WILSON, AND LUCY BYATT, introduction to *Nanoq: Flat Out and Bluesome; A Cultural Life of Polar Bears* (2006), 14

There is one animal souvenir that is redolent with the tragedy of loss yet lacks the eeriness of private sentiment. It is not a souvenir of personal remembrance but rather of biological commemoration: the extinct species. Taxidermied extinct species are the ultimate object of sad remembrance. Their presence is haunting. They exist outside time, apart from the workings of nature. Their death and stillness is of a different shade than most other pieces of taxidermy precisely because there is no wild liveliness with which to compare their immobility. They are forever caught in a melancholic aura. Perhaps the saddest objects in the world, unknowingly, unwillingly, they have become celebrities, albeit with a bleak and sorrowful fame.

Most creatures that went extinct before the twentieth century linger only as stuffed hides, if that. Without artistic taxidermy, all we would have to remember the great auk, the Labrador duck, the passenger pigeon, the Cape lion, the quagga, and all other extinct species would be a drawing, a piece of skin, perhaps a few pickled bits and pieces. Such maudlin fragments are tragic reminders that an entire species has disappeared from our earth forever. With taxidermy, at least we have some notion of the size, proportions, and presence of the species. With recently extinct creatures, perhaps some film footage exists, or at least a few photographs. Moving pictures certainly convey a creature's behaviors and movements. Photographs offer an idea of living expressions and poses. But only the actual creature can offer an encounter between you and a beast, an encounter that will never again occur without taxidermy or, for most of us, outside a natural history museum. If taxidermied extinct species spotlight previous generations' excessive collecting practices, they also ironically underscore the importance of documenting nature's forms.

As the decades and centuries pass, those lonely beasts will increasingly show their age. Taxidermy may preserve skins beyond their natural course, but it does not offer immortality. Straw pokes through. Rumps crack. Jagged tears appear as skins get older and older. Yet these creatures will never be allowed to decompose. They will never be discarded or disregarded. Any museum lucky enough to possess extinct birds or beasts will surely cherish them, ensuring their survival through the afterlife. The creatures will persist for as long as materially possible, lingering as cautionary tales, immortal and musty, bereft of their clan.

While certainly not as tragic, all old taxidermy from previous centuries is caught in a similar atmosphere of surreal timelessness. Old taxidermy exudes an aura totally unlike modern mounts, with their clean fur and uncrusted eyes. But it is not simply that old taxidermy is often cracked or malformed, or that new taxidermy is more skillfully prepared. As obvious as it sounds, old taxidermy is old, very old. It is an impossibly old creature—or at least its skin—lingering behind glass for tens of decades and sometimes more, and the passage of time is everywhere visibly palpable, if such a dual sense exists. Just as the worn surfaces of architectural ruins convey a tactile knowledge of their textured history, the torn skin on a gemsbok's neck gaping straw and clay, a Tasmanian devil's opaque black eyes set in his near-mummified face, the sun-bleached face and beak of a blue and yellow macaw, all on display at the Harvard Natural History Museum, likewise appeal to our sense of touch, but it is not a texture we need to handle in order to understand. We know instinctively what cracked, century-old skin will feel like. It is the feel of time itself traced in organic matter.

Natural history museums with eighteenth- and nineteenth-century roots have almost become time capsules themselves, and their animals are like portals to another epoch, portals that have almost closed, almost but not quite. Most museums are no longer collecting specimens for public display with the same vigor as their predecessors, which means that most of the displayed animals are decades old. They linger from an era that valued them as startling documentations of nature, yet our current age is not altogether sure what to think of taxidermy. But while the creatures at the Harvard Museum may be cultural and intellectual souvenirs, they are not merely old, inanimate husks. Behind the glass, set against bright blue, vermilion, and aqua-green walls, the creatures are flooded with light from above. The cabinets glow with a decrepit beauty of forgotten relics. The face of a tarsier is painted opaque pink. The slender loris staring out at the world, with dusty eyes and disproportionately slender arms and legs, is "like a banana on stilts," the label tells us. A ruffed lemur with black-painted lips scowls skyward. A diminutive British weasel is small enough to curl into a man's outstretched palm. Enduring, almost forgotten, from a time when natural history was a passionate pursuit and taxidermy was well loved, these creatures, dead and stuffed before even our grandparents were born, have endured beyond their age and almost beyond their scientific usefulness.

Out of step with time, old collections create an enchanting sense of secrecy and stillness. In a preserved world set apart from the scuttling speed of modern life, they offer a quiet look at nature's most beautiful forms. In fact, their tattiness, their leathery faces, gormless smiles, and broken fingers make these beasts even more visible. Most modern taxidermy is formed on prefabricated molds, which may or may not be altered by taxidermists to match the particularities of the skin. However, underlying each piece of nineteenth-century taxidermy is a body form expressly made for its particular skin. Each was uniquely prepared and is uniquely expressive. In contrast to the homogenously pristine perfection of recent taxidermy, every ancient specimen is uniquely old, uniquely scruffy and tattered. The dilapidated delicacy of old taxidermy draws us in to look at the animals more closely in order to see their individuality, perhaps to notice the soft brown eyelashes and the downy chin of a Verreaux's sifaka at the Field Museum in Chicago, preserved more than a hundred years ago, or to realize that the aye-aye's middle finger has shriveled to nothing more than a curl of smoke. In a sense, old taxidermy stresses the burden of looking at these animals, slowly and carefully, and makes us appreciate their forms both as individuals and as members of their species.

This might all sound overly sentimental, and perhaps it is. These animals are not living. They no longer have feelings or wants or urges or desires. Any pathos we might read into their inanimate husks is a romanticized human projection. However,

35 Martin d'Orgeval, *Touched by Fire*, 2008.
Photograph. Photo courtesy of the artist.

as antiques and relics, these old, lingering beasts deserve as much respect as anything else—watches, photographs, books, and bowls—that has endured for centuries. I would argue that these beasts deserve more respect, because despite the death, despite the taxidermy, they remain pieces of the creaturely existence that all animals share. And perhaps for this reason, the fire that raged through the famous nineteenth-century collection at Deyrolle in Paris on the morning of February 1, 2008, was a tragic loss not only of irreplaceable and invaluable ancient beasts but also of some part of ourselves and our longings for enduring connection.

In 1831 Jean-Baptiste Deyrolle, a renowned entomologist, founded the taxidermy establishment on the Rue de Bac, near St. Germain-des-Pres. For the next 177 years, the emporium had been an icon of dilettantish eccentricity of the sort rarely seen anymore: a black bear curled up with snowy white lambs, moose, tigers, chickens, and an albino emu gathered together around a nineteenth-century cabinet filled with shells and other exotic specimens. Deyrolle housed hundreds of thousands of butterflies, beetles, and birds collected in the nineteenth century. The fire destroyed them all. Ninety percent of the shop's collection, including most of the animals and insects, was reduced to cinders. A strong acrid smell of burned hair, horns, hooves, and wings assaulted all who entered the building the morning after.[20]

The photographic images of Deyrolle's charred animals and insects taken by Martin d'Orgeval just a few days after the fire are haunting and unforgettable. They read like crime scenes, with broken furniture and burned cabinets strewn on the floors, crumbling walls, and the creatures of a devastated ark. A zebra with a burned back, the skin of its head hanging limply, is posed against a blistered black wall. It stands on a natural history cabinet whose contents are no more. There are images of blackened butterflies, burned parrots, and a sacrificial bear with a scorched belly and a Deyrolle sign hanging from his charred, outstretched arm. "That which Man and science had taken from the natural cycle of life and death and fixed forever for our wide-eyed pleasure was partially brought back to its original destiny: the fading and disappearance that awaits any creature. Time had been made to stand still, and nature had reclaimed its rights."[21] The bleak beauty left by the fire is shocking and entrancing. The animals never seemed more alive.

The tragedy at Deyrolle is reminiscent of specimens purposefully burned by the Saffron Walden Museum because they were believed to be useless, musty Victorian relics. The blackened animals provide a counterpoint to the white bears that inspired Snæbjörnsdóttir and Wilson's exhibition of ten white polar bears in a clean, white gallery space. The destruction reminds us that these animals from a previous generation form part of our heritage of how we came to know the natural world. And perhaps it offers a searing visual metaphor of our relationship with taxidermy as a whole. All taxidermied animals have been transfigured by the fervor of human longing. Their intrinsic animal magnetism impels us to look but also causes us to regret their deaths. The animals are never just cultural objects but are rather provocative animal-things imbued with both the longing to capture animal life immortally and the longing to see the living animal again. The burned beasts at Deyrolle, charred almost beyond recognition, offer an overwhelming spectacle of beauty, death, tribute, love, and immortal longing. And so it is with all taxidermy.

NOTES

INTRODUCTION

1. Bryndís Snæbjörnsdóttir and Mark Wilson, "Provenances," in *Nanoq: Flat Out and Bluesome; A Cultural Life of Polar Bears*, exh. cat. (London: Black Dog, 2006), 98–127.

2. Bryndís Snæbjörnsdóttir, Mark Wilson, and Lucy Byatt, introduction to Snæbjörnsdóttir and Wilson, *Nanoq*, 17.

3. See Susan Stewart, *On Longing: Narratives of the Miniature, the Gigantic, the Souvenir, the Collection* (Durham: Duke University Press, 1993), 145.

4. Stephen R. Kellert, "The Biological Basis for Human Values of Nature," in *The Biophilia Hypothesis*, ed. Stephen R. Kellert and Edward O. Wilson (Washington, D.C.: Island Press, 1993), 42.

CHAPTER 1

1. Sir Hans Sloane, *A Voyage to the Islands Madera, Barbados, Nieves, S. Christophers and Jamaica, with the Natural History*, 2 vols. (London, 1701, 1725), 1:1346–47.

2. Quoted in Arthur MacGregor, "The Life, Character, and Career of Sir Hans Sloane," in *Sir Hans Sloane: Collector, Scientist, Antiquary, Founding Father of the British Museum*, ed. Arthur MacGregor (London: British Museum Press, 1994), 12.

3. Sloane, *Voyage to the Islands*, 1:1–29.

4. Zacharias Conrad von Uffenbach, *London in 1710 from the Travels of Zacharias Conrad von Uffenbach*, trans. and ed. W. H. Quarrell and Margaret Mare (London: Faber and Faber, 1934), 185.

5. Sloane's collection grew in great part by donation and from his purchase of his contemporaries' collections whole. See MacGregor, "Life, Character, and Career," 21–29.

6. Juliet Clutton-Brock, "Vertebrate Collections," in MacGregor, *Sir Hans Sloane*, 83–85.

7. MacGregor, "Life, Character, and Career," 31.

8. Not all of Sloane's creatures came from abroad. The Arctic fox, the beaver, and the Bengal crane (which died from swallowing a brass sleeve button) all lived in Sloane's garden for

several years until their unfortunate deaths. The beaver enjoyed particular freedom and was allowed to amble about the garden and swim in the fountain with fish. The elephant died of consumption near Middlesex in the south of England. The patch of lion skin, along with several other pieces of lions, including a stuffed lion whelp, was taken from lions living (and dying) in the royal menagerie housed in the Tower of London since the early thirteenth century.

9. The hermaphroditic monster is described in Lorraine Daston and Katharine Park, *Wonders and the Order of Nature, 1150–1750* (New York: Zone Books, 1998), 177.

10. This image of the known world fringed by wonders and encircled by a sea can be found in Sir John Mandeville's marvelous journal, supposedly written during his Eastern travels between 1322 and 1356: "the earth and sea is round. For it is a commonplace that Jerusalem is in the middle of the earth." See *The Travels of Sir John Mandeville*, trans. C. W. R. D. Moseley (London: Penguin Books, 1983), 129. For further reading on the medieval worldview of a topography of wonders, see Mary B. Campbell, *The Witness and the Other World: Exotic European Travel Writing, 400–1600* (Ithaca: Cornell University Press, 1988), 47–86; Daston and Park, *Wonders and the Order of Nature*, 21–66; and Stephen Greenblatt, *Marvelous Possessions: The Wonder of the New World* (Chicago: University

of Chicago Press, 1991), 26–51.

11. Daston and Park, *Wonders and the Order of Nature*, 33.

12. Quoted in ibid., 32–33.

13. Mandeville, *Travels of Sir John Mandeville*, 113.

14. Such wonders are related in ibid. Colossal diamonds were found in Ethiopia. The pepper shrubs grew on an island off the Indian coast. Self-sacrificing fish and two-headed geese were both found in Ceylon. Blue elephants, apple smellers, and unicorns could be encountered on an island called Pytan in the Far East.

15. Jacques Le Goff, *The Medieval Imagination*, trans. Arthur Goldhammer (Chicago: University of Chicago Press, 1988), 32.

16. The wonders are listed in Gervase of Tilbury's *Otia imperialia*, written in 1210. See Daston and Park, *Wonders and the Order of Nature*, 21–24.

17. Lawrence Weschler, *Mr. Wilson's Cabinet of Wonder: Pronged Ants, Horned Humans, Mice on Toast, and Other Marvels of Jurassic Technology* (New York: Vintage Books, 1996), 80.

18. Greenblatt, *Marvelous Possessions*, 20.

19. This list is aggregated from multiple sources, including Marina Belozerskaya, *The Medici Giraffe and Other Tales of Exotic Animals and Power* (New York: Little, Brown, 2006); Oliver Impey and Arthur MacGregor, eds., *The Origins of Museums: The Cabinet of Curiosities in Sixteenth- and Seventeenth-Century Europe* (Oxford: Clarendon Press, 1985); and John Tradescant, *Musæum Tradescantia-*

num, or A Collection of Rarities Preserved at South-Lambeth Neer London (London, 1656).

20. Krzysztof Pomian, *Collectors and Curiosities: Paris and Venice, 1500–1800,* trans. Elizabeth Wiles-Portier (Cambridge: Polity Press, 1990), 36.

21. Paula Findlen, *Possessing Nature: Museums, Collecting, and Scientific Culture in Early Modern Italy* (Berkeley and Los Angeles: University of California Press, 1996), 41.

22. For further reading on the importance of material things in early modern natural history, see Amy Boesky, "'Outlandish-Fruits': Commissioning Nature for the Museum of Man," *English Literary History* 58, no. 2 (1991); Adalgisa Lugli, "Inquiry as Collection: The Athanasius Kircher Museum in Rome," *RES: Journal of Anthropology and Aesthetics* 12 (1986): 109–25; and Findlen, *Possessing Nature.*

23. Findlen, *Possessing Nature,* 56.

24. See Peter G. Platt, *Reason Diminished: Shakespeare and the Marvelous* (Lincoln: University of Nebraska Press, 1997). The following discussion of Patrizi's theory of wonder is indebted to Platt's analysis.

25. Translated by Platt and quoted in ibid., 15.

26. René Descartes, *Passions of the Soul* (1649), in *The Philosophical Works of Descartes,* trans. Elizabeth S. Haldane and G. R. T. Ross, 2 vols. (London: Cambridge University Press, 1967), 1:358, 362.

27. Aristotle, *Metaphysica,* in *The Works of Aristotle,* trans. William David Ross, ed. William David Ross and John Alexander Smith, 12 vols. (Oxford: Clarendon Press, 1908–52), 8:982.

28. On the Aristotelian tradition of domesticating wonder, see Terence Cave, *Recognitions: A Study in Poetics* (Oxford: Clarendon Press, 1988), 261. See also Daston and Park, *Wonders and the Order of Nature,* particularly chapter 3, "Wonder Among the Philosophers."

29. Lorraine Daston, "Introduction: Speechless," in *Things That Talk: Object Lessons from Art and Science,* ed. Lorraine Daston (New York: Zone Books, 2004), 14–15.

30. Bill Brown, "Thing Theory," *Critical Inquiry* 28, no. 1 (2001): 24.

31. Svetlana Alpers, "The Museum as a Way of Seeing," in *Exhibiting Cultures: The Poetics and Politics of Museum Display,* ed. Ivan Karp and Steven D. Lavine (Washington, D.C.: Smithsonian Institution Press, 1991), 26.

32. To create a shrunken head you must first remove the skin from the skull, ensuring that the lips, nose (the presence of nose hair, some argue, is a sign of an authentic shrunken head), eyelashes, and all hair from the victim's head remain intact and attached. The skin is then smoked over a fire until it contracts to the size of an apple. The most famous shrunken heads are from the Ecuadorian and neighboring Peruvian Amazon. Members of the Jivaro tribe wore the shrunken head, or *tsanta,* of their enemy as a trophy to harness the powers of the victim's

spirit and to enhance the wearer's prestige and power. If the head of a slain warrior could not be obtained, the Jivaro substituted the head of a tree sloth, which many of the tribes in the region believed to be a direct ancestor of humans and endowed with human qualities. Since shrunken heads involve skinning, they are closer in kind to taxidermy than dehydrated mummies are. Yet because the goal is to shrink a quantity of skin that normally covers a human skull down to a fraction of its original size, shrunken heads cannot really be classified as taxidermy.

33. One of the few examples of spiritual taxidermy (that is, lifelike taxidermic representations of animals used in religious ceremonies) I have encountered comes from the Huichol (Wixáritari) peoples in central western Mexico, as described by Carl Lumholtz in *Unknown Mexico: Explorations in the Sierra Madre and Other Regions, 1890–1898* (New York: Dover, 1987). Lumholtz describes several uses of animal preservation among the Huichol, most notably a stuffed squirrel and a skunk used at a *hikuli* (peyote) celebration feast and dance: "Two important participants in the feast, the grey squirrel and the small striped skunk, were placed in the northwest part of the patio. Both were fairly well stuffed, the squirrel in a squatting position. They were tied to sticks stuck firmly in the ground to keep them upright. These animals play a conspicuous part in the cult.

The squirrel, which sees better than ordinary people and guards against evil, is supposed to guide the hikuli-seekers on their way. It is dressed in a curious fashion; around part of its body was wrapped a weather-stained old piece of newspaper, tied up with twine, which also kept the tail in position. There were feathers stuck under the twine, and round the neck were suspended two shining dark-green wing-covers of a beetle, and two small coloured birds of clay bought in Mexico stores. The most extraordinary ornament, however, was a large metal crucifix that hung from its neck down over its stomach" (273).

34. Paul Lawrence Farber, "The Development of Taxidermy and the History of Ornithology," *Isis* 68, no. 4 (1977): 552n8.

35. William Shakespeare, *Romeo and Juliet*, ed. G. Blakemore Evans (Cambridge: Cambridge University Press, 1984), 5.1.42–44.

36. Karl Schulze-Hagen, Frank Steinheimer, Ragnar Kinzelbach, and Christoph Gasser, "Avian Taxidermy in Europe from the Middle Ages to the Renaissance," *Journal für Ornithologie* 144 (2003): 466–67.

37. Quoted in ibid., 471.

38. Ibid.

39. Sarah Lee, *Taxidermy, or The Art of Collecting, Preparing, and Mounting Objects of Natural History for the Use of Museums and Travellers*, 2nd ed. (London: A. and R. Spottiswoode, 1821), 4.

40. James Petiver, "Appendix," in Petiver, *Musei petiveriani centuria secunda &*

tertia rariora naturae continens (London, 1698), unpaginated.

41. Ibid.

42. Sloane, *Voyage to the Islands*, 2:347.

43. Petiver, "Appendix." Glass jars with cork stoppers or sealed with paper and wax had been used widely from about the mid-sixteenth century, but it wasn't until the seventeenth that alcohol become a standard preservative. Petiver's contemporary Robert Boyle was among the first to widely advocate the use of alcohol for studying nature's intricacies and mysteries. In 1666 Boyle published his formula for embalming chicken fetuses in "Spirit of Wine" at various embryonic stages. He suggested soaking the fetus—a method applicable to the fluid preservation of any creature—in spirits for several days: "the Fætus being remov'd into more pure and well dephlegm'd Spirt of Wine, might not discolour it, but leave it almost limpid, as before it was put in." What caused the alcohol to become "phlegm'd" was protein leaching from specimens, which stained the liquid a dark opaque red. See Robert Boyle, "A Way of Preserving Birds Taken out of the Egge, and Other Small Fætuses; Communicated by Mr. Boyle," *Philosophical Transactions* 1, no. 12 (1666): 199–201.

44. René-Antoine Ferchault de Réaumur, *Divers Means for Preserving from Corruption Dead Birds, Intended to be Sent to Remote Countries, So That They May Arrive There in a Good Condition. Some of the Same Means May be Employed for Preserving Quadrupeds, Reptiles, Fishes, and Insects* (1748), trans. Philip Henry Zollman, *Philosophical Transactions* 45 (1748): 307, 311–12.

45. Ibid., 314–17.

46. John Lettsom, *The Naturalist's and Traveller's Companion, Containing Instructions for Collecting and Preserving Objects of Natural History, and for Promoting Inquiries after Human Knowledge in General* (London: E and C Dilly, 1774), 12.

47. Tesser Samuel Kuckahn, "Four Letters from Mr. T. S. Kuckhan [sic], to the President and Members of the Royal Society, on the Preservation of Dead Birds," *Philosophical Transactions* 60 (1770): 303.

48. Lee, *Taxidermy*, 5.

49. Thomas Pole, *The Anatomical Instructor, or An Illustration of the Modern and Most Approved Methods of Preparing and Preserving the Different Parts of the Human Body, and or Quadrupeds by Injection, Corrosion, Maceration, Distention, Articulation, and Modelling, &c. with a Variety of Copper Plates* (London: Smith and Davy, 1813), 182.

50. After the death of father and son, Ashmole acquired the Tradescants' collection and donated it to Oxford University in his own name. The newly named Ashmolean Museum officially opened to the public on June 6, 1683. The story of how Ashmole obtained the collection is rather troubling, beginning with the Tradescants accusing him of deception and ending with Mrs. Tradescant's body discov-

ered at the bottom of her pond. For the whole story, see Mea Allen, *The Tradescants: Their Plants, Gardens, and Museum, 1570–1662* (London: Michael Joseph, 1964).

51. Elias Ashmole, *Elias Ashmole (1617–1692): His Autobiographical and Historical Notes, His Correspondence, and Other Contemporary Sources Relating to His Life and Work*, ed. C. H. Josten (Oxford: Clarendon Press, 1966), 1823.

52. According to Thomas Pennant, the first European "to testify from ocular demonstration" that the birds had feet was the Venetian scholar Antonio Pigafetta, who was part of Ferdinand Magellan's famous first circumnavigation of the globe, making Magellan and his crew the first Europeans to visit the Spice Islands. And yet the romantic myth lived on. See Pennant, *Indian Zoology* (London: H. Hughs, 1790), 17.

53. Ibid., 13.

54. Zacharias Conrad von Uffenbach, *Oxford in 1710 from the Travels of Zacharias Conrad von Uffenbach*, ed. W. H. Quarrell and W. J. C. Quarrell (Oxford: Basil Blackwell, 1928), 27.

55. Quoted in Karen Wonders, *Habitat Dioramas: Illusions of Wilderness in Museums of Natural History* (Uppsala: Almqvist and Wiksell, 1993), 25.

56. David Freedberg, "Ferrari on the Classification of Oranges and Lemons," in *Documentary Culture: Florence and Rome from Grand-Duke Ferdinand I to Pope Alexander VII*, ed. Elizabeth Cropper, Giovanna Perini, and Fran-

cesco Solinas (Bologna: Nuovo Alfa Editoriale, 1990), 287–306. Similarly, Findlen has highlighted the imaginative possibilities inherent in exotic and strange natural phenomena as elaborated in Benedetto Ceruti and Andrea Chioco's overtly baroque catalogue of Calzolari's cabinet, published in 1622. See *Possessing Nature*, 38.

57. Francis Bacon, *The New Organon and Related Writings*, ed. Fulton Anderson (Toronto: Liberal Arts Press, 1960), 279.

58. On this point, see Horst Bredekamp, *The Lure of Antiquity and the Cult of the Machine: The Kuntskammer and the Evolution of Nature, Art, and Technology*, trans. Allison Brown (Princeton: Markus Wiener, 1995), particularly 63–80.

59. Daston and Park, *Wonders and the Order of Nature*, 236.

60. Nehemiah Grew, *Musæum Regalis Societatis, or A Catalogue and Description of the Natural and Artificial Rarities Belonging to the Royal Society and preserved at Gresham Colledge* (London, 1681), preface (unpaginated).

61. Ibid., 56, 81.

62. Ibid., preface.

63. Quoted in Lugli, "Inquiry as Collection," 109.

64. Quoted in E. Saint John Brooks, *Sir Hans Sloane: The Great Collector and His Circle* (London: Batchworth Press, 1954), 221.

65. The mocking word "nicknackatory" was used in a satirical poem by Sir Charles Hanbury Williams, written after Sloane asked him to send any

curiosity he encountered on his travels. The curiosities Williams sardonically lists include "The pigeon stuff'd, which Noah sent / To tell him when the water went." See ibid., 193.

66. On the perceived vulgarity of wondrous fragments among eighteenth-century collectors, see Daston and Park's chapter "The Enlightenment and the Anti-marvelous," in *Wonders and the Order of Nature*, 329–68.

67. See William T. Stearn, *The Natural History Museum at South Kensington: A History of the British Museum (Natural History), 1753–1980* (London: Heinemann, in association with the British Museum, 1981), 17.

68. Steve Baker, *The Postmodern Animal* (London: Reaktion Books, 2000), 98.

69. Stephen Greenblatt, "Resonance and Wonder," in Karp and Lavine, *Exhibiting Cultures*, 42.

70. Edward O. Wilson, *Biophilia* (Cambridge, Mass.: Harvard University Press, 1984), 10.

CHAPTER 2

1. William Bullock, *Six Months' Residence and Travels in Mexico, Containing Remarks on the Present State of New Spain in Its Natural Productions, State of Society, Manufactures, Trade, Agriculture, and Antiquities, &c., with Plates and Maps* (London: John Murray, 1824), 263.

2. William Bullock, *A Companion to the Liverpool Museum* (Liverpool: T. Schofield, [1800?]), 30.

3. William Bullock, *A Companion to Mr.*

Bullock's Museum: Containing a Brief Description of Upwards of Seven Thousand Natural & Foreign Curiosities, Antiquities, and Productions of the Fine Arts, 9th ed. (London: H. Reynell, 1810), 67.

4. Bullock, *Six Months' Residence and Travels in Mexico*, 273.

5. A description of the combat first appeared in the fifteenth edition of Bullock's *Companion to Mr. Bullock's Museum*, published in 1813. The entire contents of Bullock's museum, including the battle display, were sold item by item at auction in 1819. But that was hardly the end of Bullock's entrepreneurial ventures. In 1821 Bullock traveled to Mexico, making him one of the first British visitors to the country after Mexico gained its independence. He returned in 1823 with his son and acquired a large number of natural specimens and artifacts—including his hummingbirds—to show at a Mexican exhibition at the Egyptian Hall in London in 1824. By 1828 Bullock was back in America. He purchased a piece of land on the Ohio River, opposite Cincinnati, with the idea of building a utopian town named Hygeia (Greek for health), and he had a detailed city plan drawn up. The scheme failed, and Bullock returned to England in the 1830s. For more on Bullock's life, see Susan Pearce, "William Bullock: Collections and Exhibitions at the Egyptian Hall, London, 1816–1825," *Journal of the History of Collections* 20, no. 1 (2008): 17–35. See also E. G.

Hancock, "'One of those dreadful combats'—A Surviving Display from William Bullock's London Museum, 1807–1818," *Museums Journal* 79, no. 4 (1980): 172–75.

6. Bullock, *Companion to the Liverpool Museum*, 29.

7. Bullock, *Companion to Mr. Bullock's Museum*, 69.

8. Bullock, *Six Months' Residence and Travels in Mexico*, 264–65.

9. Ibid., 267–69.

10. Judith Pascoe, *The Hummingbird Cabinet: A Rare and Curious History of Romantic Collectors* (Ithaca: Cornell University Press, 2006), 38–39.

11. Bullock, *Six Months' Residence and Travels in Mexico*, 273.

12. Ibid., 273–74.

13. Gould's illustrious taxidermy career began with the "thick knee'd Bustard" he preserved for King George IV. Gould is the first known taxidermist to receive royal patronage, and the honors continued. Gould also preserved an ostrich, a giraffe, a crane, two mouse deer, and two lemurs for the king. In 1827 Gould handily beat all competitors in obtaining the post of curator and preserver of the Zoological Society of London, a position that gave him access to all of the animals that lived and died in the society's Zoological Gardens at Regent's Park. Gould's reputation, however, far exceeded his skills as a taxidermist. He was most notably a diligent ornithologist. On his return to England with the *Beagle*, Charles Darwin delivered boxes of collected specimens to the Zoological Society's naturalists for identification. Gould identified eleven species of bird, all new to science. They were the Galapagos finches, the birds that first prompted Darwin to associate geography with biology. For more on Gould, see Isabella Tree, *The Ruling Passion of John Gould: A Biography of the Bird Man* (London: Barrie and Jenkins, 1991).

14. Ibid., 175.

15. See Anne Larsen Hollerbach, "Of Sangfroid and Sphinx Moths: Cruelty, Public Relations, and the Growth of Entomology in England, 1800–1840," *Osiris*, 2nd ser., 11 (1996): 201–20.

16. Edmund Burke, *A Philosophical Enquiry into the Origin of Our Ideas of the Sublime and Beautiful* (1757), ed. James T. Boulton (1958; repr., London: Routledge, 2008), 155.

17. For a wonderful analysis of romantic collecting and hummingbirds, see Pascoe, *Hummingbird Cabinet*, 26–52.

18. John Ruskin, "Conversation with M. H. Spielman at Brantwood," in *The Works of John Ruskin*, ed. E. T. Cook and Alexander Wedderburn, 39 vols. (London: George Allen, 1903–12), 34:670.

19. David Elliston Allen, *The Naturalist in Britain: A Social History* (1976; repr., Princeton: Princeton University Press, 1994), 66. For the emotive reaction to nature, see also Carl Woodring, *Nature into Art: Cultural Transformation in Nineteenth-Century Britain* (Cambridge, Mass.: Harvard University Press, 1989), 11–15.

20. Philip Henry Gosse, *The Romance of Natural History* (London: James Nisbet and Co., 1860), v.

21. Allen, *Naturalist in Britain*, 54.

22. See R. W. Hepburn, "Contemporary Aesthetics and the Neglect of Natural Beauty," in *British Analytical Philosophy*, ed. Bernard Williams and Alan Montefiore (London: Routledge and Kegan Paul, 1966).

23. The criteria for World Heritage Sites can be read on UNESCO's website, at http://whc.unesco.org/en/criteria/ (accessed November 10, 2009).

24. Edward O. Wilson, *Biophilia* (Cambridge, Mass.: Harvard University Press, 1984), 1.

25. Annie Dillard, "Living Like Weasels," in Dillard, *Teaching a Stone to Talk: Expeditions and Encounters* (1982; repr., New York: Harper Perennial, 1992), 67–70.

26. For introductory reading on the cultures of nature appreciation, see Kate Soper, *What Is Nature? Culture, Politics, and the Non-Human* (Oxford: Basil Blackwell, 1995); and Jennifer Price, *Flight Maps: Adventures with Nature in Modern America* (New York: Basic Books, 1999).

27. Arnold Berleant, *The Aesthetics of Environment* (Philadelphia: Temple University Press, 1992), 21.

28. George-Louis Leclerc de Buffon, *Histoire naturelle des oiseaux*, 9 vols. (Paris: L'Imprimerie Royale, 1770–86), 1:v–vi, 21. All translations are my own unless otherwise indicated.

29. It was John Gould who found, or at least published, a solution to the problem of replicating hummingbirds' metallic shimmer on paper. The effect was produced by painting transparent oils and varnish colors over pure gold leaf. However, it seems that Gould learned the process from William Baily, a hummingbird specialist from Philadelphia, although Gould had very little to say on this matter. For the full controversy, see Tree, *Ruling Passion of John Gould*, 164–69.

30. Charles Waterton, *Wanderings in South America, the North-West of the United States, and the Antilles, in the Years 1812, 1816, 1820, & 1824, with Original Instructions for the Perfect Preservation of Birds, &c. for Cabinets of Natural History*, 2nd ed. (London: B. Fellowes, 1828), 117.

31. Buffon, *Histoire naturelle des oiseaux*, 6:15, 18, 20–21.

32. See Yves Laissus, "Les cabinets d'histoire naturelle," in *La curiosité scientifique au XVIIIe siècle: Cabinets et observatoires*, ed. Charles Bedel, Roger Hahn, Yves Laissus, and Jean Torlais (Paris: Hermann, 1986), 679–712.

33. Bettina Dietz, "Mobile Objects: The Space of Shells in Eighteenth-Century France," *British Journal for the History of Science* 39, no. 3 (2006): 371. See also Dietz and Thomas Nutz, "Collections Curieuses: The Aesthetics of Curiosity and Elite Lifestyle in Eighteenth-Century Paris," *Eighteenth-Century Life* 29, no. 3 (2005): 44–75.

34. See Emma C. Spary, *Utopia's Garden: French Natural History from Old*

Regime to Revolution (Chicago: University of Chicago Press, 2000), 20–22; and Emma C. Spary, "Codes of Passion: Natural History Specimens as a Polite Language in Late Eighteenth-Century France," *Wissenschaft als kulturelle Praxis, 1750–1900*, ed. Hans Erich Bödeker, Peter Hanns Reill, and Jürgen Schlumbohm (Göttingen: Vanderhoeck and Ruprecht, 1999), 105–35. Bettina Dietz writes that until the last third of the eighteenth century, the main collectors "were essentially drawn from the court nobility, the nobility of office and the circle of upwardly mobile *financiers*." Dietz, "Mobile Objects," 377.

35. Emma C. Spary, "Forging Nature at the Republican Muséum," in *The Faces of Nature in Enlightenment Europe*, ed. Lorraine Daston and Gianna Pomata (Berlin: Berliner Wissenschafts-Verlag, 2003), 167.

36. Antoine-Joseph Dézallier d'Argenville, *La conchyliologie, ou Histoire naturelle des coquilles de mer, d'eau douce, terrestres et fossiles*, 3rd ed. (Paris: Guillaume de Bure, 1780), 199.

37. Emma C. Spary, "The 'Nature' of Enlightenment," in *The Sciences in Enlightened Europe*, ed. William Clark, Jan Golinski, and Simon Schaffer (Chicago: University of Chicago Press, 1999), 295–96.

38. D'Argenville, *Conchyliologie*, 193–96.

39. Ibid., 232.

40. Ibid., 191.

41. Louis-Jean-Marie Daubenton, "Description du Cabinet du Roi," in Daubenton, *Histoire naturelle* (1749), quoted in Denis Diderot, "Cabinet d'histoire naturelle," in *Encyclopédie, ou Dictionnaire raisonnée des sciences, des arts et des métiers*, ed. Denis Diderot and Jean Le Rond d'Alembert, 17 vols. (Paris: Briasson, 1751–65), 2:491.

42. Sarah Lee, *Taxidermy, or The Art of Collecting, Preparing, and Mounting Objects of Natural History for the Use of Museums and Travellers*, 2nd ed. (London: A. and R. Spottiswoode, 1821).

43. Tesser Samuel Kuckahn, "Four Letters from Mr. T. S. Kuckhan [*sic*], to the President and Members of the Royal Society, on the Preservation of Dead Birds," *Philosophical Transactions* 60 (1770): 304.

44. Thomas Bewick, *A General History of Quadrupeds* (1790; Trowbridge, UK: Ward Lock Reprints, 1970), 479.

45. A philosopher of nature and natural simplicity, Rousseau advocated breaking free from the pressures and artificialities of society. He preferred escapes such as the wild and romantic banks of Lake Bienne, Switzerland, where the "contemplative philosopher . . . loves to ruminate at leisure on the charms of Nature, while retiring into a silence broken only by the cry of eagles, the mingled warbling of various song-birds, or the rushing of torrents which precipitate themselves from the surrounding mountains." For such a contemplative philosopher, the rigors of zoological exploration were not quite pleasant. To properly pursue natural history, Rousseau writes,

one would need a menagerie or the energy to pursue each animal in the wild. Barring that, one had to study dead animals, "separate their bones, and turn at leisure their palpitating entrails! What an assemblage does an anatomical amphitheatre exhibit!—Stinking bodies, putrid and livid flesh, blood, loathsome entrails, hideous skeletons, and pestilential vapours!—It is not among such objects, I promise you, that J. J. will seek amusement." Nothing here about taxidermy. For Rousseau, it was surely better to study the gentler arts of botany. Jean-Jacques Rousseau, *Les rêveries du promeneur solitaire* (published posthumously in 1782) (Geneva: Editions Slatkine, 1978), 5, 129.

46. This is not just a historical evaluation. Take, for example, today's food revolution. With the extraordinary explorations in biotechnology, genetic manipulation, and even cloning, when preservatives and air travel allow foods to be flown between continents, when scientific research has produced superior antibiotics to allow more animals to live in closer quarters to produce more meat, purity and simplicity are increasingly valued in the food industry. Farmers are rediscovering and cultivating old, almost forgotten breeds of animals and varieties of vegetables. Consumers pay extra for heirloom tomatoes, organically grown produce, and meat raised on small, local farms. For every step that science and technology seem to take further away from nature, some species of

biophilia draws us back to simpler, more connected encounters with the natural world.

47. Kuckahn, "Four Letters," 302–3.

48. Ibid., 312–17.

49. "Baking is not only useful in fresh preservations, but will also be of very great service to old ones, destroying the eggs of insects; and it should be constant practice once in two or three years, to bake them over again, and to have the cases fresh washed . . . which would not only preserve collections from decay much longer, but also keep them sweet." Ibid., 318–19.

50. On the taxidermic dispute between Kuckahn, Pierre-Jean-Claude Mauduyt de la Verenne, and Jean-Baptiste Bécoeur, see Paul Lawrence Farber, "The Development of Taxidermy and the History of Ornithology," *Isis* 68, no. 4 (1977): 556–67.

51. Ibid., 561.

52. Quoted in L. C. Rookmaaker, P. A. Morris, I. E. Glenn, and P. J. Mundy, "The Ornithological Cabinet of Jean-Baptiste Bécoeur and the Secret of Arsenical Soap," *Archives of Natural History* 33, no. 1 (2006): 148.

53. See Thad Logan, *The Victorian Parlour: A Cultural Study* (Cambridge: Cambridge University Press, 2001), 141–42.

54. John Woodhouse Audubon, *Audubon and His Journals*, ed. Maria R. Audubon, with zoological and other notes by Elliott Coues, 2 vols. (New York: Dover, 1960), 1:101, 105.

55. William Swainson, *Taxidermy, and Bibliography, and Biography* (London:

Longman, Orme, Brown, Green, and Longmans, 1840), 81–82.

56. Shirley Hibberd, *Rustic Adornments for Homes of Taste, and Recreations for Town Folk, in the Study and Imitation of Nature*, 2nd ed. (London: Groombridge and Sons, 1857), 5.

57. Charles Darwin, *The Autobiography of Charles Darwin, 1809–1882: With Original Omissions Restored*, ed. Nora Barlow (London: Collins Clear-Type Press, 1958), 87, 119.

58. Henry Housman, *The Story of Our Museum: Showing How We Formed It, and What It Taught Us* (London: Society for Promoting Christian Knowledge, 1881), 245–46, 25–26, 252.

59. William Henry Flower, "Boys' Museums," in Flower, *Essays on Museums and Other Subjects Connected with Natural History* (1898; Freeport, N.Y.: Books for Libraries Press, 1972), 63–69.

60. William Henry Flower, "Museum Organisation," in ibid., 17–18.

61. Waterton wrote, "Till within these few years, no idea of the true colours of the [toucan's] bill could be formed from the stuffed toucans brought to Europe. About eight years ago, while eating boiled toucan, the thought struck me that the colours in the bill of a preserved specimen might be kept as bright as those in life." The key, Waterton explained, was to remove all the veins and internal membranes inside the beak. These both turned black when dried and made the bill appear black as well.

Scraping them both away, leaving only the external horn, and filling the inside with white chalk, would preserve the colors. *Wanderings in South America*, 125–26.

62. Ibid., 332.

63. Ibid., 321.

64. Ibid., 117.

65. Charles Waterton, *Essays on Natural History*, 3rd ser., 2nd ed. (London: Longman, Brown, Green, Longmans, and Roberts, 1858), 118.

66. Charles Waterton, *Essays on Natural History, Chiefly Ornithology*, 2nd ed. (London: Longman, Orme, Brown, Green, and Longmans, 1838), 300.

67. Waterton, "On Preserving Birds," in *Wanderings in South America*, 322.

68. Ibid., 323.

CHAPTER 3

1. Nancy Ireson, "The Dangerous Exotic," in *Henri Rousseau: Jungles in Paris*, ed. Frances Morris and Christopher Green (New York: Harry N. Abrams, 2005), 143.

2. Christopher Green, "Souvenirs of the Jardin des Plantes: Making the Exotic Strange," in ibid., 42.

3. Nancy Leys Stepan, *Picturing Tropical Nature* (Ithaca: Cornell University Press, 2001), 34.

4. See ibid., 36, 46–50.

5. The exhibition was organized by Tate Modern in London and the Réunion des musées nationaux and the Musée d'Orsay in Paris.

6. Quoted in Green, "Souvenirs of the Jardin des Plantes," 30.

7. Edward Said, *Orientalism* (1979; repr., New York: Vintage Books, 1994), 21–22.

8. For a beautifully comprehensive analysis of the practices and poetics of collecting, see Susan Pearce, *On Collecting: An Investigation into Collecting in the European Tradition* (London: Routledge, 1995), particularly pt. 3, "The Poetics of Collecting."

9. For an excellent discussion of photography, big-game hunting, and taxidermy in the Victorian imagination, see James R. Ryan, *Picturing Empire: Photography and the Visualization of the British Empire* (Chicago: University of Chicago Press, 1997), 73–98. See also Michelle Henning, "Skins of the Real: Taxidermy and Photography," in *Nanoq: Flat Out and Bluesome; A Cultural Life of Polar Bears*, exh. cat. (London: Black Dog, 2006), 135–47.

10. See Chris Wilbert, "What Is Doing the Killing? Animal Attacks, Man-Eaters, and Shifting Boundaries and Flows of Human-Animal Relationships," in *Killing Animals*, ed. Animal Studies Group (Urbana: University of Illinois Press, 2006), 32.

11. In fact, however, a much earlier use of internal modeling was exhibited at the Great Exhibition of 1851 by François Comba, taxidermist at the Royal Museum at the University of Turin. Comba's European elk was declared "the *chef-d'œuvre* of taxidermy" at the exhibition. This "magnificent restoration of the European elk, which is all but breathing, leaves us no expectation of ever seeing anything better.

This perfect model of the animal, which appears to have been petrified in its own skin, retains in a striking manner all the anatomical details of the living creatures." Such high praise was due to the innovative methods of construction. According to the *Morning Chronicle*, the "model upon which the skin is placed was produced by Signor Comba, from a species of papier mâché or carton moulé, which was cast in a mould from a model in clay." "The Great Exhibition," *Morning Chronicle* (London), September 1, 1851.

12. William T. Hornaday, *Taxidermy and Zoological Collecting: A Complete Handbook for the Amateur Taxidermist, Collector, Osteologist, Museum-Builder, Sportsman, and Traveller* (New York: Charles Scribner's Sons, 1891), 147.

13. Ibid., 149.

14. Ibid., 171–72.

15. Ibid., 172–77.

16. Hornaday similarly suggested the family dog as a model for wild canines and cheekily advised that when "modeling the mouth or muscles of a gorilla or orang utan, catch the first amateur taxidermist you can lay your hands on—the wilder and greener the better—and use him as your model. Study him, for he is fearfully and wonderfully made. The way some of my good-natured colleagues used to pose for me as (partly) nude models at Ward's, when I once had a ten-months' siege with orangs, gorillas, chimpanzees, was a constant source

of wonder and delight to the ribald crew of osteologists who knew nothing of high art." Ibid., 175.

17. For the significance and symbolism of imperial hunting in the nineteenth century, see John M. MacKenzie, *The Empire of Nature: Hunting, Conservation, and British Imperialism* (Manchester: Manchester University Press, 1988); and Harriet Ritvo, *The Animal Estate: The English and Other Creatures in the Victorian Age* (Cambridge, Mass.: Harvard University Press, 1987), 243–88.

18. Philip Henry Gosse, *The Romance of Natural History* (London: James Nisbet, 1860), 221–47. For more on the intimate connection between the growth of natural history and big-game hunting, see MacKenzie, *Empire of Nature*, 25–50.

19. Green, "Souvenirs of the Jardin des Plantes," 33.

20. Ritvo, *Animal Estate*, 223.

21. Gaston Tissandier, "Les galleries de zoologie du Muséum d'histoire naturelle de Paris," *La Nature*, October 12, 1889, 311.

22. For readings of the concept of "the world as exhibition," see Timothy Mitchell, "The World as Exhibition," *Comparative Studies in Society and History* 31, no. 2 (1989): 217–36; and Carol Breckenridge, "The Aesthetics and Politics of Colonial Collecting: India at World Fairs," ibid., 195–216.

23. As briefly mentioned in chapter 2, William Bullock's museum was among the first to present taxidermied animals in a lively manner in the first decades of the nineteenth century. The various guides to his museum list several displays of animals arranged in combat. A vulture, "the most cruel, filthy, and indolent bird in the creation," was posed in the act of preying on a silver pheasant. A golden eagle, which, Bullock noted dramatically, was able to carry off children, was shown attacking a white hare. Also on display was a "Merlin killing a leveret," and, of course, "The Royal Tiger," the deadly combat between a boa constrictor and a tiger. William Bullock, *A Companion to the Liverpool Museum* (Liverpool: T. Schofield, [1800?]). Paolo Savi, a professor of zoology and a taxidermist at the University of Pisa, similarly created nearly a hundred theatrical scenes, including two hounds attacking a wild boar.

24. Quoted in Karen Wonders, *Habitat Dioramas: Illusions of Wilderness in Museums of Natural History* (Uppsala: Almqvist and Wiksell, 1993), 35.

25. "The Colonial and Indian Exhibition," *Morning Post* (London), April 22, 1886; "The Colonial and Indian Exhibition," *Times* (London), April 22, 1886; "The Colonial Exhibition," *Daily News* (London), April 22, 1886. One visitor, however, was rather less enthusiastic about Ward's taxidermy. Although taxidermist and writer Montagu Browne could not deny that the overall impression was admirable, the "critical observer," he wrote, might well observe the sort of facial faults that Hornaday warned could ruin the finest work: "the tigers

nearest the entrance were ill-managed about the heads—the tongues, thickly painted and exhibiting no papillæ, being apparently made of slabs of some material, probably clay . . . and the other parts of the mouths being somewhat shrivelled and destitute of palatal ridges and of large muscles around the teeth; but, whilst the mouths generally were bad, and the noses and the modelling and arrangement of the eyelids not good, the eyes themselves were excellent. Indeed, taking the mammals as a whole, with the exception of the eyes, the faults of the ordinary taxidermist were apparent, and the impression they left was, that there was too much paint and putty, and too little artistic modelling by proper methods." Montagu Browne, *Artistic and Scientific Taxidermy and Modelling: A Manual of Instruction in the Methods of Preserving and Reproducing the Correct Form of All Natural Objects, Including a Chapter on the Modelling of Foliage* (London: Adam and Charles Black, 1896), 14–15.

26. Rowland Ward, "The Indian and Colonial Exhibition," *Times* (London), February 6, 1886.

27. "Ceylon's Isle," *Daily News* (London), June 24, 1886.

28. Jonathan Burt, *Animals in Film* (London: Reaktion Books, 2004), 9–10.

29. Montagu Browne, *Practical Taxidermy: A Manual of Instruction to the Amateur in Collecting, Preserving, and Setting Up Natural History Specimens of All Kinds,* 2nd ed. (London: L.

Upcott Gill, 1884), 254.

30. See Diana Donald, "Pangs Watched in Perpetuity: Sir Edwin Landseer's Pictures of Dying Deer and the Ethos of Victorian Sportsmanship," in Animal Studies Group, *Killing Animals,* 50–68.

31. See Wonders, *Habitat Dioramas,* 149–60.

32. Daniel Justin Herman, *Hunting and the American Imagination* (Washington, D.C.: Smithsonian Institution Press, 2001), 8.

33. Stephen Christopher Quinn, *Windows on Nature: The Great Habitat Dioramas of the American Museum of Natural History* (New York: Abrams, in association with the American Museum of Natural History, 2006), 64.

34. John Henry Patterson, *The Man-Eating Lions of Tsavo* (Chicago: Field Museum of Natural History, 1925), 2–3.

35. Ibid., 6–7.

36. See Justin D. Yeakel, Bruce D. Patterson, Kena Fox-Dobbs, Mercedes M. Okumura, Thure E. Cerling, Jonathan W. Moore, Paul L. Koch, and Nathaniel J. Dominy, "Cooperation and Individuality Among Man-Eating Lions," *Proceedings of the National Academy of Sciences* 106, no. 45 (2009): 19040–43.

37. Patterson, *Man-Eating Lions of Tsavo,* 10.

38. Wonders, *Habitat Dioramas,* 112.

39. Ibid., 10.

40. For a good introduction to American nature writing, see Thomas J. Lyon,

ed., *This Incomperable Lande: A Book of American Nature Writing* (Boston: Houghton Mifflin, 1989).

41. This rationale dates to the mid-nineteenth century, although such early comments were usually (and oddly) emotionally neutral about the loss. For example, one English naturalist wrote in 1851, "Should civilization continue to advance as rapidly as it has done during the last fifty years, and should the human race extend itself over the face of the earth, this increase will probably lead to the destruction, and eventually to the extermination, of most races of wild animals. The largest or most obnoxious must disappear first; in proof of this we may refer to what has taken place in our own island, and it would be most interesting could we now see in the British Museum the last wolf killed in England." "Great Exhibition," *Morning Chronicle* (London), September 1, 1851.

42. William T. Hornaday, *The Extermination of the American Bison, with a Sketch of Its Discovery and Life History* (Washington, D.C.: Smithsonian Institution Press, 1889), 529.

43. Quoted in ibid., 546.

44. Donna Haraway, "Teddy Bear Patriarchy: Taxidermy in the Garden of Eden, New York City, 1908–1936," *Social Text* 11 (1984–85): 24.

45. Donald Crawford, "The Aesthetics of Nature and the Environment," in *The Blackwell Guide to Aesthetics*, ed. Peter Kivy (Malden, Mass.: Basil Blackwell, 2004), 306–24.

46. Malcolm Budd, *The Aesthetic Appreciation of Nature: Essays on the Aesthetics of Nature* (Oxford: Oxford University Press, 2002), 5, 9.

47. Ibid., 91.

48. T. J. Diffey, "Experiencing Nature and Experiencing Art," in *Art and Experience*, ed. Ananta Ch. Sukla (Westport, Conn.: Praeger, 2003), 52.

49. This question of authenticity can, admittedly, become confused when pieces of animals are rearranged or combined. The polar bear at the center of Mark Dion's 1995 installation *Ursus maritimus* is not in fact a bear but a bear made from the skin of goats. This knowledge disrupts our perception of the thing on display and pushes our experience away from authenticity toward something else, something far stranger than even taxidermy usually conveys. Here I am interested in the confrontation between viewer and the preserved skin of an animal crafted into a semblance of its former liveliness.

50. Yeakel et al., "Cooperation and Individuality," 19042.

CHAPTER 4

1. Harriet Ritvo, *The Platypus and the Mermaid, and Other Figments of the Classifying Imagination* (Cambridge, Mass.: Harvard University Press, 1997), 10.

2. Works on this subject include Tony Bennett, *The Birth of the Museum: History, Theory, Politics* (London: Routledge, 1995); Sharon Macdonald,

ed., *The Politics of Display: Museums, Science, Culture* (London: Routledge, 1998); Susan Sheets-Pyenson, *Cathedrals of Science: The Development of Colonial Natural History Museums During the Late Nineteenth Century* (Kingston: McGill-Queen's University Press, 1988); and Carla Yanni, *Nature's Museums: Victorian Science and the Architecture of Display* (London: Athlone Press, 1999).

3. For an overview of Linnaeus's background and contributions to systematic nomenclature, see William T. Stearn, "The Background of Linnaeus' Contributions to the Nomenclature and Methods of Systematic Biology," *Systematic Zoology* 8, no. 1 (1959): 4–22.

4. Linnaeus, introduction to *Systema naturae*, quoted in Stephen Asma, *Stuffed Animals and Pickled Heads: The Culture and Evolution of Natural History Museums* (Oxford: Oxford University Press, 2001), 116.

5. To counteract the chaos of names in popular circulation, Linnaeus chose names that were as simple and as easy to remember as possible. Did the creature have a defining feature? Did it occur exclusively in a particular geography? Did it remind him of someone or something? Who was the first collector of the species? For example, Linnaeus named the common bumblebee *Bombus hortensus*, from the Latin *bombus*, meaning a humming or buzzing sound, and *hortus*, meaning garden. He named the snapping turtle *Chelydra serpentina*, from the Greek word for water serpent, *chelydra*, and the Latin *serpentine*, meaning snakelike, a reference to the turtle's long, snaking neck. Naming is serious work, but naturalists are often less than serious in their choices—inside jokes, puns, and jabs are frequently incorporated into scientific nomenclature. The entomologist Terry Erwin named three carabid beetles *Agra schwarzeneggeri* (in reference to the males' markedly developed, biceps-like middle femora), *Agra sasquatch* (for its big feet), and *Agra vation*. There is a genus of mites named *Darthvaderum*, a snail from the Fijian island of Mba named *Ba humbugi*, and a genus of mollusks called *Ittibittium*, so named because they are smaller than the genus *Bittium*.

6. Ritvo, *Platypus and the Mermaid*, 14.

7. For a late Victorian discussion of types, see Charles Schubert, "What Is a Type in Natural History?" *Science* 5, no. 121 (1897): 636–40.

8. Linnaeus offered a list of human varieties: *americanus, europeanus, asiaticus, africanus, sylvestris, ferus,* and *monstrosus,* the last three names designating orangutans, wild children (the sort raised in the woods by wolves), and humans with bodily deformations, respectively.

9. The example is drawn from the English naturalist William Swainson. As Swainson explains, "One [naturalist], arguing from the flight of bats, looks on it as that animal which constitutes the true passage from quadrupeds and birds. Another, looking to its

general aspect, is disposed to place it among mice, fortified by the general name given by the French to the whole tribe of *chauve souris*. A third, chiefly influenced by the peculiarity of its teeth, arranges it in the same group as monkeys, and each, acting on his respective inferences, fashions his system accordingly. Now, as to the facts connected with the individual structure . . . of the bat, all these naturalists would agree; because such facts can be verified by their personal observation. . . . But here unanimity ceases. They proceed to inference; and each, laying a peculiar stress upon some one fact more than upon others, makes it a principle of his own arrangement. This is the true cause of the number and the mutability of zoological systems." Swainson, *A Preliminary Discourse on the Study of Natural History* (London: Longman, Rees, Orme, Brown, Green, and Longman, 1834), 153.

10. For an overview of the taxonomic debates, see Paul Lawrence Farber, *Finding Order in Nature: The Naturalist Tradition from Linnaeus to E. O. Wilson* (Baltimore: Johns Hopkins University Press, 2000); Asma, *Stuffed Animals*; Ritvo, *Platypus and the Mermaid*; and Mario A. Di Gregorio, "In Search of the Natural System: Problems of Zoological Classification in Victorian Britain," *History and Philosophy of the Life Sciences* 4, no. 4 (1982).

11. An interesting aside: hippos, you will notice, are no longer related to horses,

as they were in Linnaeus's ordering. The word hippopotamus literally means "river horse," from the Greek *hippo*, meaning horse, and *potamus*, meaning river. This ancient correlation was ruptured in 1848, when even-toed hoofed animals were divided from the odd-toed. Largely based on their similar molar structure, hippos and pigs were believed to be cousins. However, molecular research in the 1980s and the subsequent discovery of two new fossil (extinct) mammal species have determined that the hippo's closest living relatives are actually whales. The common ancestor of hippos and whales branched off from ruminants after the divergence of the rest of the even-toed ungulates. Whales later returned permanently to the ocean, while hippos remained semiaquatic.

12. William John Burchell, *Travels in the Interior of Southern Africa*, 2 vols. (London: Longman, Hurst, Rees, Orme, Brown, 1822, 1824), 1:138–39.

13. After Burchell's distinction, this species was commonly known as the dauw rather than as a zebra in much mid-nineteenth-century zoological literature. For example, see Charles Hamilton Smith's *Natural History of Horses*, ed. William Jardine (London: Henry G. Bohn, 1866), 329.

14. Burchell, *Travels in the Interior of Southern Africa*, 1:138–39.

15. John Edward Gray, "A Revision of the Family *Equidæ*," *Zoological Journal* 1 (1824–25): 241.

16. Naturalists have long debated the

exact positioning of the quagga—was it more closely related to the horse or to the zebra? Almost a century after the last quagga died, DNA testing of samples taken from several taxidermied quaggas finally resolved the debate in the 1980s. The quagga was a subspecies of the plains zebra. Moreover, since the quagga was distinguished and named before the plains zebra, according to the laws of classification its name should be upheld. Accordingly, the quagga's scientific name is *Equus quagga quagga*, while the plains zebra is known as *Equus quagga*. Richard Lydekker, *Catalogue of Ungulate Mammals in the British Museum* (London: British Museum, 1916), 22–23.

17. Émile Oustalet, "Une novelle espèce de zèbre: Le zèbre de Grévy (*Equus grevyi*)," *La Nature*, June 3, 1882, 12–14.

18. T. E. Buckley, "On the Past and Present Geographical Distribution of the Large Mammals of South Africa," *Proceedings of the Scientific Meetings of the Zoological Society of London* 44, no. 1 (1876): 282.

19. Angel Cabrera, "Subspecific and Individual Variation in the Burchell Zebra," *Journal of Mammalogy* 17, no. 2 (1936): 89–112.

20. Debra Bennett, "Stripes Do Not a Zebra Make, Part 1: A Cladistic Analysis of *Equus*," *Systematic Zoology* 29, no. 3 (1980): 272–87. For detailed discussions of zebra taxonomy, see C. P. Groves and Catherine H. Bell, "New Investigations on the Taxonomy of the Zebras Genus *Equus*,

Subgenus *Hippotigris*," *Mammalian Biology* 69, no. 1 (2004): 182–96; and Cabrera, "Subspecific and Individual Variation."

21. As Andrew McClellan has written about the cultural transformations at work in the postrevolutionary Louvre, "collections were rearranged in accordance with the principle of *representativeness* rather than that of *rarity*. . . . This change is tied up with and enables a functional transformation as collections, no longer thought of as means for stimulating the curiosity of the few, are reconceptualised as means for instructing the many." Such comments are equally pertinent to the reformation of natural history museums. The question of representativeness, as Tony Bennett writes, "contrasts markedly with the principles of curiosity which, since the objects are valued for their uniqueness, and since, therefore, no object can stand in for another, can assign no limits to the potentially endless proliferation of objects which they might contain." Andrew McClellan, *Inventing the Louvre: Art, Politics, and the Origins of the Modern Museum in the Eighteenth Century* (Cambridge: Cambridge University Press, 1994), 39; and Bennett, *Birth of the Museum*, 42.

22. Emma C. Spary, "Forging Nature at the Republican Muséum," in *The Faces of Nature in Enlightenment Europe*, ed. Lorraine Daston and Gianna Pomata (Berlin: Berliner Wissenschafts-Verlag, 2003), 172.

23. William Swainson, *Taxidermy, and*

Bibliography, and Biography (London: Longman, Orme, Brown, Green, and Longmans, 1840), 1.

24. This distinction between mounted and stuffed animals is also used by modern taxidermists to distinguish between the stuffed animals of early taxidermists—in which the skins were literally stuffed out with materials—and the modern techniques of mounting skins on anatomically correct sculptural forms.

25. Swainson, *Taxidermy, and Bibliography, and Biography*, 84–85.

26. Charles Darwin to Thomas H. Huxley, October 23, 1858, in *The Correspondence of Charles Darwin*, vol. 7, *1821–1857*, ed. Frederick Burkhardt and Sydney Smith (Cambridge: Cambridge University Press, 1985), 176.

27. Charles Darwin to J. D. Hooker, October 29, 1858, ibid., 177.

28. "Memorials Presented to the British Government in 1858," published as appendix 6 in ibid., 525–27.

29. For example, see Karen Rader and Victorian Cain, "From Natural History to Science: Display and the Transformation of American Museums of Science and Nature," *Museum and Society* 6, no. 2 (2008): 152–71.

30. Quoted in Saffron Walden Museum Society, "Annual Report of the Saffron Walden Museum Society, 1959–1960" (April 28, 1960), 7.

31. Spencer's taxidermy purge is not a unique episode. The International Committee for Museums and Collections of Natural History has established a working group on the art of taxidermy and its cultural heritage importance in the hope of raising awareness about the loss of many natural history collections around the globe. The group's website states that as museums "modernize," taxidermied animals are frequently the first items to be removed: "When fire, earthquakes and wars destroy the world's historical and cultural heritage, it might not be possible to do anything, but when that destruction is undertaken by the very people employed as guardians of our heritage, then it is a criminal act and we must all despair for the future of our collections. It is especially difficult to understand the fact that those causing the disastrous damage call themselves scientists when, due to a lack of scientific and historical rigour, they burn or otherwise destroy historical evidence . . . both through the destruction of irreplaceable specimens and the context in which they were displayed." http://www.ggwinter.de/icom/fmus.htm.

32. Stephen R. Kellert, "The Biological Basis for Human Values of Nature," in *The Biophilia Hypothesis*, ed. Stephen R. Kellert and Edward O. Wilson (Washington, D.C.: Island Press, 1993), 42.

CHAPTER 5

1. William Adolph Baillie-Grohman, *Fifteen Years' Sport and Life in the Hunting Grounds of Western America and British Columbia* (London: Horace Cox, 1900), 49.

2. Ibid., 24.

3. See Garry Marvin, "Wild Killing: Contesting the Animal in Hunting," in *Killing Animals*, ed. Animal Studies Group (Urbana: University of Illinois Press, 2006), 25–26.

4. Roger King, "Environmental Ethics and a Case for Hunting," *Environmental Ethics* 13 (1991): 62.

5. William Adolph Baillie-Grohman, *Camps in the Rockies, Being a Narrative of Life on the Frontier, and Sport in the Rocky Mountains, with an Account of the Cattle Ranches of the West* (London: Sampson Low, Marston, Searle, and Rivington, 1882), 127. Hereafter cited parenthetically in the text.

6. See Susan Stewart, *On Longing: Narratives of the Miniature, the Gigantic, the Souvenir, the Collection* (Durham: Duke University Press, 1993), 135–36.

7. This emotional focus on *how* an animal died (and not merely the fact of an animal's death) lies at the heart of the varying reactions to products made from different animals. Consider three pairs of shoes, one made from a cow, one from a seal, and one from a Cape buffalo. The general assumption would be that the cow was killed as much for its meat as for its hide in an industrial meatpacking plant; that the seal was slaughtered in the wild primarily for its coat; and that the buffalo was stalked and passionately pursued for the sheer dangerous excitement of the hunt and not principally for either its skin or its meat. All of the shoes are made from an animal, yet our understanding as to how each animal died strongly influences our reaction to the resulting product.

8. Marvin, "Wild Killing," 17.

9. Angela Singer, e-mail to author, March 18, 2011.

10. Charles Landis, introduction to William Adolph Baillie-Grohman, *The Land in the Mountains, Being an Account of the Past and Present of Tyrol, Its People and Its Castles* (London: Simpkin, Marshall, Hamilton, Kent, 1907), xxiii.

11. Matt Cartmill, *A View to a Death in the Morning: Hunting and Nature Through History* (Cambridge, Mass.: Harvard University Press, 1993), 29–30.

12. Marvin, "Wild Killing," 19.

13. Cartmill, *View to a Death in the Morning*, 52–75.

14. William Adolph Baillie-Grohman, "The Chamois," in *Big Game Shooting*, ed. Clive Phillipps-Wolley, 2 vols. (London: Longmans, Green, 1894), 2:77, 82.

15. Landis, introduction to Baillie-Grohman, *The Land in the Mountains*, xvi–xviii.

16. Ibid., xxix.

17. For example, see Rowland Ward, *The Sportsman's Handbook to Practical Collecting, Preserving, and Artistic Setting-Up of Trophies and Specimens Together with A Guide to the Hunting Grounds of the World* (London: Rowland Ward, 1900); and Joseph H. Batty, *Practical Taxidermy, and Home Decoration; Together with General Information for the Sportsman* (New York: Orange Judd, 1885).

18. John M. MacKenzie, *The Empire of Nature: Hunting, Conservation, and British Imperialism* (Manchester: Manchester University Press, 1988), 28–30. See also Harriet Ritvo, "The Thrill of the Chase," in Ritvo, *The Animal Estate: The English and Other Creatures in the Victorian Age* (Cambridge, Mass.: Harvard University Press, 1987), 243–88.

19. Daniel Justin Herman, *Hunting and the American Imagination* (Washington, D.C.: Smithsonian Institution Press, 2001), 158.

20. Jennifer Price, *Flight Maps: Adventures with Nature in Modern America* (New York: Basic Books, 1999), 12.

21. Batty, *Practical Taxidermy*, xii.

22. Ibid., xi.

23. See, for example, Melissa Milgrom, "Cool, Dead, and Stuffed," *Daily Beast*, March 11, 2010, http://www.thedailybeast.com/blogs-and-stories/2010-03-11/cool-dead-and-stuffed/?cid=topic:mainpromo1 (accessed March 14, 2010). See also Penelope Green, "The New Antiquarians: Cultivating a Late Nineteenth-Century Style at Home," *New York Times*, July 30, 2009.

24. Celeste Olalquiaga, *The Artificial Kingdom: On the Kitsch Experience* (Minneapolis: University of Minnesota Press, 1998), 5.

25. Herman, *Hunting and the American Imagination*, 272.

26. See Susan Sontag, "Notes on 'Camp,'" in Sontag, *Against Interpretation and Other Essays* (1961; repr., New York: Farrar, Straus and Giroux, 1967), 285.

27. Jean Baudrillard, *The System of Objects*, trans. James Benedict (London: Verso, 2002), 18, 76.

28. Morgan Mavis, e-mail to author, March 23, 2011.

CHAPTER 6

1. Nicholas Howe, "Fabling Beasts: Traces in Memory," in *Humans and Other Animals*, ed. Arien Mack (Columbus: Ohio State University Press, 1995), 229–30.

2. Ibid., 243, 244.

3. John Berger, "Why Look at Animals?" in *Selected Essays of John Berger*, ed. Geoff Dyer (New York: Vintage International, 2001), 263.

4. See Alan Bleakley, *The Animalizing Imagination: Totemism, Textuality, and Ecocriticism* (New York: St. Martin's Press, 2000).

5. In popular language, "grotesque" suggests something abhorrent, ugly, or unpleasantly bizarre, although the term's historical and artistic meaning is more complex. The word comes from the Latin for *grotto* and is used in art history to describe excessively baroque architectural detailing that interlaces garlands and fantastic human and animal figures. Likewise, in literature the term indicates something that is comic and at the same time horrible or hard to take, something queasy and unsettling yet simultaneously amusing. See Wolfgang Kayser, *The Grotesque in Art and Literature* (New York: Columbia University Press, 1957).

6. The piece was bought by Lord and Lady Bangor and is still displayed in Castle Ward, County Down, Northern Ireland.

7. "The Comical Creatures from Wurtemburg," *Morning Chronicle* (London), August 12, 1851.

8. The tale is too lengthy to tell in full, but a brief synopsis gives a good idea of the sly fox's devious ways. All animals appear at a tribunal except Reineke the fox, who is accused of many dark deeds. The wolf accuses him of blinding his children. The dog tells how Reineke stole his sausage. The cock tells how the fox ate his brood. A bear is sent out to bring the fox to court, but Reineke outsmarts him. A cat is sent, but again Reineke conceives an evil plan, and the cat stumbles home with only one eye. Using his wiles and fearsome eloquence, Reineke finds a way to save his own skin by capitalizing on the other animals' weaknesses, greed, and hunger. The unscrupulous fox variously maims some animals, sentences others to death, eats still others, and generally causes grief and pain to everyone in the forest.

9. "The appearance of the Wurtemberg animals at the Exhibition came fortunately *apropos* to our assistance: a few years ago it was rare to find a person who had read the Fox Epic . . . but now the charming figures of Reineke himself, and King Lion, and Isegrim, and Bruin . . . had set all the world asking who and what they were, and the story began to get itself known. The old editions, which had long slept unbound in reams upon the shelves, began to descend and to clothe themselves in green and crimson. Mr Dickens sent a summary of it around the households of England. Everybody began to talk of Reineke." James Anthony Froude, "Reynard the Fox," in Froude, *Short Studies on Great Subjects*, 2 vols. (London: Longmans, Green, 1867), 1:263.

10. David Brogue, *The Comical Creatures of Wurtemberg, Including the Story of Reynard the Fox* (London, 1851); untitled book review, *Examiner* (London), August 2, 1851.

11. "Comical Creatures from Wurtemburg." In fact, the publication was so popular that a pirate edition appeared, and the printers were brought to trial by David Brogue.

12. Ibid. See also "Walks Through the Crystal Palace No. XIII," *Aberdeen Journal*, August 13, 1851.

13. "The Great Exhibition," *Morning Chronicle* (London), September 1, 1851. The article's highest praise, however, went to a European elk prepared by François Comba from the Musée royal de l'Université de Turin. This *"chef-d'œuvre"* of taxidermy was "all but breathing" and left viewers with "nothing to wish, except that we could see it placed in the British Museum, to scare into better shape those monstrous libels upon the forms of animal nature which there daily misinform the ignorant, and distress the eyes of the learned." As such, the works of English taxidermists were all too

deserving of the "undignified name of 'stuffing.'"

14. Montagu Browne, *Practical Taxidermy: A Manual of Instruction to the Amateur in Collecting, Preserving, and Setting Up Natural History Specimens of All Kinds*, 2nd ed. (London: L. Upcott Gill, 1884), 15.

15. Ibid., 254, 249.

16. Nigel Rothfels, introduction to *Representing Animals*, ed. Nigel Rothfels (Bloomington: Indiana University Press, 2002), vii.

17. The word itself is derived from the Latin *spectare* (to look, to look at) and the shifty prefix *ex*, meaning outside, deprived of, removed, thoroughly, deeply, to trigger or to initiate. In the case of anthropomorphic taxidermy, traditional narratives and values are partly imagined, partly experienced.

18. Thomas Bewick, *A General History of Quadrupeds* (1790; repr., Trowbridge, UK: Ward Lock Reprints, 1970), iv.

19. As Jenny Uglow has rather poetically written, Bewick's *History of Quadrupeds* grew from a sensibility that "gave birds names like their own—Jackdaw, Tom Tit, Robin Redbreast, Jenny Wren, Willy Wagtail. They knew that dogs had different dispositions, that pigs had cunning, that cows had their own slow kind of reason. They knew, too, that men could be just as devious and cruel as foxes and quite as filthy as swine. In a different way, men and women of 'sensibility,' who believed that true humanity rested less in reason than in an open emotional response to the world, from delight in a piece of music to sympathy with the poverty of a child, had no doubt that animals felt pain and could suffer. *Quadrupeds* certainly took this stance." Uglow, *Nature's Engraver: A Life of Thomas Bewick* (London: Faber and Faber, 2006), 182.

20. See Rose Lovell-Smith's wonderful essay "The Animals of Wonderland: Tenniel as Carroll's Reader," *Criticism* 45, no. 4 (2003): 383–415. The *Times* article on children's books appeared on December 26, 1865.

21. E. W. Collins, *Guide Book and History of Potter's Museum and Exhibition*, 8th ed. (n.p., n.d.), 2.

22. Spot, the dog that killed the rats, was also stuffed and on display in Potter's Museum, along with the following extraordinary narrative: "During corn threshing this dog was accidentally covered with straw and remained imprisoned until it was discovered, still alive, twenty-one days later. Then, it was accidentally shot, but again escaped death. Twelve months later it jumped out of a stable window in pursuit of a rat, and broke its shoulder bone; consequently it had to be destroyed." Ibid., 28.

23. See Katharine M. Rogers, *Cat* (London: Reaktion Books, 2006), 90–105.

24. Collins, *Guide Book and History of Potter's Museum*, 2.

25. Susan Stewart, *On Longing: Narratives of the Miniature, the Gigantic, the Souvenir, the Collection* (Durham: Duke University Press, 1993), 54, 57.

26. For an extended discussion of Victorian nature, nostalgia, and modernity,

see Celeste Olalquiaga, *The Artificial Kingdom: On the Kitsch Experience* (Minneapolis: University of Minnesota Press, 1998).

27. Idiots' artist statement, http://www.idiots.nl/news/index.php#ABOUT (accessed March 1, 2010).

28. Steve Baker, *The Postmodern Animal* (London: Reaktion Books, 2000), 52–53.

29. See Stewart, *On Longing*, 3–4. See also Maureen Quilligan, *The Language of Allegory: Defining the Genre* (Ithaca: Cornell University Press, 1979).

CHAPTER 7

1. Susan Pearce, *On Collecting: An Investigation into Collecting in the European Tradition* (London: Routledge, 1995), 243.

2. For a wonderful reading of "Un coeur simple," see Julian Barnes, *Flaubert's Parrot* (London: Jonathan Cape, 1984).

3. Of all the incorruptible parts of the body that might serve as relics, hair was the quintessential Victorian bodily souvenir. Hair mementos crystallized the essence of a dead or absent loved one into something permanent and tangible, something elegant, not ghoulish. As Christiane Holm observes, the rise of Victorian mourning jewelry coincides with a change in attitudes toward death. The focus of mourning shifted from the mourned to the grieving experience of the mourners. Likewise, Marcia Pointon notes that hair jewelry and other death mementos focused the mourners' attention away from the grim realities of death—"the nauseous corruption of the corpse"—and toward their own sadness and loss. See Christiane Holm, "Sentimental Cuts: Eighteenth-Century Mourning Jewelry with Hair," *Eighteenth-Century Literature* 38, no. 1 (2004): 139–43; and Marcia Pointon, "Materializing Mourning: Hair, Jewellery and the Body," in *Material Memories*, ed. Marius Kwint, Christopher Breward, and Jeremy Aynsley (Oxford: Berg, 1999), 39–71.

4. David Lowenthal, "Material Preservation and Its Alternative," *Perspecta* 25 (1989): 72.

5. See Susan Stewart, *On Longing: Narratives of the Miniature, the Gigantic, the Souvenir, the Collection* (Durham: Duke University Press, 1993), 132–45.

6. Keith Thomas, *Man and the Natural World: Changing Attitudes in England, 1500–1800* (Oxford: Oxford University Press, 1983), 110–11.

7. Kathleen Keet, *The Beast in the Boudoir: Petkeeping in Nineteenth-Century Paris* (Berkeley and Los Angeles: University of California Press, 1994), 40.

8. Quoted in ibid., 89–90.

9. "Episode 5: The Lifelike Pet," *Fun*, December 13, 1882, 248.

10. For a similar, although factual, narrative of a stuffed pet, Harold White offers a ridiculous story of Dante Gabriel Rossetti and his wombat in his lecture "Rossetti's Wombat: A

Pre-Raphaelite Obsession in Victorian England," given at the National Library of Australia, Canberra, April 16, 2003. The lecture is published online at http://www.nla.gov.au/grants/haroldwhite/papers/atrumble.html (accessed November 16, 2009).

11. Marc Shell, "The Family Pet," *Representations* 15 (1986): 136–37.

12. As Erica Fudge has noted, a linguistic twist allows us a greater distance between the animal in the field and the animal on the table. We do not actually eat cows and pigs but beef and pork. For more on how we put pets into a separate category from the rest of the animal world, see Fudge, *Animal* (London: Reaktion Books, 2002), 27–34.

13. "A Weekend Tribute to Lacie, Our Beloved Pet," posted on the client appreciation page of Pet Preservations, February 7, 2004, http://www.petpreservations.com/story1.html (accessed March 12, 2010).

14. See Perpetual Pet's gallery of client appreciation letters and images, http://www.perpetualpet.com/Gallery/ (accessed March 12, 2010).

15. "Another Experience with Pet Preservation," posted on the client appreciation page of Pet Preservations, http://www.petpreservations.com/story2.html (accessed March 12, 2010).

16. Dana C., "Another Experience with Pet Preservation," December 22, 2003, ibid.

17. For more on Balto's life and afterlife, see my chapter "Balto the Dog," in *The Afterlives of Animals: A Museum Menagerie*, ed. Samuel J. M. M. Alberti (Charlottesville: University of Virginia Press, 2011), 92–109.

18. After Rogers's death in 1998 and the death of his wife (Dale Evans) in 2001, the museum was moved in 2003 to Branson, Missouri. However, their son has since closed the museum.

19. Kim Dennis-Bryan and Juliet Clutton-Brock, *Dogs of the Last Hundred Years at the British Museum (Natural History)* (London: British Museum, 1988).

20. For more on Deyrolle and the fire, see Pierre Assouline, *Deyrolle pour l'avenir* (Paris: Gallimard, 2009).

21. Martin d'Orgeval, "Still Life," *Drawbridge* 16 (2009): 16.

INDEX